The Triune of Life Reggie Gold's Philosophical Legacy

THE INSTITUTE CHIROPRACTIC is dedicated to the publication of important books and media, which shed new light on topics such as chiropractic history and philosophy, spirituality, enlightenment, philosophy, Integral Theory, and subtle energies. The White Book Chiropractic Series is designed to bring forth important works from the history and philosophy of chiropractic, publish original new works, and inspire dialogue. Membership in The Institute Chiropractic is open to chiropractors and chiropractic students. Membership includes extensive online learning, scholarly discussion, and professional connections with the leading chiropractors around the world, those dedicated to acknowledging the profession's history, fostering a discipline of philosophy in the profession, and leading chiropractic into the future.

MORE TITLES FROM THE INSTITUTE CHIROPRACTIC

PALMER CHIROPRACTIC GREEN BOOKS
The Definitive Guide (2018)
Timothy J. Faulkner, Joseph Foley, Simon Senzon

THE COMPLETE CHIROPRACTOR
R. J. Watkins, DC, PhC, FICC, DACBR (2017)
Stevan Walton

EARLY HISTORY OF CHIROPRACTIC
The Palmer's and Australia (2014)
Rolf Peters

THE SECRET HISTORY OF CHIROPRACTIC
D.D. Palmer's Spiritual Writings: Second Edition (2014)
Simon Senzon

THE CHIROPRACTIC CHART
Ralph W. Stephenson (2017)

The Triune of Life Reggie Gold's Philosophical Legacy

Edited by
Simon Senzon

THE
INSTITUTE
CHIROPRACTIC

Asheville, N.C.

First Edition 2022

Published in the United States
by The Institute Chiropractic
218 E. Chestnut St. Asheville, N.C. 28801

Simon Senzon, b. 1971.
The Triune of Life: Reggie Gold's Philosophical Legacy.
Volume 18 of The Institute Chiropractic Books.

Includes bibliographical references.
"The Triune of Life: Reggie Gold's Philosophical Legacy features the 60th anniversary of Reggie Gold's classic chiropractic philosophic treatise *The Triune of Life*, accompanied by his iconic lectures and "The Third Paradigm" article set within a historical context by the people who knew and spent time with him."
-Provided by publisher.

ISBN 978-0-9862047-7-7 (Pbk)

For current information about all releases from
The Institute Chiropractic, visit the web site at:
www.institutechiro.com

DEDICATION

To Reggie.

Your legacy continues.

ACKNOWLEDGMENTS

Thank you, Irene Gold, for being a part of this book's history and supporting the republication of Reggie's *Triune of Life* and other classics in celebration of his philosophic legacy.

A very special thank you to Dan Lemberger for helping make this book possible, and work with me in the development and delivery of the manuscript.

Editorial thanks go to Leslie Peters.

Thank you to Stevan Walton and Timothy Faulkner for offering feedback on the triune history section.

Also thank you to *Dynamic Chiropractic* for authorizing the reprinting of the "The Third Paradigm," and to Special Collections and Archives, Palmer College of Chiropractic for the use of some of the images on pages 59-69.

Lastly, enormous gratitude goes to all of the chiropractors who wrote a section of this book to share their experiences with Reggie. It is an honor to capture these historical stories as part of the record and bring more contextual light to Reggie's contributions to the profession and chiropractic philosophy.

Foreword
Irene Gold

Reggie graduated from Palmer College in December of 1957 and returned to his family home in New Jersey. Because Palmer was not accredited in New Jersey at that time, he traveled to the closest nearby state, New York. His car broke down in my hometown, Spring Valley, and the rest is history.

Reggie met a real estate broker who had a store in the middle of town. He somehow convinced the broker to give him one-half of the store. As you can see in this book, Reggie could be very convincing, especially when the topic was chiropractic. When he arrived in my town, there were no chiropractors, no licensure, and no advertising (because it was illegal). No one had any idea what a chiropractor was supposed to do.

How do you build a practice under those circumstances? You take your spine, walk up and down the main street, and let people stop you and ask what you are doing with that spine! You visit every shop on the main street and speak to every owner and shop worker to let them know what chiropractic is and why they need to come to you.

Within two years, he was teaching Chiropractic Philosophy at the Columbia Institute of Chiropractic, now known as New York Chiropractic College. He worked for one dollar a year because everyone had to give back to Chiropractic. Four years later, he was placed on a leave of absence because the school wanted to go in the direction of the American Chiropractic Association (ACA), and the school deemed that his philosophy class was no longer necessary.

Never deterred, Reggie decided to hold a layman lecture on April 30th, which all current patients were expected to attend. As a result of this one lecture, we started 250 new families in May. We opened the office seven days a week and had to hire help to cover the explosion of new families in the office.

Reggie loved spreading and communicating the chiropractic message wherever and whenever he could. While at Columbia, Reggie represented the school for all the state license renewal programs. After leaving Columbia, we decided to open our home/office once a month to chiropractic students and doctors for philosophy talks. Every month,

50 to sometimes over 200 people gathered for these talks, some sharing their stories in this book.

When he was asked to give up this considerable practice and help start a new college, Sherman, in South Carolina, it took no more than 10 seconds to say "yes." When Sherman began, no one knew Thom Gelardi. But Reggie, from his years of speaking on chiropractic philosophy all over the world, was well-known to many chiropractic students and doctors. Reggie was responsible for bringing most of the 63 students that started in Sherman's first class to the school.

I could go on and on about his whole life being dedicated to what he felt was best for chiropractic. I think the entire idea of this book is not just historic, but also to let everyone know that no matter what you are doing now, you can do more to help ChiropracTIC.

Here is one of my favorite Reggie quotes:

> "If you are not out to change the world, your whole life is a total waste of time, filled with missed opportunities."

Don't miss the opportunities to share and grow chiropractic around the world. Reggie's and our shared legacy, depends on you.

Introduction
Simon Senzon and Dan Lemberger

There have been many great chiropractors in the history of chiropractic, but only a handful of chiropractic greats – the legends who, generations later, people still talk about. Those are the ones who leave a legacy, and Reggie Gold is one of these chiropractic giants.

The year 2022 marks the 60th anniversary of Reggie finishing his PhC thesis, *The Triune of Life* (1963), at Palmer College of Chiropractic. His contributions to chiropractic in the form of this philosophic treatise, as well as his true gift of the spoken word and lecture, have inspired three generations of chiropractors, and will influence generations to come. Reggie's simple and clear chiropractic message helped develop the modern philosophy of chiropractic and shift the direction of the profession towards non-therapeutic objectives.

To celebrate Reggie and his historic contributions to chiropractic, we republish this master work here as the central focus of this text. The mission of The Institute Chiropractic (TIC) is to establish an accurate history of ideas for the chiropractic profession to build on, to bring a common set of knowledge to a wide base of chiropractors worldwide. *The Triune of Life: Reggie Gold's Philosophical Legacy* is the flagship for this mission because it delivers pivotal texts and introduces novel insights with unique first-hand accounts.

Reggie's contribution to chiropractic far transcends *The Triune of Life* (1963). Reggie was known worldwide for his oration, so we also include two of his most iconic lectures, "The Valley of the Blind" (1972) and "The Lay Lecture" (1987), as well as his short article "The Third Paradigm" (2000). The book also includes essays from 44 chiropractors from all over the world: Argentina, Australia, Chile, Israel, Japan, Mexico, New Zealand, Scotland, South Africa, South Korea, Spain, the United Kingdom, and the United States. The authors include practicing chiropractors, technique developers and teachers, founders and leaders of professional organizations, chiropractic philosophy instructors, and former and current chiropractic college administrators and presidents from nine schools - all a testament to the impact Reggie made on the profession.

The vision of this project was to offer more than Reggie's writings and lectures, and to set them within a historical context and capture the impact his philosophical developments made on the people who knew him, spent time with him, and listened to him from the audience. The historical moment from Reggie's second generation to the third and fourth generations, included a transition in the profession, from one dominated by singular leaders, the chiropractic greats, to the modern, decentralized leadership of the profession today. Through all of this transition and change, Reggie was a thought leader who helped pivot the chiropractic profession.

The chiropractors contained herein were invited to contribute essays celebrating Reggie's ideas on *The Triune of Life*, as well as share anecdotes, experiences, and lessons learned from him. These contributions are priceless because they establish primary historical accounts of one of the most dynamic and revolutionary phases of chiropractic history, from those who continue to carry the torch for vitalistic, non-therapeutic chiropractic. Central to all the contributions are insights on practicing chiropractic simply, philosophically, and successfully - a legacy that Reggie left to the profession.

This book is undertaken with permission from Irene Gold, wife of Reggie and a mentor in her own right to thousands of chiropractors worldwide.

Philosophy, History, and Practice of Chiropractic

The Triune of Life: Reggie Gold's Philosophical Legacy covers three broad areas: (a) the philosophy of chiropractic, (b) chiropractic history, and (c) the practice of chiropractic. The book includes an objective history and serves as a document of primary and secondary accounts about a revolution in chiropractic's history of ideas and practice, one that is often misunderstood and misrepresented in the chiropractic literature. Looking forward, it conveys a new sense of purpose and understanding for chiropractors and chiropractic students.

As a work of philosophy, this book is a tribute to the influence of Reggie's life and work, especially his *Triune*. In that text, Reggie focused on Stephenson's (1927) model of the triune of life, because he found in it the "crux of the entire philosophy" (p. 6). In Reggie's view, the triune of life is the essence of the philosophy of chiropractic; it also stands on its own as a philosophical argument as the "heart and soul of Chiropractic philosophy" (p. 6). He proposed that "failure to understand the triune of life must inevitably result in failure to understand the entire philosophy of which it is a cornerstone" (p. 6). This book adds to that insight by highlighting the many ways the triune has been implemented and influences chiropractic practices around the world.

Reggie's *Triune* was written at the start of his incredible career as a chiropractic thought leader. His other lectures and essays in this book offer a glimpse into Reggie's approach, viewpoint, and his clarity of purposeful communication. The philosophical contributions, which are portrayed throughout this book, might be summed up in at least three ways: (a) the linguistic distinctions essential to emphasizing the role of vertebral subluxation, (b) the philosophical emphasis on the body's living processes as organizational, and (c) the focus on human potential as central to chiropractic's purpose.

As a work of history and practice, the book includes primary sources in the form of Reggie's writings, a short history of the chiropractic triune, and many stories of Reggie's influence on the profession through which hundreds of thousands, and - more likely millions - of chiropractic patients have been impacted. In addition to the numerous personal stories and experiences of people who spent time with Reggie, this book also includes secondary accounts from some who never met him, yet were still impacted by him profoundly.

This republication of Reggie's core teachings, along with the many incredible tributes to his life and work, initiate a new era of philosophy in chiropractic. We hope this book inspires a critical study and application of the *Triune* and its associated works for future generations.

Manuscript Philosophy and Design

Our vision for this book was to capture the essence of Reggie's message, which was eloquently conveyed through a few pivotal writings, but mainly through the spoken word at his lectures. All authors in this book were inspired by hearing Reggie speak or listening to recordings of his talks, or both. Many of the authors mention reading the *Triune*, but it was hearing Reggie that transformed most people initially. For those vitalistic chiropractors old enough to listen to things on tape cassettes, it is rare to find one who didn't listen to Reggie on cassette, and yes, we do understand future generations will never get this thrill.

The book is organized into four sections, each beginning with Reggie's words and culminating with new writings from chiropractors influenced by him. Section one republishes the 1998 second edition of

The Triune of Life. We chose to use this edition because Reggie stated this was the most complete version of it and personally edited it. However, since the second edition did not include the original reference list, we have also included the references from the reprinting in 1977 by the International Chiropractic Association. The second and third sections of this book begin with transcriptions of Reggie's "The Valley of the Blind," and "The Lay Lecture." Section four republishes "The Third Paradigm," a provocative late classic from Reggie, often talked about in chiropractic circles. These are intermingled with the stories told by chiropractors who knew or were influenced by him, to connect each section to the vitality that Reggie delivered speaking live, and to interweave for the reader how Reggie's talks impacted the profession.

Reggie's spoken lectures, "The Valley of the Blind" and "The Lay Lecture," were chosen to represent his essential teachings and were transcribed for this book. By reading these lectures in text, rather than hearing them as the spoken word, the reader may gain insights and view certain gems of Reggie's eloquence in new ways. Transitioning from spoken word to written text, minor punctuation or grammatical changes were made to make these lectures more readable. No changes were made to meaning or content of any significance, only to clarify readability.

To bridge the emphasis in Reggie's spoken word to text, in "The Valley of the Blind," Reggie emphasizes the first part of the word *dis-ease*, which is the traditional chiropractic way of describing disharmony or pathophysiological changes in the body. Such usage dates to D. D. Palmer's original advertisements in the 1880s (Senzon, 2019). For the transcription, Reggie's use of dis-ease and dis-order are hyphenated. Additionally, for the modern reader some of Reggie's examples, such as famous names like Howard Cosell and Len Bias may not be recognizable. Other instances like referencing LBJ, the initials of the 36th U.S. president Lyndon Baines Johnson, reflect the years spanned by Reggie's legacy. If some of these speeches were given today, Reggie might have obviously chosen different historical reference points. Lastly, rather than revising or editing out statements that might be viewed as politically incorrect today, we present the full text as they were spoken in the 1970s. It is hoped that readers can take any such statements *with a grain of salt*, in the context of the time, and look past any dated analogies or examples to the essential message in each talk.

In order to capture the dialogue that Reggie inspired with his recorded talks, as well as his regular talks around the globe, we chose a more colloquial quality for the book; many of the essays read like talks or spoken word. For these essays, we ask the reader to imagine you are sitting in the audience, listening to stories and insights about Reggie, his life and work, and learning about chiropractic in its purest and simplest form. Or maybe imagine you were at a Reggie talk, and another audience member shares with you their favorite Reggie experience.

One theme from the anecdotes and essays presented here is that Reggie made the complex simple. Another theme is that people often learned about Reggie from a friend or mentor saying, "You need to listen to Reggie." This book is just that: 44 authors (including the two of us) beckoning to every chiropractor and chiropractic student; *study this book, and your perspective on chiropractic and how you choose to practice might be transformed, along with your life and the lives of those around you.*

The essays capture each author's unique voice and include a wide range of styles. First- and second-person perspectives were encouraged to capture the "we" that is the chiropractic culture. To follow that approach and keep each voice distinct, the essays were lightly edited for consistency of grammar and punctuation, but not content, which is each author's own. Additionally, we did not systematize capitalization for Innate Intelligence or Universal Intelligence. Some of these essays are written by those who never met Reggie and only listened to his talks, others sat at his feet for years and decades, yet these two terms and the overall message throughout the book are congruent. Trying to dictate how terminology was written would have detracted from this congruity. Following Reggie's example, who mostly went by Reggie and often said, when called Dr. Gold, "Dr. Gold is my wife," we keep author bylines to name only, excluding their postnominals DC or MChiro; all authors of this book are people, chiropractors writing about chiropractic, and one of their mentors was Reggie Gold.

Anecdotes and Insights from Simon and Dan

As graduates of Sherman College in the late 1990s, both of us were taught philosophy by several of Reggie's students including Bill Decken, Val Pennachio, and David Koch. Dan had the privilege to take Thom Gelardi's final philosophy class before Gelardi retired as president of the school. Simon had the privilege to act as research assistant to the president when Koch took over as president of Sherman. This position led to bi-weekly one-on-one discussions about Simon's research on the Green Books and systems science. Both of us also studied with Donny Epstein, another of Reggie's students, and we took national board review courses with Irene Gold, Reggie's incredible wife (Thank you Irene!). It was a rich time to be on Sherman's dynamic campus. Reggie visited often, and was often featured at all-school assemblies, and philosophic events around Sherman.

From Dan

It took me several years after starting chiropractic school to realize that Reggie Gold influenced the reason I had my first chiropractic adjustment at the age of seven or eight years old, even though he was not the one to deliver it. It all happened in the late 1970s in Spring Valley, NY…

A friend of my parents told them about a chiropractor who they just had to go see, named Jack Dippolito. We lived about 20-30 minutes away from Spring Valley, and we probably drove past a few dozen chiropractic offices to get there across the old Tappan Zee Bridge on Saturday mornings. Jack had a "different" kind of chiropractic practice, and a fee system that incentivized bringing the entire family for care. He saw a lot of people—so many, in fact, that when we walked into the office, we had to take a number and wait, similar to what you did at the butcher counter or bakery. Later I found out Jack had been an associate in Reggie's office, before Reggie moved to South Carolina. He had opened his own practice and taken Reggie's influence, deciding to see families and children.

Another unique feature of the practice at the time, was that no one was allowed to start care unless they attended the introductory talk, a lay lecture, as I would later learn it was called. So before starting care, my parents took me with them to the class, partly because there was no babysitter, and part I think because they were told to bring me with them. The only thing I remember from that talk was someone showing a picture of the Earth, and some mention of how chiropractic helped make people more whole, and thereby the world was better. No, I did not decide there on the spot that I was destined to be a chiropractor. But as a child I heard the chiropractic story. A seed was planted. My parents heard the story, and it made sense to them to bring me to make sure I had my spine checked and adjusted, to give me the best chances in life. Sure, they had challenges and pains, but they brought me so that I wouldn't end up in the same shape they did. It sounds a lot like the story Reggie tells in his talks of not leaving your kids at home to rot, while you come here to get adjusted. Legacy is others remembering the message, even when you're gone.

To me, and to many people in this book that he impacted, Reggie's greatness was in his communication. I remember seeing Reggie speak for the first time at Sherman College Lyceum. Here's this guy standing on the stage, one leg on chair, speaking with a calm, intense certainty. He didn't overload you with jargon or complexity. He filled you with simple-to-understand and compelling truth. He was provocative, yet entertaining. He would build his talk in a realization crescendo of common sense. As he echoed his "Think dammit. Think," to us it wasn't an insult, it was a motivation, a call to action.

Chiropractic is for the generations; young and old can benefit from chiropractic care. This book is for the chiropractic generations, the future generations who will never have the experience to see Reggie speak live. My hope is that this book kindles a passion for chiropractic like Reggie's in the hearts and minds of those who have never met him, and rekindles the memories and excitement for those of us who did, and ignites a flame for us all to carry the light of chiropractic in the future.

From Simon

After reading all of the essays for this book several times, I reflected on my time with Reggie and I realized that I took him for granted while I was at Sherman. Irene helped me get through boards, which was a feat for someone who is not a natural test-taker; to her I am forever grateful. Yet Reggie seemed to be always around. He was a rock at Sherman even though he only visited occasionally. I have great memories of his talks from the FSCO Triune Seminar and the first inclusion of a philosophy forum as part of IRAPS. Even though I was a new graduate, I presented two papers at the conference and got to participate on the philosophy panel with Reggie. The essays in this book also helped me to better appreciate my first visit to speak at New Beginnings, a program created for Reggie to teach. I went on after Reggie, which I don't recommend.

These experiences of my early chiropractic career relate to my unique background compared to most chiropractors. By the time I arrived at chiropractic college, I had just completed my master's degree in philosophy and was teaching an Introduction to Philosophy class for undergraduates at Limestone College in Gaffney, South Carolina. My master's thesis cited D.D. Palmer's (1914) *The Chiropractor*, and explored the body-mind-soul connection. Thus, I brought philosophy with me to chiropractic and learned from Reggie and his students in a very informed way.

This book has also helped me to understand how Reggie's work underpins my own in important ways. I used to think that my first published papers built upon the works of my teachers and mentors, Ralph Boone, Graham Dobson, Donny Epstein, and David Koch. Now I realize more than ever that I was learning from Reggie's students. My first papers explored the unique distinctions made by Reggie and the school of thought he inspired (Senzon, 1999, 2003). I demonstrated that the emphasis on the chiropractic principle of living systems as intelligent, self-organizing, and self-healing has an organizational dimension with roots in 20th century systems science (Senzon, 2015). Reggie differentiated the subluxation as not only an anatomical and neurological aspect but also an organizational aspect (Senzon, 2018).

By focusing on the organizational aspect of the Palmers' definitions of Innate Intelligence, Reggie's school of thought made a new differentiation within the philosophy of chiropractic (Senzon, 2000). In that regard, I argued that the Palmers' committed a category error in their original definition because the same term, Innate Intelligence, was used to define different categories of being: spirit, soul, and life (Senzon, 2011). This approach offers an important way to distinguish straight schools of thought within the philosophy of chiropractic. Ultimately, because of this book and the accounts from Reggie's students, I better understand how my thinking can be traced to Reggie's *Triune*.

My favorite memories about Reggie are the Sunday program at Sherman's Lyceum every year. Reggie would moderate the stage and speakers would tell their own chiropractic story. At the end of the program, everyone would sing "Carry It On." It was a special time. Personally, I have chosen to carry on what I've learned from Thom, Reggie, Irene, and their students, which has led to my practice for the last 21 years, the completion of my PhD thesis, and TIC. Thank you, Reggie; we are carrying it on.

Suggestions on How to Read This Book

We recommend you read this book three times. The first time, just read through it and be wowed by the philosophy, the history, and the incredible impact of Reggie Gold on his students and the profession worldwide. The second time, study how Reggie's ideas and communication style impacted the viewpoints of the authors in this text; notice the similarities from story to story and let those sink in. For the final reading, own it so that you can implement it in your life and practice. Let the first reading be like a powerful wave washing over you; for the second reading, catch a wave for a moment and feel the exhilaration of surfing. For the third reading, ride the curl of the wave from start to finish, merge with it, complete it as you would a full breath of life.

References

Boone, W. (1996). The advancement of vertebral subluxation research and clinical care. *Journal of Vertebral Subluxation Research, 1*(2), 1–2.

Boone, W., & Dobson, G. (1996a). A proposed vertebral subluxation model reflecting traditional concepts and recent advances in health and science. *Journal of Vertebral Subluxation Research, 1*(1), 19–36.

Boone, W., & Dobson, G. (1996b). A proposed vertebral subluxation model reflecting traditional concepts and recent advances in health and science: Part II. *Journal of Vertebral Subluxation Research, 1*(2), 23–32.

Boone, W., & Dobson, G. (1996c). A proposed vertebral subluxation model reflecting traditional concepts and recent advances in health and science: Part III. *Journal of Vertebral Subluxation Research*, 1(3), 19-36.

Epstein, D. (1996). Network spinal analysis: A system of health care delivery within the subluxation-based chiropractic model. *Journal of Vertebral Subluxation Research, 1*(1), 51-59.

Epstein, D., Senzon, S., & Lemberger, D. (2009). Reorganizational healing: A paradigm for the advancement of wellness, behavior change, holistic practice, and healing. *JACM, 15*(5), 475-487. https://doi.org/10.1089/acm.2009.0043

Gold, R. (1963). *Triune of life*. Palmer School of Chiropractic.

Gold, R. (1966). *Triune of life* (First reprint). International Chiropractic Association.

Gold, R. (1971). *Triune of life* (Second printing). International Chiropractic Association.

Gold, R. (1972). The valley of the blind. Palmer College of Chiropractic.

Gold, R. (1977). *Triune of life* (Third printing). International Chiropractic Association.

Gold, R. (1987). The layman lecture. Recorded as part of the Chiropractic Expert Series.

Gold, R. (1998). *Triune of life* (Second edition). Sherman College of Straight Chiropractic.

Koch, D. (1997). Has vitalism been a help or a hindrance to the science and art of chiropractic? *Journal of Chiropractic Humanities, 6*, 18–22. https://doi.org/10.1016/S1556-3499(13)60065-0

Senzon, S. (1999). Causation related to self-organization and health related quality of life expression based on the vertebral subluxation model, the philosophy of chiropractic, and the new biology. *Journal of Vertebral Subluxation Research, 3*(3), 104–112.

Senzon, S. (2000). An integral approach to unifying the philosophy of chiropractic: B. J. Palmer's model of consciousness. *Journal of Integral Studies, 1*(2).

Senzon, S. (2003). What is life? *Journal of Vertebral Subluxation Research*, June; 1–4.

Senzon, S. (2011). Constructing a philosophy of chiropractic: Evolving worldviews and premodern roots. *Journal of Chiropractic Humanities, 18*(1), 10–23. https://doi.org/10.1016/j.echu.2011.09.001

Senzon, S. (2015, December 24). Chiropractic and systems science. *Journal of Philosophy, Principles & Practice of Chiropractic*, 9–20.

Senzon, S. (2018). The chiropractic vertebral subluxation Part 8: Terminology, definitions, and historicity from 1966 to 1980. *Journal of Chiropractic Humanities, 25*, 114-129. https://doi.org/10.1016/j.echu.2018.10.006

Stephenson, R. (1927). *Chiropractic textbook* (Vol. 14). Palmer School of Chiropractic.

In Memoriam
Rolf Peters

REGGIE R. GOLD, DC, PhC, FPAC
Philosopher of Chiropractic
16 DECEMBER 1925 – 24 MARCH 2012

This is an unashamedly personal memento to a dear friend and college flatmate. The accompanying portrait is one of a series of studies I made of Reggie in 1957, because I prefer to remember him in his prime rather than later portraits which showed the ravages of time.

Reggie was born on 16 December 1925 in London and died 24 March 2012 at his home in Bala Cynwyd, PA.

Our story begins in early January 1955. At that time, I was living in a rooming house on 14th Street in Davenport, and the room across the hall was occupied by Thom Gelardi. Reggie arrived and asked me to join him as a flatmate in a second-floor apartment he had leased on Ripley Street.

What a strange combination we made. I was German, had served in the U.S. Army during the Korean conflict, never fired an angry shot and left military service with the rank of Corporal. And there was Reggie, a combat veteran of World War II, who had served in the British Paratroopers and held the rank of Major, the youngest Major in the British Armed Forces.

Reggie possessed a photographic memory. Anything he read was automatically recorded in his brain. Ask a question on anatomy and he would quote Gray's Anatomy, page number, and verbalise what paragraph two contained. He used this ability to hold study sessions prior to exams for groups of classmates.

He worked at the Putnam Museum designing and building exhibits and, on many evenings, gave dinner parties in various homes selling cookware by using a single burner and cooking complete meals by stacking the various pots on top of each other.

On campus his car was the only new Cadillac. He had purchased it in his previous line of selling cemetery plots in New York and New Jersey.

Like many of our classmates Reggie belonged to Toastmasters Club 1917. Being able to speak on any subject, both pro and con, he won two consecutive Toastmasters District 19 annual speech contests.

At graduation time Reggie was both class president and Valedictorian. While most of us returned to our homes after graduation and started to set up practices, Reggie stayed behind at the college, where he studied chiropractic philosophy which culminated in his thesis *The Triune of Life* which earned him the PhC degree and then established a highly successful practice in Spring Valley, New York.

Reggie supported Sherman College since before its founding in 1973. He retired from his Spring Valley practice to help Thom Gelardi develop the college and served as dean of the college and philosophy instructor and contributed his time to fund raising and recruiting students. *The Triune of Life* became the main philosophy text at Sherman College and has been read and treasured by generations of chiropractors and students.

Reggie left Sherman College in the late 1970s and helped establish and serve as president of another straight chiropractic college - ADIO Institute of Straight Chiropractic in Pennsylvania.

He travelled the globe spreading the chiropractic message and was responsible for inspiring hundreds, perhaps thousands, of people of all ages to pursue a career in chiropractic. He was a popular guest lecturer at Sherman College and played a vital role in the college's student recruitment efforts. In 1989 he was named Sherman College Career Advisor of the Year. He freely donated his time to visit the college to address and inspire the student body, represent the college at career fairs, and assist the college's fund-raising efforts. Additionally, he has contributed a great deal of financial stability of the college and has provided for the college's future in his estate planning.

Reggie's strong communication skills, visionary insight and unfailing dedication to the chiropractic principle continually drew him into the spotlight. In 1990 Sherman College honored him by dedicating that year's Lyceum program to him and naming him Chiropractor of the Year. Among his numerous awards and honors he has received the International Humanitarian Award presented by the World Congress of Chiropractic and the Doctor of Chiropractic Humanities degree from Sherman College. He was named a Fellow of the College of Straight Chiropractic by the Federation of Straight Chiropractors and Organizations. The Palmer University system honored him with the highest award they can bestow: Fellow of the Palmer Academy (FPAC) in 1972.

In the early 1970s Reggie visited Australia for the first time, spent some time with us in Wagga Wagga, then we moved on to Melbourne, where Reggie gave a series of lectures both to the profession and to the general public. For some unknown reason Reggie needed to be adjusted and in his suite at the Sheraton Hotel in Melbourne we used a number of telephone books to act as a headpiece, and I toggled his Atlas. He commented that it was one of the best adjustments he had received in quite a while.

Over the years we usually ran into each other at Palmer Homecomings, where he used to lecture on philosophy to students at the home of the Delta Sigma Chi fraternity.

When in 2007 we met again at the 50th reunion of our class at Homecoming in Davenport we were astounded to see how many of our classmates had passed away.

Reggie is survived by his wife of 50 years, Dr. Irene Gold.

Growing up in New York City, Irene Gold developed a strong interest in her own education and put herself through college, initially earning a degree as a Registered Nurse from Fifth Avenue Hospital in NYC. She worked in numerous areas of nursing for fifteen years after graduation from nursing school. The RN was followed by a BS in Nursing Education, and a MA in Health Education.

After meeting and marrying Reggie Gold, the most dedicated and outspoken chiropractor and chiropractic philosopher of all time, Irene's education grew to include that field as well. Irene graduated from Columbia Institute of Chiropractic (now New York Chiropractic College) with her Doctor of Chiropractic in 1974.

Prior to conducting board reviews, Dr. Irene taught in several different chiropractic colleges for a number of years; first for Columbia Institute, then Sherman College of Straight Chiropractic, and finally ADIO Chiropractic College. Her years at Sherman College included several years as academic dean.

The board review classes started at Sherman College in 1975 as a way to help the students pass the National Board. The Irene Gold Associates organization became incorporated in 1978 in the state of Pennsylvania. She takes great pleasure in having successfully prepared many thousands of doctors for licensure since that time.

Now the question arises, who can and will arise to try and fill the shoes of one of the greatest Chiropractic Philosophers of all time?

Reggie, you are going to be missed by thousands. Vale, until we meet again in the great beyond.

**Reprinted with permission from Chiropractic Journal of Australia*

Tribute to Reggie Gold
Joe Strauss

Reggie Gold was a chiropractor, a philosopher, a teacher, and motivator, but he was also my mentor and friend. His life was inextricably woven into the profession of chiropractic. At this, the republication of Reggie's classic work, *The Triune of Life*, I am personally reminded of the impact that *The Triune of Life* and Reggie had on a nineteen-year-old, first quarter chiropractic student ... me! I learned my chiropractic from Reggie. I continued to learn from this amazing man over the years, and I owe much of my understanding of our amazing chiropractic philosophy to him. It was my privilege and delight to write a biography of Reggie Gold in 1997, after countless hours of sitting with Reggie, tapping his brain, and ultimately putting pen to paper. I asked him what he would like the title of his biography to be. He suggested *Reggie: Making the Message Simple*. And so it is! That is his legacy.

The chiropractic philosophy, indeed, at first appears to be very simple, in fact, to many it seems to be too simple. But the more you understand and develop the chiropractic philosophy, the more complex, the more interesting and exciting its principles and ramifications become. Most importantly, the more you understand it, the more applicable it is to life. It allows for a fuller understanding and expression of this complex phenomena that we call the human experience. Eventually it moves into metaphysical areas that we cannot truly comprehend. We have barely begun to understand the ramifications of our philosophy.

Just as with the human body and the chiropractic philosophy, Reggie, the man, was complex upon investigation. His message, from which he rarely deviated, was clear and fundamental, and yet we will probably never fully understand the man, his desires in life, his ideas, feelings, and goals. We do know that he was distinctive in that his life revolved around one thing—chiropractic. To understand Reggie and his life is to understand the development of straight chiropractic for at least as long as he had been associated with it. Who was the man, Reggie Gold? What drove him? Like the human body and the philosophy, there were parts of Reggie as a human being that no one could understand, perhaps not even himself. (Taken, in part, from *Reggie: Making the Message Simple*, p. 14.)

In the *Introduction* to Reggie's biography, I included several pages of excerpts from letters of gratitude from those who had chosen to acknowledge the profound effect he had on their lives. Among those comments were expressions of gratefulness for his kindness, his generosity, and the respectful and thoughtful way he not only answered questions but how he helped chiropractic students and chiropractors alike to find their own answers. Words were shared that expressed the profound impact of his teaching and gratefulness for his wisdom. He created enthusiasm and love for the chiropractic philosophy, and his listeners are forever grateful. One wrote, "Thousands of DC's help thousands more patients because of you." Another wrote, "Thank you for being all that you are and reminding me of all that I may yet become." Yet another wrote, "Thank you for speaking at ... I'm afraid you hit me right between the eyes. I have allowed the dimmer switch of negative feedback to dampen my vision and mission. Thank you for the wake-up call." I could go on, but if you want to read all the quotes, you need to get the book!

Reggie wrote inside my copy of his biography, "B.J. said 'Conflicts Clarify.' If he were around today, he would say 'Joe Strauss clarifies.' Thanks Joe. Reggie 3-22-1997." And that is what I have attempted to do over the years, based on the sure and solid foundation of unadulterated chiropractic philosophy from the lips of this man, Reggie Gold. Thank you, Reggie!

From his roots in the East London borough of Bow, Reggie's life was marked by overcoming obstacles, both personally and professionally, and a burning desire to succeed in the face of adversity. He overcame his cockney intonation but retained just enough of his English accent to endear himself to any listener, and he became, in the opinion of many, the most articulate speaker in the chiropractic profession.

The account of his life is both fascinating and inspirational, filled with a sense of hope and grit. Reggie was born in 1926, between the wars. From living in a "slum" and being a "sweeper" in a pawn shop at age eleven, dropping out of school with the equivalent of a sixth-grade education, experiencing the Blitz, the German bombing campaign of London between September 7, 1940, and May 11, 1941, joining the military, earning a commission in an elite Highland Regiment (which had rarely ever had a Jewish officer in its ranks), being a self-admitted "loner" and an "outcast" because of his Jewish heritage, Reggie emerged as a man who was willing to stand alone with his ideas and to be set apart because of them. He was a leader in every sense of the word. True leaders do not really care what other people think about them; that is how they are able to stretch people's thinking and lead them. He eventually became the spokesman for chiropractic.

To Reg, there was no such thing as a lost cause. He often said there is no such thing as an incurable disease until the patient is dead. Similarly, there is no such thing as a lost cause until there is no one left to fight for it. Reggie never had a fear of being that person. His famous "obituary" speech, given at Palmer Homecoming, offers a glimpse of the man's willingness to be out in front all alone, taking on the most powerful enemies, including the two that hurt straight chiropractic the most: apathy and status quo. That fictional obituary follows:

> Headline: Last Practicing Chiropractor Dies at age 97
>
> Today in Spring Valley, New York, Dr. Reginald R. Gold, Chiropractor passed away at age 97. He is survived by a wife who is also a chiropractor and retired from active practice several years ago. This ends an era in American history. Chiropractic started in Davenport, Iowa in 1895 and there followed a long and bitter struggle for survival against the combined might of organized medicine and the pharmaceutical industry. In the beginning it seemed as if the dedication and devotion of the chiropractors and the logic of their cause would be enough to overcome their monumental foe and to replace it as the world's number one healing art. But sometime during the 1960's or 1970's the tide gradually turned against the chiropractors. More and more chiropractors realized the hopelessness of their self-appointed task of saving the world. One by one they crumbled under the pressures of society and gave up fighting for their lost principle. They took instead the easier path of working for their personal acceptance and for status in the community. One by one their radical leaders died off or were deserted by their followers. And with each successive move away from their radical and unaccepted theories, the chiropractors became more and more a part of the established health team. Seven years ago, in the year

> 2015 just 120 years after its birth, chiropractic officially died, as almost all of its remaining few practitioners were formed into a paramedical group to aid doctors of physical medicine in manipulation. A few who failed to qualify continued to practice illegally under their defunct chiropractic licenses. The last of these, Dr. Reginald R. Gold passed away last Monday. The funeral was unattended.

Wow! That is chilling, is it not?

We are delighted to celebrate Reggie's life and legacy in *The Triune of Life: Reggie Gold's Philosophical Legacy*. May Reggie's observation of the apathy and status quo of those in the profession in 1963 not be realized in our future!

THE TRIUNE OF LIFE

The Triune of Life
Reggie Gold

Philosophy

In the study of any philosophy it is necessary to examine not only the individual segments of that philosophy but also the effect of each segment upon the next. The philosophy can have meaning only if studied as a cohesive whole. Parts taken out of context tend either to confuse the issues and·present distortions or, at best, to permit only limited understanding.

Every once in a while, however, a segment can be found which, standing alone, appears so complete in and of itself as to be both a statement of the entire philosophy and an explanation of it. It can be understood without reference to the other segments and yet acts to give those segments meaning and depth. It is, in fact, the crux of the entire philosophy.

If Chiropractic philosophy can be said to have any such self-sustaining segment, that part must be the **Triune of Life.** It and it alone can be sequestered from the whole and yet remain a totality within itself. It is at once a simple statement of the essence of the philosophy and, at the same time, an explanation without which the remainder would have no reality. Failure to understand the Triune of Life must inevitably result in failure to understand the entire philosophy of which it is a cornerstone. The student finds himself confronted with a maze of apparently unrelated facts, meaningless hypotheses and bewildering paradoxes.

As soon as this triune is understood, the paradoxes are resolved, the hypotheses take on meaning, and the facts become cohesive. Thus, from disrelationship emerges cohesion; from complexity, simplicity; and from confusion, clarity.

The Triune of Life, then, should be an area of concentrated study, for it embodies the heart and soul of Chiropractic philosophy.

The art and science of Chiropractic, while inseparable from the philosophy, necessarily confine themselves to the human body. The philosophy of Chiropractic, on the other hand, is much broader in scope. It deals not only with the body, or material substance, but also with immaterial factors.

The Triune of Life explains the relationship between the material and the immaterial, and more particularly, the link uniting them. These, in fact, are **the three components of the triune: intelligence, matter and force.**

In this thesis intelligence, matter and force will be examined in considerable detail. Each will be studied individually and in relationship to each of the others. The Triune of Life will be dissected, studied and reassembled to show the purpose and function of each part and the philosophical significance of the integrated whole. From the study of this vital phase of Chiropractic philosophy certain conclusions will be drawn by the process of deductive reasoning. These conclusions will then be offered as axioms for the purpose of gathering a measure of understanding of the Chiropractic principle.

Perhaps at this time a slight digression is in order to see why Chiropractic prefers deductive to inductive reasoning. The word "deduce" means to "derive by logic" (Webster). *Deductive reasoning* is the process of studying known facts and self-evident truths and, from them, arriving at inescapable conclusions which are then presented as axioms. Deduction goes from the general to the specific. After study of the general has led to logical axioms, specific areas are examined in the light of those axioms.

Inductive reasoning proceeds on an entirely different basis. Induction is the study of specific individual parts and, from them, drawing conclusions about the whole. It assumes that what is true of any part is necessarily true for all parts and for the sum of the parts. It also assumes that what is true at one time for one set of circumstances remains true even when the circumstances change.

Chiropractic is based upon a major philosophical premise. The major premise is the starting point from which all deductions are made. All conclusions are drawn from fact number one. Fact number one: **the major premise of Chiropractic is that there is a Universal Intelligence in all matter, constantly giving to it all of its properties and activities, thus maintaining it in existence.** If this is a truth it explains many things which bewilder the mechanistic mind. To use this premise as the cornerstone for an entire philosophical concept, however, its validity must be demonstrated.

Proof is an ethereal thing. In fact, proof can exist only in its own acceptance. It is possible, for example, to deduce, from seeing that the ground is wet, that it has been raining. To prove that fact to someone who refuses to look outside is impossible. So it is with any proof. In order to constitute proof, the argument and evidence presented must first be accepted. Since acceptance is an individual act by an individual mind, this means, in essence, that one can only prove something to oneself. Nothing can ever be proven to another person. He can be shown logic and if it makes sense to him he has, in effect, proven it to himself. Any proof can be rejected by the simple expedient of refusing to use any of the five senses or, having used them, refusing to accept as logical the deductions thereof.

The presentation of a philosophical thesis is, in effect, an attempt to show others the logic of one's own arguments and to have that logic accepted. To try to inject one's philosophy into a closed mind is a hopelessly frustrating experience. Therefore, this exposition will devote itself to a simple presentation of evidence in the hope that the conclusions are inescapable.

While it is essential to prove a philosophy or premise to oneself before accepting it, general acceptance by others is irrelevant. A philosophy does not become valid when a great number of people accept it. Nor does it become invalid just because a great number reject it. Its validity can only be measured in terms of its acceptability in the mind and reason of one individual person.

In considering the validity of the Triune of Life, it is well to remember that not only is proof a very tenuous thing but that proof of intangibles is infinitely more tenuous than proof of tangibles. Since two thirds of the triune are intangible and only one third tangible, the task is an imposing one.

Universal Intelligence

Every good dictionary offers some half dozen or more different definitions of the word "intelligence." *Modern usage tends to equate intelligence with the power or ability to reason.* Older and more stable usage suggests the "power of the infinite mind" (Webster). Perhaps, rather than defining the word, it would be better to understand its function. As in studying the body, anatomy is a stepping stone to the study of physiology, the mechanical being important only because it serves the functional, so in etymology the practical purpose of the word is prime.

The **purpose of intelligence** is to organize and to maintain organization. Organization is the prime manifestation of intelligence, and intelligence the sole cause of organization. The two are totally interdependent. Thus, if the presence of intelligence is to be proven, it is necessary only to demonstrate what may be called "active organization" - *active* to prove presence and *organization* to prove intelligence.

The major premise of Chiropractic states: "There is a Universal Intelligence in all matter, constantly giving to it all of its properties and activities, thus maintaining it in existence." Since all of Chiropractic philosophy is based upon this vitalistic viewpoint, to accept the philosophy it is essential to accept the premise. Conversely, acceptance of the premise makes full acceptance of the philosophy a simple progression of logic.

Bearing in mind that proof exists only in the recognition of the facts and logic presented, and that proof of an intangible is infinitely more tenuous than proof of matter, it merely remains to present evidence of the major premise in a logical sequence. Those who endorse this premise do so because they prove it to themselves by concurring with the validity of its logic.

To study the universe as a whole is a task obviously beyond the scope of a finite human mind. The finite, or limited, cannot comprehend the infinite, or unlimited. It is impossible for the human mind even to visualize limitless time or limitless space, far less the innumerable complexities which fill that time and space. Of necessity, therefore, the study must be made and the evidence presented from some small and reasonably comprehensible portion of the whole.

Perhaps the smallest and least complex particle of matter is a good starting point. Let the atom, then, be the first object of study, and see if it does not prove the existence of organization and thereby the existence of intelligence.

The atom consists of a number of tiny units of electrical energy. In its nucleus there are positively charged units called protons and a number of neutrons which carry no charge. Electrons, or negatively charged particles, maintain a constant and consistent pattern of orbit around the nucleus. The nature of the matter is determined by the number of electrons present and the pattern or ring formation of the orbit.

Albert Einstein proved that matter and energy are one. *Matter* exists as such only as long as the electrons are maintained in organized orbit. It is the organization, or more specifically the intelligence which causes the organization, that maintains the matter in existence, by uniting its component parts together in an electrical bond. These component parts are not matter but units of electrical energy. If the organization is ever disturbed, the cohesive force is lost and the units separate with tremendous force as pure energy. It is only by organization of the electrical units that all of the matter in the universe is prevented from becoming one gigantic atomic explosion. Organization, then, is essential to the very existence of matter. Without it matter would not be, and the universe as we know it would disintegrate.

Organization, however, is an effect and therefore must have a cause. It has already been shown that organization is always a manifestation of intelligent action. Universal Intelligence is the cause of the organizing state of the universe. It is therefore the cause of all matter. It is accurate, then, to state that all matter is created and maintained in existence by the organizing activity of Universal Intelligence. This is a rephrasing of the major premise of Chiropractic.

On a larger scale, a study of any of the myriad examples of nature shows a delicate balance in the harmonious interrelationship of component parts. This harmonious balance is further evidence of an organization so vast and complex as to stagger the imagination. If ever any part of the balance of nature is disturbed, the entire structure is weakened.

History is rife with examples of man's attempts to alter nature to suit himself. Each time he has paid the penalty. He attempted to destroy the coyote because it attacked his poultry, only to find that field rodents, which are the natural prey of coyotes, multiplied excessively. Without their natural enemy to keep their numbers in check these rodents overran the countryside, destroying thousands of bushels of crops annually. Finally man had to import and release coyotes to restore the balance he had destroyed. Similarly, in an attempt to destroy bacteria, man is breaking down a vital component of the nitrogen cycle by which saprophytes convert organic wastes into the inorganic state for utilization by plant life. If he ever succeeds in destroying all bacteria, he will destroy all life.

So it is throughout nature. A series of checks and balances exists, maintaining the ultimate perfection of coordinated harmony. This harmony must be either the result of organization by a Universal Intelligence or a random and undisciplined series of coincidences. No third explanation is possible.

Coincidences do, of course, occur. To deny this possibility would be ridiculous. But for innumerable trillions of coincidences to accidentally coordinate and combine to maintain the universe in balanced harmonious perfection, is a little too much for the logical mind to accept. It is totally illogical to assume that such delicate equilibrium is the result of accident rather that intelligent organization.

No one would think of looking at DaVinci's *The Last Supper* and denying that its artist ever existed, or of hearing a Beethoven symphony and suggesting that it composed itself by accident. How then, by any stretch of the imagination, can one listen to the symphonic harmony of the universe and deny its composer? How can one observe its balanced artistic beauty and suppose that it happened by accident?

To deny organization in the universe as a manifestation of Universal Intelligence is to deny all logic and all reason, and to fall back on insupportable superstition.

Innate Intelligence

Since the topic under discussion is the Triune of Life, an effort must now be made to establish a relationship between Universal Intelligence and life. As has been shown, Universal Intelligence is that which maintains in existence all matter, whether living or not.

It manifests itself through a series of universal laws, which are immutable, and universal forces, which are unswerving and without solitude for the environment in which they work. One might well ask, then, how living things are able to survive through countless generations when the very nature of universal forces is destructive toward structural matter. The answer, like the answers to so many vital questions, is basically simple. An understanding of it, however, is essential to an understanding of Chiropractic philosophy.

All matter may be divided into two great categories: animate or living things, and those which are inanimate or have no life.

Living things exhibit certain basic manifestations called the "signs of life," which are:

1. Assimilation
2. Excretion
3. Adaptability
4. Growth
5. Reproduction

Inorganic matter and organic matter which is no longer living do not exhibit these signs.

It will be noted that each of the above is the result of organization and is therefore an effect of an intelligent cause. This is why living things are called organisms and living matter, organic. The words "organic" and "organism" indicate that the matter involved is "organized in a pattern of mutual interdependence." (Oxford).

The cardinal difference between the animate and the inanimate is the state of organization present. The inanimate is organized on a level no higher than the molecular. It is therefore maintained in existence but is incapable of manifesting any of the signs of life. It does not, for example, adapt to changes in the environment and therefore is at the mercy of the elements. Molecules of inanimate matter may become bonded together, by accident or design, to form masses with varying degrees of resistance, but as natural elements act upon them, they are gradually broken down again to the molecular level. Each molecule exists as an independent entity without dependence upon any other.

Living matter, on the other hand, consists of molecules which are bonded together in an organized pattern. Each molecule exists not as an independent unit but as part of a coordinated unit.

The molecules each serve a definite purpose in the overall structure, united not by accident but by masterful design. All of the molecules present are organized for mutual interdependence, with the various properties of each contributing to the biological integrity of the functioning whole.

When acted upon by the elements, all matter is broken down to the lowest level of its organization. Inanimate matter is reduced to molecules but not to atoms, because the atoms are organized and bonded into molecules. In living matter the molecules themselves are organized into cells, and the cells into tissues, and the tissues into organs, and the organs into systems. Finally, all of the systems are united into the total organism, or living thing. This total integration and inter-activity of all the molecules demonstrates the presence of a much higher degree of organization than in inanimate matter. It is this higher level of organization that permits adaptation to take place, with the individual properties of all molecules being selectively utilized for survival of the whole.

If animate matter has a higher degree of organization than inanimate matter, it necessarily follows that it also has a higher degree of intelligence. The more complex the organizational task, the greater the intelligence needed to accomplish it. There can be no denying that living things are more highly organized than nonliving things. Therefore, they must have some additional organizing intelligence.

Inanimate matter is organized energy. Animate matter has the additional capacity to reorganize intelligently in order to adapt to an ever-changing environment; to survive. When it ceases to reorganize and adapt, it is no longer alive. The difference between life and non-life, then, is the ability of the living to reorganize itself intelligently. It has an inborn or innate intelligence to accomplish this reorganization.

It should be clearly understood that reference is not being made here to the human mind. As far as is known, a blade of grass or an amoeba has no ability to reason. Yet, the inter-function of their component parts is as intelligently organized as that of man, the most complex of nature's creatures. A tulip bulb planted upside down produces a stem which curves 180 degrees to pierce the surface of the ground and thrust upward toward the sunlight. This is intelligent action, neither random nor haphazard, but a definite adaptive response to circumstances.

It is true that man is a reasoning creature, but that ability to reason is the product of a totally different type of intelligence. It is essential to differentiate between the two. It is to make the distinction between them that Chiropractic philosophy uses two different terms.

The power to reason and to decide upon a course of action in accordance with that reason, the ability to remember, the faculty to form value judgements, are all manifestations of an intelligence which man himself controls. This is called the "educated mind." Its quality and quantity vary greatly from person to person. It can be enhanced by learning or damaged by illness. It deals with external matter.

The inborn wisdom of any living thing, which maintains its parts in active organization for the purpose of function, is called Innate Intelligence. This is the intelligence responsible for all things internal. It makes the upper teeth grow downward and the lower teeth grow upward. It increases the heart rate when we walk upstairs. It regulates the action of some 250 different glands simultaneously. It maintains and coordinates dozens of organs, hundreds of muscles, thousands of miles of blood vessels, and countless trillions of cells. It never sleeps. It cannot be injured. It is as great in the moron as in the genius. It is always present 100 percent in every living thing from the most complex down to the simplest unicellular particle of life.

It is this Innate Intelligence which forms one of the three facets of the Triune of Life. It could be defined as "that expression of Universal Intelligence which exists in all living things, the specific localized intelligence by which living things assemble universal matter and adapt universal forces into a state of active organization."

Webster defines life as the "vital force, whether regarded as physical or spiritual, the presence of which distinguishes organic from inorganic matter." That which is living remains so by organized function. The Innate Intelligence is responsible for this organized function. There can be no life without it. It is the life force, the cause of all living function.

Although the presence of Innate Intelligence is actual and demonstrable, its location has to be theoretical. The brain is the organ through which coordination is maintained. All motor and trophic impulses originate there, and all sensory impulses are interpreted there. It seems reasonable to assume, therefore, that the brain is the place in which Innate Intelligence is located. In actuality, however, there can be no specific location for Innate Intelligence. Being immaterial, it does not occupy space. To say that it is located in the brain would be to deny that it is located anywhere else. Paradoxically, it is everywhere, yet has no location at all.

The human mind, being finite, is unable to comprehend the infinite. Yet such is the nature of man's quest for knowledge that he tries to understand that which is beyond his comprehension. In so doing he necessarily distorts it by bringing it down to the confined limits of his imagination. He tends to visualize Innate Intelligence as some anthropomorphic figure sitting up in the brain pulling wires, pressing buttons and giving orders to all body parts by means of a complete telephone system. It is this type of distortion of truth that causes much misunderstanding of Chiropractic and is no doubt responsible, in part at least, for rejection of the entire philosophy by many lay people and chiropractors alike. In actuality, they are rejecting not the philosophy but their own distortion of it.

Acceptance demands either understanding or faith. Chiropractic is not a religion. It is not based on faith. It is a philosophy, and therefore its self-proof must be based upon understanding. To understand an intangible is admittedly difficult, yet the reality of dozens of intangibles is accepted by all schools of thought.

Electricity is an intangible. It is not directly observable by any of the five senses. Yet it is a very real thing, the presence of which is easily demonstrable by its manifestations.

The same is true of the educated intelligence. Nobody has ever seen one, or heard it, or smelled or tasted or touched it. Yet nobody ever thought to question whether there is such a thing. By the very act of questioning, they would be using and thereby demonstrating their own educated intelligence.

Innate Intelligence is similarly demonstrable by studying its manifestations. Could the perfection of interrelated harmonious functioning of the human body be random and coincidental? If not, the only alternative is that there is, inborn within that body, an organizing intelligence.

There is one major difference between the educated intelligence and Innate Intelligence, and that is the quality of perfection. Since it is a part of and yet apart from Universal Intelligence, Innate Intelligence must be as perfect as the perfection of creativity itself. It is always 100 percent present and functioning 100 percent as the active organizing force of every living thing.

This characteristic of infallibility is an important one for it means, in essence, that the body, by the wisdom within it, always knows what is best for perfect function. There is an innate awareness of every innate need. It further means that Innate Intelligence will always act in the best interest of that body at all times, limited only by the matter with which it has to work and the time available for such work. It is, in fact, the doctor of the body, with the great advantage over all other doctors of begin right 100 percent of the time.

Hans Selye, MD, in his great book, *The Stress of Life*, records the findings of a lifetime dedicated to researching the dynamics of life. He states that life is a constant process of adaptation. Indeed, adaptation can be said to be the most significant of life's processes. This is not to suggest that other functions are insignificant or that life could go on without them. It means, rather, that all functions can be considered as forms of adaptation.

The ability to change function instantly in response to need is a tangible demonstration of the difference between the living and the nonliving. A living body, when cut, moves instantly to initiate repair processes, as well as the many other responses needed to adapt to the new situation. Every single change in internal or external environment demands a corresponding adaptive change by the living organism. Failure to make that change results in the same destructive effect on living matter that universal forces have on nonliving matter.

Adaptation, to be totally effective, must be perfect not only as to character but also as to time. A change that does not occur at the specific moment of need does not fulfill its purpose. In fact, the net result of such a change may be destructive rather than constructive. Adaptation is a constant function of Innate Intelligence. Since the internal environment changes in thousands of ways every second of life, adaptive response must also be as constant and as rapid. By this method and only by this method can the intelligence of the body fulfill its purpose of maintaining coordinated function, with each part doing its job for the benefit to the whole unit.

Matter

Adaptation, then, is the expression of the organization of life. But it is not life. Innate Intelligence alone is not life but rather the intangible basis for life. The tangible basis for life is matter. The immaterial, or intangible, can no more be said to be life than can the matter, or tangibles. Nobody would suggest that matter is life. It is an essential part of life but no more than that. The same is true of intelligence. Life itself is a composite of the two, consisting of the expression of the one through the other. Life is defined by Chiropractic as "the expression of intelligence through matter." Obviously, both must be present for life to exist.

It was shown earlier that all matter is maintained in existence only through atomic organization by Universal Intelligence. All matter therefore expresses intelligence. If life is "the expression of intelligence through matter," then all matter has life in the broad sense, for it all expresses the intelligence that created and maintains it. A clarification must now be made to differentiate between this broad sense and the narrower meaning of popular usage. It is true that in the broad sense all matter can be said to have life because it expresses the intelligence of creativity. It has also been shown, however, that the organizational state of that which we call living matter is at a much higher level. The difference lies at the level of organization and with the key words: adaptability and reorganization.

By popular usage the word "life" connotes that which is not only maintained in existence by Universal Intelligence but is also responsive to an Innate Intelligence. The presence or absence of an Innate Intelligence is the determining factor of differentiation between the living and the nonliving. The matter is structurally the same; the organization is different.

Matter is defined chemically as anything which has weight and occupies space. Any particle of matter can be divided and subdivided into smaller and smaller pieces until it finally reaches that state where any further subdivision would necessitate changing the basic electrochemical structure of the substance. If that basic electrochemical structure consists of single atoms, the substance is called an element. If the basic unit consists of two or more dissimilar atoms, the substance is called a compound, and the basic unit is a molecule.

Chemically speaking, an organic compound is one containing atoms of carbon. In this thesis, however, the word "organic" refers to living matter or matter which has once been living. This represents no difference of opinion with accepted scientific thought, merely a reference to the fact that carbon-containing compounds are formed by chemical reactions which take place only in living matter. Every carbon-containing compound found in nature is or was at one time part of the cell structure of some form of animal or plant life.

When two or more dissimilar substances are bonded together physically they form a mixture which can be broken down with comparative ease. When they are bonded together electrochemically they form compounds which can then be broken down only as the result of another electrochemical reaction.

Compounds, then, are stable substances which can be formed or split only by chemical reaction. This perhaps gives some insight into one of the most interesting phenomena of the living body. The various glands and organs of the body function as complex chemical factories. Each one manufactures a multitude of different organic compounds for the body's use.

The newborn infant contains within it everything it will ever need throughout life, with the exception of food, water and oxygen. As food is taken into the gastrointestinal tract it undergoes a series of chemical reactions. The first of these is the analysis and breakdown of the food into its component elements which are then transported through the serous circulation to various glands and organs. Here they are selectively resynthesized into such compounds as the body needs. In this manner all body chemicals and all body tissues are made. That which was eaten for lunch yesterday is today walking, talking flesh and blood. From a ham and cheese sandwich with lettuce and mayonnaise on rye bread and a glass of milk, the body manufactures bile, adrenaline, lymph, blood, eye tissue, liver tissue, brain tissue, and all of the other multitude of complex body structures.

From dead, inert matter, living cells arise by the application of the intelligence that is within.

Obviously, in order for the glands and organs to function perfectly and to manufacture chemical compounds of correct quality there must be an adequate intake of elements. This means that food intake must not only meet minimum requirements as to quantity but also be of correct elemental quality or type.

The body is extremely economical in its use of matter. It wastes nothing which may be of value. Even that which is a toxic by-product of some cellular function may be utilized as an essential substance by another cell in a distant part of the body. Normal muscle activity, for example, produces lactic acid which is toxic to the muscle cells and, if allowed to accumulate, will cause tetanic spasm. Lactic acid, however, properly broken down and resynthesized in a complex series of biochemical reactions, is a vital substance for heart physiology. When muscle activity increases, heart action also increases in order to supply more blood for the muscles. The extra muscle activity produces the additional quantities of lactic acid which the extra heart action demands. Thus the laws of demand and supply maintain perfect reciprocal armony within the living body.

After death, when chemical reactions in the body are governed only by unadapted universal laws, there is no such reciprocal harmony. Lactic acid accumulates in the muscles producing a total tetany known as *rigor mortis.*

In life, all of the matter of the body responds to the governing intelligence of the body, thereby expressing or giving action to that intelligence. The body itself, of course, is composed entirely of matter. The matter, or material substance, of the body is the form through which Innate Intelligence expresses itself. It is the second constituent of the Triune of Life.

Force

In the foregoing paragraphs, the two vital constituents of the living body have been discussed. A body without intelligence would be a corpse. It would have no life. It would be unable to adapt to changes in its environment and therefore could not survive. It would be inanimate clay. Matter without Innate Intelligence is not alive.

Similarly, Innate Intelligence without matter must be considered not alive. It would have no presence. Rather it would be an ethereal or spiritual manifestation without corporeal entity. There can be no life without matter.

From this it might seem that life is the coincidental presence of matter and intelligence. However, the mere presence of both is not sufficient. Bacteria are alive and therefore indicate the presence of intelligence. In a dead body there are bacteria, Therefore, in a dead body there is to be found both matter and intelligence existing coincidentally. But the body is still not alive. In order for there to be life there must be matter and intelligence and a link to unite the two. Only in this way can matter express intelligence and intelligence be expressed through matter.

Life, it must be remembered, is not the presence of intelligence and matter, but the expression of intelligence through matter. Hence, intelligence plus matter still need a link to unite them for there to be life.

The link which unites the two is *force.* Force completes the Triune of Life and is just as essential as the other two factors. That which in Chiropractic is called "force" is called "energy" in the study of physics. The two are synonymous and interchangeable. There are two forms of energy: kinetic and potential. Kinetic energy is energy in action, or in motion. It is applied energy. Potential energy on the other hand is energy which is tied up or stored.

The energy of force which unites Universal Intelligence with matter is potential. It is that which maintains atoms in existence and also forms the electrical bond between atoms in a molecule. If a molecule is divided by chemical reaction, potential energy is released to become kinetic energy, usually in the form of heat.

The living body, like all other matter, is composed of atoms and molecules and is therefore a storage-house for potential energy. It is also a vast laboratory wherein chemical reactions are constantly taking place which convert potential energy into kinetic energy. The body is, in fact, a subsource of kinetic energy. It takes in potential energy in the form of food and converts it to kinetic energy by physiological chemistry.

All matter is the result of Universal Intelligence. Energy and matter are interchangeable by the formula $E=mc^2$. Therefore, all energy is the result of Universal Intelligence. Rephrased, this means that Universal Intelligence is the sole source of force. This point is of particular importance, because it gives some insight into the nature of force. Universal Intelligence is, by definition, perfection. Thus, that which it creates and maintains is perfect. All matter is perfect and all force is perfect.

Universal forces are the generalized forces of the universe. They are governed by universal laws. They are absolutely not adapted to constructive purpose and will therefore act to destroy structural matter. They can, however, be adapted. The mission of Innate Intelligence is to adapt universal forces for use in the body. The function of Innate Intelligence is to create forces to fulfill this mission.

The function of intelligence is to create force. The function of Innate Intelligence is to create innate forces. Innate forces are adaptive. Their purpose is to adapt universal forces for the body's use.

A universal force may be beneficial or harmful to the body. An innate force is always beneficial. That is its purpose. Its action upon universal forces is to change them, if possible, to their exact opposite so that they work according to the laws of adaptation.

Innate forces are forces arranged by Innate Intelligence for use within the body. They are universal forces assembled or adapted for dynamic functional purposes: to cause tissue cells to function or to offer resistance to environmental force. They may be used for the adaptation of other universal forces which have not yet been adapted, or to balance, annul, check, augment or otherwise adapt them, or adapt to them.

Resistive forces are those innate forces which are called into being to oppose the invasion of external forces into the body. They may be physical or chemical in nature, and are specific to resist a specific invasive force.

Invasive forces are universal forces which invade and act upon the body in an unadapted or destructive manner. They, too, may be physical or chemical in nature and call forth a specific response from innate forces.

When an external invasive force meets with an internal resistive force, the result is a concussion of forces which may be constructive and usable by the body or destructive and unusable by the body. When resistance is low, the concussion tends to be more destructive.

The principle of a Chiropractic adjustment is to intentionally introduce a specific, limited, external invasive force to the spine. This meets with the internal resistive force of the body, and the resultant concussion of forces is used within the body by Innate Intelligence to correct vertebral subluxation. This is a classic example of *force* being used by *intelligence* to affect *matter*. It also shows how external forces are adapted for use within the body.

An incorrectly applied adjustive thrust would also meet with an internal resistive force but, in this case, the resultant concussion of forces may not be utilizable by Innate Intelligence. It would then either be neutralized to have no effect or would overcome the innate resistance and have a destructive effect. Ill timed or unbalanced resistive forces may result in subluxations, luxations, sprains, torn tissue or fractures. Such a mishap could occur, for example, by walking down five steps when only four exist, or by applying great strength to lift something thought to be heavy when in reality it was very light. This would be using more resistive force than the occasion called for, causing an unbalanced concussion. It should be noted that these unbalanced or improper resistive responses are always due to mistakes by the educated mind. Innate Intelligence, being perfect, makes no mistakes. Only educated, or imperfect, mind can err.

To err is indeed human, and if man were "only human" as he so often claims in order to excuse his mistakes, he could not long survive. The mind that forgets to wind the alarm clock at night could not safely be entrusted with the trillions of regulatory tasks of running a human body. Universal Intelligence, therefore, assigns this task to a part of itself within each living thing and equips it with whatever forces are necessary to accomplish the job. These innate forces are the link between intelligence and matter, and permit the intelligence to express through the matter. They are the third constituent of the Triune of Life.

Mental forces are those innate forces which are generated in the brain and travel via nerves to all parts of the body. They are also called mental impulses and, incorrectly, nerve impulses. While it is true that they travel via neural pathways, they originate in the brain as an intangible result of mental processes, and should therefore properly be called mental impulses. The rays of the sun are not called atmosphere rays just because they travel through the atmosphere. They originate from the sun and are named accordingly. So should it be with mental impulses or mental forces.

Science has long sought to classify the nature of mental impulses, but since they are neither physical nor chemical no answer has yet been found. The method of neural transmission of mental forces is described as an electrochemical phenomenon and has been understood by neurophysiologists for some time. But to understand their prime mode of transmission is not to understand the forces themselves. Recent experiments with "thought waves" at Duke University have shown that although nerves are a major pathway for the transmission of mental forces they are by no means the only pathway.

Chiropractic is deeply involved with the neural transmission of mental impulses, and more specifically with the interference to that transmission which is an integral part of vertebral subluxation. The innate forces generated within the body are always 100 percent, since they are a result of a perfect intelligence. They can fail in their appointed mission only when their transmission is blocked. Even when they are overcome by external invasive forces, it is not because of a lack of perfection of the innate force but because of the limitations of the adaptive powers of the body. They are still 100 percent perfect within those limits.

It was stated earlier that Universal Intelligence is the sole source of all force. This means that Universal Intelligence is the source of innate forces. Since Universal Intelligence is perfection and each of its products and effects is similarly perfect, this means that innate forces are always perfect.

Perfection of the Triune

By definition, everything in the universe, both tangible and intangible, is the result of Universal Intelligence. This means that all matter, all intelligence and all forces are the result of Universal Intelligence. They are, therefore, all perfect for their purpose 100 percent of the time. The only possible cause of imperfect action, then, is the superimposed influence of some secondary intelligence. That secondary intelligence is the human intellect, or the *educated mind,* with which man is endowed. Why man was given command of an intelligence which can result in imperfect action and the free will to decide when to use it is a subject on which many philosophers have pondered and expounded. It is a subject too vast to be treated adequately as a side issue of this particular exposition and no attempt to do so will be made.

Suffice it to note that all manifestations of Universal Intelligence are necessarily perfect. Thus, even the imperfections of educated mind must be perfect for their purpose.

Innate Intelligence is perfect yet it cannot adapt to maintain the body in life if any vital organ is destroyed, or if two-thirds of the body's blood is suddenly removed, or nutritional or oxygen intake is cut off. Innate Intelligence has limitations of adaptability because the matter which expresses it has limitations of adaptability. Similarly, innate forces have limitations of resistance and adaptability. When any of the aforementioned limitations is surpassed, it is not as a result of imperfection of any of the triune but rather as a result of the perfection of the limitations granted to them and placed upon them by their creator. Universal laws govern all matter and all force. They are a prime manifestation of Universal Intelligence. They are immutable and inviolable. Man cannot intentionally or unintentionally break a universal law. If he acts contrary to a law, it will not be broken; he will.

The living triune, then, is perfect as to quality and quantity but has certain limitations within which it must work. Like all other effects of Universal Intelligence, it can exist only within the framework of universal laws.

Innate Intelligence is always 100 percent in living matter. It is perfect as to both quality and quantity in health and in dis-ease. It is either present 100 percent or absent 100 percent. It is the difference between life and death. There is no in between. Even in terminal illness the intelligence is working at 100 percent perfection with whatever it has available right up to the moment of death.

Innate forces, being produced by Innate Intelligence, are similarly 100 percent. They may vary as to quality and quantity but only at the dictates of Innate Intelligence. They are always 100 percent of what is needed by any body cell at any given moment. They do not lessen in dis-ease or impending death, though blockage of their transmission may render them ineffective.

Matter, then, is the only part of the triune which can be less than 100 percent. This pertains qualitatively as well as quantitatively.

The word "health" means "hale" or "whole." For a body to be healthy, therefore, it must be whole. This is to say that each of its components, tangible as well as intangible, must be present 100 percent. If a body is deprived of any part or parts through surgery, accidental trauma, pathology or congenital defect, it can never again experience total health. Innate Intelligence, through its use of innate forces, will utilize the parts that are left with the best possible economy to function as perfectly as the imperfect matter will allow, but total health demands totality of matter.

Health, then, becomes a relative factor. Total health, having a prerequisite of total matter, must be irrevocably gone when a part or parts are permanently removed from the whole. This limitation of matter does not lessen the task of Innate Intelligence. To the contrary, it increases the difficulty of adaptation and places greater stress than ever upon the remaining parts. Total health is then inevitably lost, and all that remains is relative good health, that is to say, the best possible state of organized function under the circumstances.

It is said that a person is healthy when all of the component parts are working together in harmonious mutual function in response to a single control. If the matter is 100 percent then health can be 100 percent. If the matter is only 90 percent then the best that can be expected is 100 percent harmonious inter-function of that 90 percent. This is *relative health.*

Ill-health, or *dis-ease,* is the state wherein, regardless of the percentage of body parts present or absent, those that are present are lacking in mutual harmonious inter-function.

One hundred percent health is 100 percent organization of 100 percent of matter. Relative health is 100 percent organization of less than 100 percent of matter. Dis-ease is less than 100 percent organization regardless of the percentage of matter.

The word "function" means purpose. Since all matter, all intelligence and all force are manifestation of Universal Intelligence, or *intelligent creation,* each must serve some intelligent purpose. That purpose is its function.

The function of intelligence is to create force.
The function of force is to unite intelligence and matter.
The function of matter is to express force.

It can be seen from the above listed functions that life is a coordinated fulfillment of these functions. One hundred percent of life, or 100 percent health, is the 100 percent coordinated fulfillment of these functions. In order for the functions to be coordinated, the principle of "time" is involved. The sixth principle of Chiropractic philosophy states that "there is no process which does not take time." This fact is so self-evident as to require no proof. However, to accept it as fact is not necessarily to recognize its importance. Adaptation, the very essence of the mission of Innate Intelligence, is a process, and like all other processes it takes time. Coordination takes time. Creation of innate forces takes time. Transmission of those forces through matter takes times. If the time factor is imperfect, either increased or decreased, the resultant function will be imperfect. If hydrochloric acid from the oxyntic cells of the stomach is produced too soon there is hyperchlorhydria at the moment of need. If it is produced too late there is hypochlorhydria at the moment of need. Perfect function demands perfect timing. The result of vertebral subluxation is to alter the time it takes to transmit mental impulses from brain to tissue cells. The result must be imperfect function.

It has been shown that, of the three components of the triune, only matter can ever be less than 100 percent. It would then appear to follow that the only cause of imperfect total function is a deficiency of matter. This, however, is not true. It has also been shown that even when matter is deficient, relative health can remain at 100 percent of its potential.

The concern of Chiropractic is for those cases where health is at less than 100 percent of its potential regardless of the amount of matter present. Chiropractic is concerned not with the degree of matter present but with the degree of the expression of Innate Intelligence through that matter. Intelligence is always 100 percent. Force is always at 100 percent. How then can dis-ease, or lack of expression, occur?

Again the answer is a simple one, yet is the basis for all Chiropractic practice. The answer is that interference to the transmission of innate forces can and does occur. This and this alone is the cause of imperfect expression and resultant dis-ease.

Obviously, whether or not innate forces can be interfered with is a prime question. If they cannot, then there is no cause of dis-ease. Since there can be no effect without a cause, this would mean that dis-ease could not exist.

Transmission of Force

Article 122 states:
"The cause of Dis-ease is interference with transmission of mental impulses."

There is a tendency today to suppress or deny this flat statement of provable fact and to suggest that vertebral subluxation, which is the physical representation of interference to transmission, is *a* cause rather than *the* cause of dis-ease. This attitude of compromise is the result of failing to understand the term "dis-ease," and equating it with the medical term "disease."

The word "disease" implies an entity, a presence of something which has affected the body adversely. There are some 1,860 named diseases, as of this writing, each different and demanding different medical treatment. Dis-ease, on the other hand, denotes the absence of an entity. The entity that is absent is coordinated, organized function, or relative health. Disease, the indefinable presence of symptoms, can be manifested when the body is functioning perfectly. This takes place during retracing and also during the repair process after the cause has been corrected, but before repair is complete. During that time function is perfect for that body in its current state of unwholeness, but symptoms may persist.

Conversely, dis-ease can be present when there is no disease. When vertebral subluxation is extant, but before the resultant tissue damage has reached the identifiable symptomatic stage, there is, of course, dis-ease, or incoordination, but no disease.

When Chiropractic states that interference with transmission is *the* cause of dis-ease, it refers specifically to *dis-ease* and not disease. Perhaps modem chiropractors should consider using the word "disharmony" to replace the old term "dis-ease" and so avoid confusing it with the medical entity of "disease."

Those who would state that a knife wound or other external trauma produces dis-ease forget that all tissue present is still functioning at 100 percent of its potential unless and until interference to transmission occurs. Therefore, while a wounded body may manifest symptoms of disease, there is no dis-ease if the transmission of innate forces is unimpaired.

Poisons, on the other hand, may produce both disease and dis-ease. The disease or symptomatic changes occur as a result of direct tissue damage (reduction of the quality and/or quantity of matter.) The disease occurs as a result of chemical interference to transmission. It must be remembered that the cause of dis-ease is not vertebral subluxation but interference to the transmission of mental impulses. The art and science of Chiropractic deals with the location and correction of vertebral subluxations, and certainly vertebral subluxation is a common, and perhaps the most common, cause of nerve interference. But nerve interference, and therefore dis-ease, can be caused by other factors.

A severed nerve due to accident or surgery, nerve tissue destruction from a poison, intentional nerve blockage used in anesthesia, and synaptic dysfunction caused by ingestion of aspirin or other drugs are all possible causes of interference to transmission. Each of these, by virtue of the interference, will result in dis-ease. Chiropractic, however, deals with only the correction of vertebral subluxation and not with these other causes of dis-ease.

Dis-ease is incoordination or malfunction of that matter which is present and functionable, not a lack of matter or a lack of the functionability of matter. It is true that 100 percent health demands 1 00 percent quality and quantity of matter. But less than that 100 percent quality or quantity of matter results not in dis-ease but merely in the body having less to work with. The cause, and the *only* cause, of dis-ease is interference with the transmission of mental impulses between the brain, or coordinating center, and the tissue cells of the body.

Perhaps a study of force in general and interference in general will lead to a better understanding of specific innate forces and specific interference to those forces.

The only source of force is Universal Intelligence. Universal forces are unadapted for constructive purposes. They are manifested in myriad ways. Food, drink, heat, weather, electricity and sunlight are examples of the manifestations of universal force. They may be harmful to the body or, when adapted, beneficial to it. Their transmission may be either direct, by radiation, or indirect, by conduction or convection via some form of matter.

They are always subject to some form of interference. Examples of such interference to universal forces are:

- A tree blocking the sun's rays, producing shade.
- A rheostat reducing the passage of electricity.
- A grounded and shielded booth breaking a magnetic field.

Such examples could go on almost indefinitely. They are to be seen by the thousands every minute of the day and can be physical or chemical in origin.

It is significant to note that all universal forces, while able to travel by means of radiation, travel faster and more directly by conductive or convective means.

The bolt of lightening which strikes a house is merely taking the most effective mode of transmission. Telephone communication is less likely to fade than is radio communication. Electricity travelling via a copper wire is more likely to reach its destination at a usable strength than if radiated.

Furthermore, different forms of universal force, or energy, exhibit a preference for different types of conductive materials. Due to the properties of the matter, some are better used to conduct various types of energy than others. Water, for example, is a fine conductor for electricity but a very poor conductor of heat.

It is also significant to note that conducted or convected forces are more easily interfered with than those which are radiated. This is due to the confining nature of the conductor or convector. To block radio waves is more difficult than to block telephone wires. The wide spread of radio waves means that some will go around the blockage unless it too is extremely widespread. A lead shield to stop x-rays must be much bigger than the x-ray film or the bucky grid, because the waves spread in an ever-increasing cone from the point of emanation. Electric impulses when transmitted through air similarly disperse, whereas when they are transmitted through copper wire they confine themselves mainly to that medium and do not spread.

In the living body innate forces conform to the same laws that govern all other universal forces. They are transmissible by radiation as well as by conduction and convection.

They, too, are subject to interference by either chemical or physical means.

It has been shown that all matter is capable of conducting force or energy. Specifically, the innate force referred to as a "mental impulse" is transmissible by any type of body tissue. Cartilage, having a high percentage of inert matrix in proportion to its living cellular structure, is the body's worst conductor but is still a conductor. Bone is also a fairly poor conductor. Blood, muscle tissue, and particularly heart muscle, which is described as a neuromuscular tissue, are high up on the list of efficient conductors. Nerve tissue, of course, being especially designed for the purpose of conducting mental impulses, is the conductor of all. It is the main mode of transmission of mental impulses. It is the physical means by which intelligence and matter are linked. It is also the place where interference to transmission takes place.

In order to understand how interference to transmission takes place, it is first necessary to understand more about transmission itself.

Scientific research has evolved several theories of nerve impulse transmission. The most commonly accepted is that the transmission is electrochemical. Each nerve fiber has as its outermost layer a semipermeable membrane which is positively charged on its outer surface and negatively charged on its inner surface. The permeability, however, is selective. That is to say, the positive ions are able to pass through this membrane while the negative ions remain on the other side. This results in a polarized state, or a difference in electrical potential between the two sides of the membrane (Helmholtz's double layer). When the nerve is stimulated there is, according to this theory, a physical and chemical change which results In an increase in the permeability of the membrane. This allows a flow of negative ions to pass from the outside of the membrane to the inside where they combine with their positively charged counterparts and create a state of electrical neutrality. The neutral or depolarized state irritates/stimulates the adjacent segment of membrane which in turn increases its permeability. Thus a wave of irritability/ stimulation passes unidirectionally along the nerve, with the synapses acting to ensure monopolarity, carrying the impulse wave to its ultimate destination.

Soon after the depolarization has taken place, constructive forces are set to work to restore the membrane to its original conditions so that it is prepared to transmit the next impulse as and when needed.

In the event of a vertebral subluxation, interference to transmission occurs. This fact is demonstrable by means of the electroencephaloneuromentimpograph, although the actual dynamics of the interference must remain theoretical until the phenomenon of transmission is fully understood.

If the above theory of membrane depolarization is correct, then a simple explanation of interference may be as follows.

The vertebral subluxation, being a small local sprain, produces inflammation as does any lesion. Swelling or local edema is a characteristic part of inflammation. The edema is an excess of extracellular fluid, which of necessity changes the permeability of the membrane. The excessive permeability permits an untimely interchange of the sodium and potassium ions, thereby depolarizing the membrane and rendering it incapable or less capable of normal function depending upon the amount of damage done.

It will also be noted that the improper depolarization from a vertebral subluxation has the same electrochemical potential as does a proper functional depolarization. It too may release energy which affects the adjacent point in the fiber, causing thereby the improper conduction of an impulse.

The foregoing is by no means the only acceptable theory of the physiology of vertebral subluxation. Certainly, the effect of the lesion upon the hormonal production of the nerve cannot be ignored. Neither can the compression factor which must occur when body tissues in an osteologically confined space are compressed by reduction of the bony lumen of the foramen.

Interference to the transmission of mental impulses can occur at the level of the nerve root, where it passes through the intervertebral foramen, or at the level of the spinal cord itself. This latter type of interference, produced directly or indirectly by the vertebral subluxation, has far greater injury potential than does the former. Whereas injury at the nerve root level can directly affect only the limited number of nerve fibers of that root, injury at the cord level can affect any of the billions of fibers which comprise the cord. This does not mean, however, that nerve root damage is even relatively unimportant. On the contrary, since every body cell is dependent upon the efficient function of all others, to deprive one of its proper nerve supply is to injure them all. In all cases, "nerve interference" must be interpreted as "nerve impulse alteration," not as a deficit. Indeed, more damage may result from an excess of force than from a deficit.

It must further be remembered that interference can occur on the afferent as well as the efferent side of the safety-pin cycle. If the brain is at any time deprived of knowledge of the circumstances of any of the body's parts, it cannot intelligently act to bring about adaptive changes.

For perfect function the link between intelligence and matter and between matter and intelligence must be 100 percent intact. If an impulse arrives a split second later than its proper time, it is an improper impulse for that moment. Thus, if a vertebral subluxation does not completely stop the passage of a given impulse but merely slows it down, or for that matter, speeds it up, it cannot fail to produce malfunction or dis-ease.

It is this transmission of force which is the prime, and indeed only, concern of Chiropractic.

Medical practice concerns itself with matter. Christian Science and Ontology, to name but two, concern themselves with intelligence. Chiropractic concerns itself with the link or communication between the two. It was to emphasize this that B.J. made his famous pun:

Christian Science - always mind-never matter.
Medical Science - always matter-never mind.

Health

Health is wholeness, or 100 percent expression of intelligence through matter. When the Triune of Life is perfect, health is perfect. When intelligence, which is always 100 percent, is unable to express 100 percent, it is because force, the link, is interfered with or unable to be properly transmitted. It can also be stated that health is harmony: the maximum state of organization in which every cell is harmoniously functioning to fulfill its purpose for the benefit of the entire organism. It is a state of supreme order.

Dis-ease is nothing more nor less than a lack of organization or order. Thus, malfunction is dis-order. There is no such thing as a stomach disorder or a blood disorder because the stomach and the blood have but one purpose: the total being. The total being is either in orderly, organized harmony or in dis-ease.

Dis-ease, dis-harmony or dis-order are all one and the same thing. They are but the functional manifestations of a single fact. The Triune of Life has been violated. The intelligence is unable to express 100 percent through the matter because the link between them, the vital force, has been interrupted. Unless and until the Triune of Life is restored to its natural perfection, life must, of necessity, be diminished. This is the principle of Chiropractic.

Bibliography from the First Edition

Stephenson, R.W., D.C., Ph.C.; *Chiropractic Textbook*; Vol. XIV; Palmer School of Chiropractic; 1927.

Palmer, B.J., D.C., Ph.C.; *The Philosophy of Chiropractic*, Vol. V; Palmer School of Chiropractic; 1919.

Fulton, John, M.D.; *The Textbook of Physiology*; W.B. Saunders Company; 1955.

Loethout, William D., Ph.D., Tuttle, W.W., Ph.D.; *Textbook of Physiology*; C.V. Mosby Company; 1952.

Seyle, Hans, M.D.; *The Stress of Life*; McGraw-Hill Company; 1954.

Speransky, A.D.; *A Basis for a Theory of Medicine*; International Publishers Company; 1943.

Young, L.E., Porter, C.W.; *General Chemistry*; Prentice Hall, Incorporated; 1954.

Websters - New International Dictionary.

New Oxford Dictionary; Oxford University Press; 1954.

A History of the Chiropractic Triune
Simon Senzon

Reggie Gold's (1963) PhC thesis, *The Triune of Life,* is one of the seminal works of philosophy in the chiropractic profession. The book you are reading, *The Triune of Life: Reggie Gold's Philosophical Legacy,* is a testament to the impact of the *Triune* and Reggie, who transformed the profession. Legacy is measured by how a text or a teacher influences subsequent generations. Reggie's *Triune* has inspired three generations of chiropractors (Table 1) to deepen their philosophical understanding and develop tools to communicate chiropractic simply, clearly, and logically. This chapter establishes the historical context from which the *Triune* emerged. This chapter, and other contributions to this book, can serve as a foundation to further develop triune studies in the chiropractic profession.

Table 1
Intellectual Generations of the Chiropractic Profession

Generation	Time period
1st	1913–1946
2nd*	1947–1980
3rd*	1981–2014
4th*	2015–2048

Note. From Senzon (2018a).
* Generations influenced by Reggie Gold's *Triune of Life,* first presented in his 1963 thesis.

The method for this chapter includes a search of the gray chiropractic literature, which was then organized historically. Gray literature is not controlled by big publishing houses and is usually published outside of the mainstream. This is the domain of the chiropractic triune. Presented here is a history of the facts and theories about the triune as it relates to the philosophy of chiropractic. This chapter consists primarily of excerpts from original texts and does not include a critical assessment of the primary and secondary sourced documents about the triune. As such, this chapter's historical timeline serves to contextualize the republished works of Reggie Gold and the amazing accounts from those who met him and were mentored by him. Each author in this book is part of the history, as is each reader.

Context for a Timeline of the Triune in Chiropractic

Establishing the historical context for triune in chiropractic is vital because of the impact on the profession and its different definitions in the writings of D.D. Palmer, B.J. Palmer, R.W. Stephenson, and Reggie Gold. In fact, the chiropractic literature includes many references to the term "triune" and there is a thread of congruence between the different definitions. However, understanding how the term has been used and how it has evolved throughout chiropractic history allows the next generation to build upon it with academic rigor, philosophical depth, and historical accuracy. Before exploring the chiropractic use of the term, it is useful to briefly consider it in relation to Western philosophy, religion, and how D.D. Palmer may have encountered the term.

Triune in Western Philosophy and Religion

The first triune in Western philosophy begins with Plato. For example, Plato's *Phaedrus* depicts reason, the highest function of the soul, as the charioteer, which is pulled by the body's internal drives: will and appetite (Plato, c. 370 BCE/1972). Harmony occurs when all parts work together, and disharmony occurs when the soul can't control the bodily forces. This tripart union has been viewed as the "triune soul" (Gebser, 1949/1985, p. 198) of spirit, soul, and body and the first integration within Western philosophy of body, mind, and spirit (Senzon, 1994). Additionally, Plato's *Timaeus* could be viewed as the origin of a distinction between Universal Intelligence and Innate Intelligence or the universal Good individualized into the plurality of creation (Senzon, 2011). The most well-known triune in the West is the Christian Trinity, which also has roots in ancient Greek philosophy (Santrac, 2013).

The triunes of Western philosophy and religion are foundational to the triunes found in writings about Spiritualism and magnetic healing. It is through these movements that D.D. Palmer most likely encountered the triune.

Spiritualism, Magnetic Healing, Osteopathic Philosophy, and D.D. Palmer's Triune

D.D. Palmer was a Spiritualist and a magnetic healer before he developed chiropractic. Spiritualism was the third-largest religious movement in the United States in the latter half of the 19th century. The movement combined a belief in the afterlife and spirit friends with a viewpoint sourced in Mesmer's paradigm that magnetic trance states were related to the energetic ether linking the universe together. Mesmer's practice and theory were the origins of hypnosis and magnetic healing (Albanese, 2007).

As a young man, before he is to find Spiritualism, D.D. Palmer studies for five years to become a minister in the Advent Church of Soul Seekers and then decides Spiritualism is a more logical path for him to follow. At age 28, D.D. Palmer (1872) writes a letter to the editor at the *Religio-Philosophical Journal*, in which he describes this personal transformation. In the letter, which is a tribute to the clairvoyant abilities of his first wife, Abba Lord Palmer, he refers to a "mesmeric sleep," where the "spirit or intelligence" (p. 6) can leave the body during a magnetic trance state. In the letter, he mentions that he has been attending Spiritualist circles and lectures for five years.

The *Religio* includes Abba Lord prominently, including advertisements and letters to the editor. In one letter, dated April 8, 1871, Abba Lord highlights how much she loves the "Religio" and describes her feelings about being a newly married medium:

> Brother Jones: Welcome! 'did I say to the dear RELIGIO, as it came last night to my home, and I greet it as an old friend, and bearer of sweet messages from thee-laborers in the cause of truth, that bring peace and joy to my soul. Thrice welcome is it now, because I can say it is received by husband and myself at *our* home; yet in the past, it has cheered my lonely life, made my purpose stronger, by its stirring and earnest words of kindness and counsel to live the life of a medium, which has been no easy task, and at times, one of humiliation...
>
> Mediums ought to live above envy, strife and vain-glory, aiming to work more harmoniously and zealously in the cause of truth, letting their acts be such that the world may

> know they have communed with angels. (A.L. Palmer, 1871, p. 6)

Several of the advertisements for Abba Lord's clairvoyant practice are published on the same pages as articles defining the term triune (Child, 1871b, 1871c, 1871d). This suggests that D.D. Palmer is likely to have seen the articles and may have been influenced at this early stage of his thinking on such topics.

Articles from two authors in the *Religio-Philosophical Journal* stand out because their writings about the triune are congruent with various chiropractic definitions. The first author is Henry Child (1871d), who writes,

> Through the varied conditions of earth-life, and the earlier conditions of spirit-life, man has been like a wandering comet; now he begins to move in his appropriate orbit as a planet, and the light which has hitherto been vague and uncertain, becomes clear and distinct. He is still a triune being, having an eternal physical, a mental and soul nature. (p. 5)

Another article by Child (1871a) is published on the same page as the "Medium's Directory" listing Abba Lord in New Boston, Illinois. Child proposes a new triune to replace trinities of Buddhism, Hinduism, Parsee, and Christianity: "electricity, light, and heat" (p. 3). He relates light to motion as an ethereal level, heat as material, and electricity as the balancer of life linking the other two. Child (1871c) also writes of the triune as body, mind, and spirit and proposes that the mental level is the "connecting link" of the triune (p. 5), joining the physical and soul (Child, 1871e).

The second author is Emma Hardings Britten. Her lecture *On the Spirit-Circle and the Laws of Mediumship*, delivered at Cleveland Hall in London on July 2, 1871, is published in the journal the same year. The lecture states, "The spirits inform us … that we are triune beings" (Britten, 1871, p. 2): matter, life, and spirit. Britten describes life as a universal element that permeates all matter, such as atoms, dust, flowers, and organisms. This concept of universal life is similar to one of R.W. Stephenson's (1927a) 33 principles, to be published more than 50 years hence in his *Chiropractic Textbook*. D.D. Palmer (1910) seems to have integrated these ideas, because he later writes of Universal

Intelligence in all matter and the soul as the intelligent life, which is the connecting link between the physical and the spiritual.

D.D. Palmer's conception of the triune may also have been influenced by the books he was reading. For example, two books he owned include similarities to his writings on the human aura and the link between spirit and matter. One of the books, *Vital Magnetism* by E.D. Babbitt (1874), will be included in D.D. Palmer's Traveling Library: the books he had bound together for ease of study when traveling (Senzon, 2014). Babbitt, "a prominent Spiritualist" (Jones, 1871, p. 5), is involved with the *Religio-Philosophical Journal* through contributions and advertisements (Babbitt, 1871, 1872). In his book, Babbitt (1874) describes the link between soul and body as the "life aura" (p. 19), a combination of vital magnetism and vital electricity. Another influential book for D.D. at this time is W.F. Evans' (1866) *Esoteric Christianity*, which cites Plato and describes the triune man as spirit, soul, and body. Evans also writes of a "Universal Life Principle, which is the intelligent, animating force of the world and of the human body" (p. 92). Evans is an influential proponent of Mind Cure (Albanese, 2007). A copy of Evans' book, signed by D.D. Palmer, is preserved in The Palmer Family and Chiropractic History Museum (personal communication, J. Knaak, June 15, 2015). The books by Babbitt and Evans include instructions for patient care using hands-on magnetic healing and mental cure, respectively. By 1886, D.D. Palmer, who has been learning by self-study for 14 years, will advertise himself as Dr. Palmer, vital healer, and started caring for patients full-time with his magnetic cure (Waters, 2013).

Another magnetic healer involved in Spiritualism at this time is A.T. Still, the founder of osteopathy (Albanese, 2007). There is no evidence that Still and Palmer met (Hart, 1997). However, D.D. Palmer was well-read in the osteopathic literature and likely influenced by it (Senzon, 2019), which includes influence from Still's theory of triune man. For example, nine months before using the term triune for the first time (D.D. Palmer, 1909b, p. 30), D.D. Palmer (1909c) cites Still's (1892) textbook, *The Philosophy and Mechanical Principles of Osteopathy*. In the book, Still writes of the triune man by first questioning how the will is controlled. He concludes:

> Man is triune when complete ... first the material body, second the spiritual being, third a being of mind which is

> far superior to all vital motions and material forms, whose duty is to wisely manage this great engine of life. (Still, 1892, p. 15)

This definition of the triune is reminiscent of Plato's metaphor of the charioteer, with reason guiding will and appetite. It also shares similarities with the many triune definitions described above.

And yet, even in the context of these various definitions of triune, D.D. Palmer's integration of these ideas is unique. For example, in Robert Fuller's (1989) book *Alternative Medicine and American Religious Life*, he proposes that D.D. Palmer made innovative contributions to the discourse of his era:

> Palmer's claim to originality lies in his interest in discovering the precise physiological routes through which the individualized segments of divine spirit, Innate, directs the life process within the individual. Palmer asserted that Innate generates life impulses through the medium of the brain, which in turn transmits them along nerve pathways to their different peripheral endings. (p. 22)

This insight by Fuller is crucial to fully appreciate the impact of D.D. Palmer's triune on the chiropractic profession. D.D. emphasizes the transmission of the life force: the intelligence expressed as health and normal function, conducted through the nervous system. Vertebral subluxation interferes with this expression of health. Thus, the practice of chiropractic, the chiropractic adjustment of vertebral subluxation to restore normal function, is central to D.D. Palmer's paradigm. His paradigm might be summarized in three parts: his perspective on the triune relationship connecting spirit, life, and body; his theory of vertebral subluxation and neurologically mediated health expression; and the chiropractic adjustment as the practice that brings forth the paradigm.

The First Triune in Chiropractic: D.D. Palmer's Paradigm

Before exploring how the term *triune* is used in the more recent chiropractic literature, it is essential to consider the origins of the triune concept, especially in the works of D.D. Palmer. Ultimately, understanding D.D. Palmer's use of triune in the context of his theory, practice, and moral viewpoint allows us to understand his paradigm more completely. This is crucial because D.D. Palmer's paradigm underpins the philosophy of chiropractic and the evolution of the use of triune in the chiropractic literature.

1909: D.D. Palmer First Uses the Term Triune

In September 1909, D.D. Palmer publishes a short article titled "Monstrosities," which deals with embryonic development gone awry or leading to "great congenital deformity" (D.D. Palmer, 1909b, p. 30), a topic D.D. has written about before, dating back to some of his earliest writings on Innate (Senzon, 2019). However, in this article, he expounds on the connection between spirit, soul, and body and uses triune for the first time. He describes the soul as the link between the spiritual and the physical, "the symphisis [sic] which makes a triune of spirit, soul and body" (p. 31). In his textbook, to be published the following year, D.D. Palmer (1910) expands on this concept that the soul is the "intelligent life," the vital link that unites spirit and body (p. 56). For D.D. Palmer, it is the connecting link that unites the spiritual and the physical, without which the two domains are "distinct from each other" (p. 691). Table 2 depicts five ways D.D. Palmer describes this triune.

Table 2
D.D. Palmer's Triune Definitions

Immaterial	Bond of Union (p. 56)	Material
Innate	Soul	Body
Innate	Intelligent life	Body
Immaterial	Vital	Material
Spirit	Soul (life of the body)/intelligence	Body
Spiritual	Connecting link	Physical

Note. From D.D. Palmer (1910, p. 691).

D.D. Palmer establishes this triune as central to his philosophy and links it to his moral vision. In the two paragraphs that follow the description of the triune in the original article, D.D. (1909b) writes about his moral duty as a chiropractor. The sentences about his "right and bounden duty" (p. 31) are taken from his new definition of chiropractic.

1909: D.D. Palmer Defines Chiropractic

D.D. Palmer's new definition of chiropractic is first published in March 1909. Besides the fact that he includes part of this definition in "Monstrosities," the definition is important to include in this discussion of his triune because it grounds the perspective of his philosophy - which views spirit, soul, and body as a unity—to the practice and theory of chiropractic. D.D. Palmer's (1909a) definition of chiropractic is as follows:

> *Chiropractic as a Philosophical Science* is founded upon the knowledge of functions performed by Innate in health and disease. When this controlling intelligence is able to transmit mental impulses to all parts of the body, free and unobstructed, we have normal action, which is health.
>
> Innate's desire, directing its vital energy, is transmitted thru the nervous system to specialize the co-ordination of sensation and volition.
>
> Displacement of any part of the skeletal frame, may press against and thereby cause impingement of nerves, which are the channels of communication, decreasing or intensifying their carrying capacity, creating either too much or not enough function, an aberration known as disease; the affection depending upon the shape of the bone, the amount of pressure, age of patient, nerves impinged and the individual make-up.
>
> *Chiropractic as an Art* adjusts by hand all displacements, subluxations of the 300 articular joints, more especially those of the vertebral column, for the purpose of removing nerve impingements, which are the cause of deranged functions. The long bones and the vertebral processes are used as handles by which to adjust displacements of the hard tissue of the skeleton; by so doing, normal transmission of nerve force is restored.
>
> Vital functions are personified physical expressions; normal amount is health. Every vital act is controlled by Innate Intelligence, managed thru the nervous system in

> proportion as the lines of communication are free and unobstructed.
>
> Knowing that our physical health and intellectual progress of Innate (the personified portion of Universal Intelligence), depends upon the proper alignment of the skeletal frame; therefore, we feel it our right and bounden duty to replace any displaced bones, so that the physical and spiritual may enjoy health, happiness and the full fruition of our earthly lives. (p. 63)

This definition introduces D.D. Palmer's latest development of chiropractic theory, which includes an insight that the pathophysiological process is dependent on multiple factors associated with each individual patient. This viewpoint evolves into the chiropractic theory of momentum of disease (Drain, 1946; B.J. Palmer, 1913a; Stephenson, 1927a). D.D. Palmer's (1909b) article on monstrosities includes the last sentence of this definition, thus connecting his perspective (the triune) to his theory, practice, and moral viewpoint. He will expand on this moral view in his final lectures in 1913 (Foley, 2016), which are published posthumously as "The Moral and Religious Duties of a Chiropractor" (D.D. Palmer, 1914). It is useful to consider these ideas together as D.D. Palmer's paradigm and especially important when interpreting other chiropractic definitions of the triune, because D.D. Palmer will stop using the term the following year.

1910: D.D. Palmer Stops Using the Term "Triune"

Interestingly, D.D. Palmer republishes "Monstrosities" in edited form in his textbook, replacing his 1909 "triune of spirit, soul and body"(p. 30) with "triplet":

> The breath of life is evidence of the union existing between spirit and body the intelligent life, known in the Good Book as the soul, the symphisis [sic] which makes a triplet of spirit, soul and body. The vegetative function, guided by intelligence, constitutes life—the soul. (D.D. Palmer, 1910, p. 631)

Earlier in the book, D.D. explains why he does not like the term "triune," but he never mentions that he used it the year before. Instead, he critiques the inclusion of the word "triune"—referring to spiritual, mechanical, and chemical—on a chiropractor's business card D.D. states that it is sacrilegious to use the term because it refers to the trinity of the "Godhead" (D.D. Palmer, 1910, p. 107). After this critique, he never uses the term again.

1910: D.D. Palmer Critiques One of B.J.'s Early Triune Models

It may seem hypocritical that D.D. Palmer condemns a term he had used only months before. However, when understood in context, we could infer D.D. Palmer's motives. For example, 1909 is the height of his public feud with his son, B.J. Palmer (Senzon, 2019), when D.D. focuses his energies on criticizing other chiropractors and elucidating his chiropractic paradigm. D.D. Palmer considered these *adjustments* to other chiropractors' ideas. These critiques culminate in his textbook, which includes "The Chiropractor's Adjuster" on the spine of the book (D.D. Palmer, 1910). Thus, D.D. Palmer's critique of the triune on the chiropractor's business card may have been a veiled attack on B.J. After all, in B.J.'s 1909 textbook, *Philosophy of Chiropractic* or Vol. V, he writes, "Man is a triunity (1) *spiritual*, which moves the (2) *mechanical*, thereby producing the (3) *chemical*" (B.J. Palmer, 1909b, p. 280). It is likely the business card owner was a student of B.J.'s, which leads D.D. to write, "To entertain a thot of uniting spirit and mechanical and chemical entities shows a lack of comprehension of terms" (D.D. Palmer, 1910, p. 108). B.J. (1909b) proposes several other early triune models, aspects of which are also critiqued by his father.

B.J. Palmer's central triune model, however, is actually congruent with D.D. Palmer's perspective: the unity of spirit, matter, and intelligent life. For example, as part of his critique of the business card, D.D. Palmer (1910) writes,

> The living body is subject to vital force, the expenditure of which is known as energy. It is not feasible to unite a spiritual entity to chemical action; the laws of chemistry and kinematics are incongruous.
>
> Man is not a machine—a mechanical contrivance run by mechanical power. The bodily functions are carried on by an energy known as vital force. Mental impulses are not power; they do not run the body. They are a production of

> Innate, spirit. Power and mental impulses are not synonymous. Man is not a machine—he is not subject to the laws which govern inanimate matter. Vital force furnishes the energy—impulses direct them. Impulses are not made, they are created. (p. 107)

This quote is important because it highlights D.D. Palmer's organismic viewpoint and demonstrates his theory that mental impulses are created and not defined as power. B.J. Palmer's model generally agrees with this although he proposes that mental impulses are created in the brain cell and then expressed as power at the tissue cell. Ultimately, it is D.D. Palmer's triune model that is central to the original chiropractic paradigm, as it is destined to be expanded upon and integrated throughout chiropractic theory and practice for more than a century to come.

B.J. Palmer's First Triune Models: Cycles and Complexity

Between 1906 and 1911, B.J. Palmer publishes six textbooks as Volumes 1 through 6 (B.J. Palmer, 1907, 1908a, 1908b, 1909b, 1911; D.D. Palmer & B.J. Palmer, 1906). By 1920 he updated each text, some with multiple editions (Faulkner et al., 2018). The subsequent editions include the latest ideas such as his multiple and complex triune models.

1907–1908: The Origins of B.J. Palmer's First Chiropractic Triune Model

In 1907, B.J. Palmer publishes his first solo-authored textbook as Volume 2 of the new Green Book series. The text contains original lectures on chiropractic, with innovative theories that build upon D.D. Palmer's chiropractic paradigm. The most significant contribution from this text is B.J.'s cycle of life, which emphasizes a three-part path: creation, transmission, and expression. It refers to the *creation* of the mental impulse within the brain cell, *transmission* of that impulse over the nerves to the periphery, and the *expression* of that impulse as power and healthy function at the tissue cell. B.J. (1909b) refers to these three aspects of the cycle as "life's three primary principles" (p. 402). When the cycle between these three principles is interfered with by vertebral subluxation, normal function cannot be expressed. The chiropractic adjustment restores the circuit so that the mental impulse can be expressed as normal function. The model is successfully argued at the landmark Morikubo trial in 1907 to demonstrate one aspect of chiropractic's distinct science (Senzon & Myers, 2019). B.J.'s cycle of life will go on to become a cornerstone of chiropractic theory for decades.

This new three-part pathway of the cycle of life exemplifies D.D. Palmer's perspective because it is an embodied approach to the unity of the spiritual, mental, and physical, mediated through the nervous system. Thus, the model captures the uniqueness of chiropractic as described above by Fuller (1989).

B.J. sees this new model as a major breakthrough because it captures the moment of creation, whereby the intelligence is unified with the physical through action; he considers the creation of the mental impulse as a sacred act of creation itself. Ultimately, the expression at the tissue cell, the embodiment of the intelligence in action, is how creation is expressed. The depth and non-fanatical breadth of B.J. Palmer's (1909b) perspective is captured in this quote about the relationship between the mental and the physical:

> Chiropractic is the first science that harmonizes the two. We maintain just as steadily, as the Christian Scientist, that all is mental first, *but it must be physically interpreted,* it must show its expression *in the body*, and have a definite path and a precise something to send through that which performs mental thoughts. Chiropractors, step by step, analyze the existence from God to physical function. We are not fanatic upon the mental aspect, nor are we clinging, alone, to the physical, ignoring everything else. Remember that, in and all around us, all the time, is this intelligent power or force, that this is the individuality, who places power in contact with physical, and our mental mind, thru brain, receives and places it through a transformation brain impulse. This latter is God personified in you and I. Brain impulse is unseen and unfelt in itself, cannot be sensed in any form, yet it is the exemplification of all that is pure, holy and righteous. It must have expression through a physical medium, which is our body. It has reached the form of impulse and while still power, internally manifested, it

> passes through nerves and from them causes action in muscles, which is mechanical action. This function, the outward expression, would be, if normal, a counterpart of the original principle. Man cannot assist nor give advice to Innate, therefore Christian Science is wrong; at base the M.D. is one-sided because either or both hold fast to only *one-half of the unit.* That is why Chiropractic is the only *philosophical study; it unites the two, makes of it a completeness.* I know of nothing which is *so definite in conclusions* and briefly given as the diagram upon the board. (p. 61)

It is unclear what diagram B.J. is referring to. However, less than a year after Volume 2 was published, in the lectures from the winter of 1908 (published the next year as Volume 5) he includes 37 diagrams in the 158-page chapter called "Cycles" (B.J. Palmer, 1909b). Figure 1 traces the cycle of life from the brain cell to the tissue cell and back, which was codified by Stephenson (1927a) as *the safety pin cycle.*

Figures 1 and 2

B.J. Palmer's Simple Cycle and Creation, Action, Impression Cycle

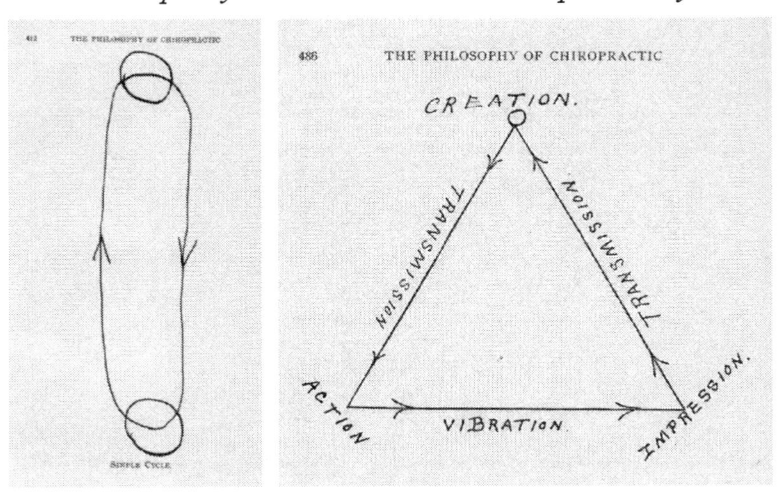

Note. Figures 1 and 2 are from B.J. Palmer (1909b), pages 412 and 486, respectively.

Figure 2 depicts a triad of creation, action, and impression, which captures the fullness of the cycle. This diagram exemplifies the entire model because, for B.J., it is the raw vibrations from the environment, which are impressed upon the senses and transmitted to the brain for interpretation, that are the source of the transformation. (This is the afferent half of the cycle, which begins with the impression from the tissue cell, the internal environment.) The creation of a mental impulse is when the intelligence merges with the raw energy, transforming it, which is then transmitted to the tissue cell for action. Successful function means that Innate Intelligence embodied the appropriate action to adapt to the environment. These ideas were expanded upon in complex detail as Volume 5.

1909: B.J. Palmer's Use of Triunity in Philosophy of Chiropractic *(Volume 5)*

In Volume 5, which is published and shipped on May 22, 1909 (Faulkner et al., 2018), B.J. Palmer (1909b) introduces the triune that D.D. will later critique: spirit, mechanical, and chemical. When discussing his insights about Innate Intelligence accessing the power, energy, and force of Universal Intelligence, B.J. describes the progress of the "triune man" (p. 358). He considers this a new breakthrough of thinking in regard to the "science of medicine" and the "*inner life of man today*" (p. 368). However, his essential contribution to triune studies during this series of lectures is his writing on "triunity" (p. 404).

B.J. Palmer (1909b) critiques religious and psychological doctrines that rely on things like spirits and the spirit realm. To him, embodiment is central. The link connecting physical and immaterial is of the utmost importance. For example, he writes, "But 'just how' to connect the *three phases into one* scientific or philosophical completeness — a triunity — has always been the conundrum that has never been solved until this lecture places the solution before you" (p. 405). For decades after this statement, B.J. Palmer will claim that chiropractic solves this oldest philosophical problem (Faulkner et al., 2018). In another description of the triunity, B.J. (1909b) writes, "What we have before us tonight is the study of a circuit to be entirely based upon intellectual creation, immaterial transmission through a material agent and physical expression of an immaterial power" (p. 408). By combining union and triune in the term triunity, he conveys a new level of depth about the chiropractic triune.

B.J. Palmer (1909b) suggests that chiropractic was born of the link between creation and transmission, which are glued to expression.

Expression leads to the final steps of function, or action of the tissue cell and coordination, which is successful adaptation. Thus, he writes that the cycles "complete the triunity of purpose" (p. 485), exemplified in what the second edition of Volume 5 refers to as the *restoration cycle.* The restoration cycle demonstrates how the correction of vertebral subluxation leads to the restoration of transmission, which then leads to coordination (Figure 3).

Figure 3

The Restoration Cycle from the First Edition of Vol. 5 (B.J. Palmer, 1909b)

488 THE PHILOSOPHY OF CHIROPRACTIC

PHYSIOLOGICAL CHANGES OF THE ABNORMAL CYCLE UNDER ADJUSTMENT OR RESTORATION OF INCOÖRDINATION TO COÖRDINATION.

Efferent Half.

1. Universal Intelligence.
2. Innate Intelligence.
3. Mental.
4. Creation.
5. Brain Cell.
6. Transformation.
7. Mental Impulse.
8. Propulsion.
9. Efferent Nerve.
10. Transmission.
11. Concussion of forces (awkwardly applied.)
12. Subluxation.
13. Interference with transmission.
14. Tissue cell.
15. Reception.
16. Excess or lack of personification.
17. Excess or lack of expression.
18. Excess or lack of function.
19. Incoördination (disease).

Afferent Half.

1. Universal Intelligence.
2. Innate Intelligence.
3. Mental.
4. Creation.
5. Brain Cell.
6. Transformation.
7. Mental Impulse.
8. Propulsion.
9. Efferent Nerve.
10. Transmission.
11. Adjustic concussion of forces.
12. Innate contraction of forces.
13. Subluxation adjusted.
14. Restoration of transmission.
15. Tissue cell.
16. Reception.
17. The circuit re-established.
18. Normal personification.
19. Normal expression.
20. Normal function.
21. Coördination (health).

Note. This figure is taken from J. H. Craven's personal copy of the first edition of Volume 5 (p. 488), which includes some handwritten corrections that would be integrated into the second edition (Palmer & Craven, 1916).

The restoration cycle is derived from the *normal complete cycle* (NCC), which is also introduced in Volume 5. This cycle demonstrates how the levels of Universal Intelligence, Innate Intelligence, and the Mental level are steps of this complex cycle (Figure 4). These levels of the cycle are illustrated by curved lines at the top of the diagram of the NCC (Figures 5). B.J. theorizes a sort-of step-down transformer, whereby a process unfolds from Universal Intelligence to Innate Intelligence to Mental, and then to the brain cell, where the creation of mental impulse occurs. Mental impulses are subsequently transmitted to the tissue cells. The other side of the cycle mirrors this process, with transmission coming from the environment—the domain of Universal Intelligence, which organizes all matter (B.J. Palmer, 1909b).

Figure 4

The Steps of the Normal Complete Cycle

NORMAL COMPLETE CYCLE.

Efferent Half		Afferent Half	
1.	Universal Intelligence.	1.	Coördination.
2.	Innate Intelligence.	2.	Tissue cell.
3.	Mental.	3.	Vibration.
4.	Creation.	4.	Impression.
5.	Brain Cell.	5.	Afferent nerve.
6.	Transformation.	6.	Transmission of vibration.
7.	Mental Impulse.	7.	Brain Cell.
8.	Propulsion.	8.	Reception.
9.	Efferent nerve.	9.	Mental.
10.	Transmission.	10.	Mental Interpretation.
11.	Tissue cell.	11.	Sensation.
12.	Reception.	12.	Ideation.
13.	Physical Personification.	13.	Innate Intelligence.
14.	Expression.	14.	Intellectual adaptation.
15.	Function.	15.	Universal Intelligence.
16.	Coördination.		

Note. The Normal Complete Cycle is taken from J. H. Craven's personal copy of the first edition of Volume 5 (p. 415), which includes some handwritten corrections that would be integrated into the second edition (Palmer & Craven, 1916).

Figure 5
Diagram of the NCC

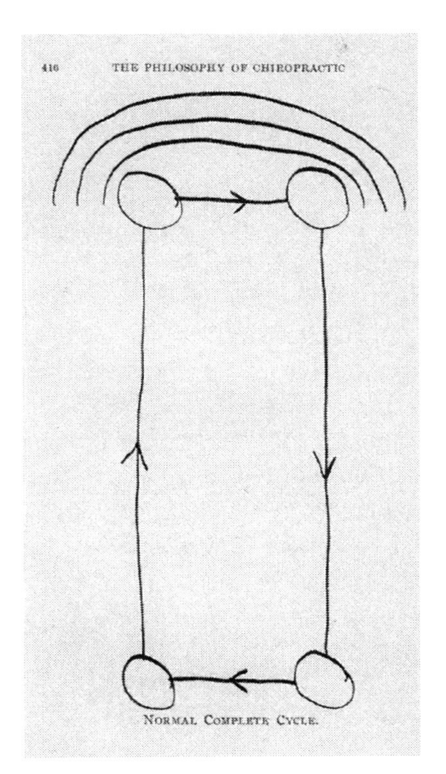

B.J. Palmer (1909b) conveys the essential unity of the triune with the term "oneness" (p. 449). Use of this term is especially interesting because he uses "oneness" when describing two dimensions of the triune, the material and immaterial:

> When we use the words, harmony or inharmonious, coordination or incoordination, we do so with the thought in mind of the triunity existing between the points of creation and the point of expression. There must be a oneness between these three immaterialities (creation, transmission, and expression) and the three materialities (brain cell, never fiber, and tissue cell) to have health. (p. 449)

Thus, B.J. Palmer's description of the two dimensions adds to the complexity of his model: each dimension includes two triunes going in opposite directions, all within one cycle. Directionality and dimensionality were essential to B.J. Palmer's model.

B.J. Palmer's Early Writings: Influential Uses of the Term Triune

Another important way that B.J.'s triune model impacts the profession into the 1920s is his new definition of chiropractic, published in the March 1909 issue of *The Chiropractor*. Perhaps this new definition is a response to D.D.'s (1909a) definition also published in March of the same year. B.J.'s updated definition includes a new paragraph on the history of chiropractic, which emphasizes his new developments to chiropractic theory. The definition was well publicized; it is included in new editions of Vols. 2 and 3 and will be published in several issues of *The Chiropractor*, adopted by *Encyclopædia Britannica* (B.J. Palmer, 1913c), and used as part of the New Jersey chiropractic law in 1920 (FHN, 1920). The new historical definition includes the term triune twice (B.J. Palmer, 1909c):

> CHIROPRACTIC HISTORICAL - The first accidental crude Chiropractic adjustment of a vertebra was given In September, 1895, by Dr. D.D. Palmer. Neither the art, nor the science was formed at this time. Its growth remained practically dormant till 1903, since which time, his son, B.J. Palmer, has developed it into a well defined non-therapeutical philosophy, science and art that has no resemblance whatever to any therapeutical method. Health (equality) is restored by completing the mental and physical circuit; restoring the currents of cycles of mental impulses acting thru the material agency; to replace the full quota of positive with an equivalent negative; permitting the reconveyance of the intelligent immateriality into the mechanical corporeal; to reconstruct the normal psycho physical unit; to make as one the triunity of creation, transmission and expression; to re-establish equilibrium between the abstract and concrete, all of which is induced by replacing specific disordered concrete mechanical anatomy which permits adjustment between that one law

of two principles—cause and effect—the rules and manner of declaration of which are unique and unlike any theories of stimulative or inhibitive movements or applications used by any other school.

DEFINED—Chiropractic is a name given to the study and application of a universal philosophy of biology, theology, theosophy, health, disease, death, the science of the cause of disease and art of permitting the restoration of the triune relationships between all attributes necessary to normal composite forms, to harmonious quantities and qualities by placing in juxtaposition the abnormal concrete positions of definite mechanical portions with each other, by hand, thus correcting all subluxations of the three hundred articulations of the human skeletal frame, more especially those of the spinal column, for the purpose of permitting the re-creation of all normal cyclic currents thru nerves that were formerly not permitted to be transmitted, thru impingement, but have now assumed their normal size and capacity for conduction as they emanate thru intervertebral foramina—the expressions of which were formerly excessive or partially lacking—named disease. (inside front cover)

1913: The Momentum Triune of Force, Matter, and Time

In 1913, B.J. is still expanding triune models. For example, he refers to the triune of spiritual, mechanical, and chemical as three laws in action. The spiritual uses the power of mental impulses to unite and regulate the other two, which leads to perfect health (B.J. Palmer, 1913b, p. 13). In this year, B.J. publishes an article called "Momentum," where he writes, "Momentum introduces three things-force, matter, and time" (B.J. Palmer, 1913a, p. 45). The theory of momentum relates to how much time it might take for each individual patient to be restored to normal function. This theory can be traced to D.D. Palmer's paradigm, highlighted in his 1909 definition of chiropractic mentioned above and will be carried forward in the discourse by B.J.'s students (Drain, 1927; Stephenson, 1927a). Interestingly, in the same issue of *The Chiropractor* as the article on momentum, a letter to the editor from Lee Edwards, MD, DC (1913) is published. The letter discusses adjustment of subluxations in cases of epilepsy and describes the element of time as one of the key factors in conveying a correct prognosis to patients. Edwards concludes, "Force, matter and time are the three components of the cycle of life, and we must deal with it as such" (p. 74). It is possible that Edwards's letter inspires B.J., the publisher of *The Chiropractor*, to write "Momentum" and develop this new perspective on the triune because B.J. published the letter in the same issue as his new essay. By 1922, B.J. would write,

> You see the thought I am trying to get to is the fundamental upon which Chiropractic rests, the triune story of force, matter and time. There is no health; no normal function unless force, matter and time are working coordinately. If any one of these is unbalanced, we have disease of the triune relation of the three. (p. 4)

This new triune is significant because force and matter will become two components of Stephenson's (1927a) classic triune of life and perfection of the triune, published as Principles 4 and 5 of his landmark deductive argument set within 33 principles. Time is incorporated into Principle 6, which tells us that this new momentum triune captures a combination of vital chiropractic principles.

1916: B.J.'s Triune of Matter, Mind, and Time

In the second edition of Volume 5, B.J. Palmer (1916) includes a new chapter called "Poisons: Man-A Triune Chemical Analysis," which is republished in each subsequent edition and excerpts will appear in *The Chiropractor* several years hence (B.J. Palmer, 1923, 1927). In the chapter, he introduces "matter, mind, and time," as a "triune state," which he equates to "generation, transmission, and expression" (p. 283). This new interpretation of the triune also emphasizes the time it takes for normalization of functions. For example, diseases are normalized through chemical changes leading to a normal expression of functions. He writes, "The Chiropractor goes to the basis of matter, mind and time; or generation, transmission and expression by the adjustment of cause, which neutralization process flows from inside to the outside" (p. 284). By integrating mind with matter and time, B.J. expands the complexity of his triune models, again (Table 3).

Table 3
B.J. Palmer's Triune Models, 1907–1916

Year	Components of the triune 1	2	3
1907	Creation	Transmission	Expression
	God		Physical function
	Mental		Physical/body
	Mental Mind	Intelligent power or force	Physical through brain
1909	Creation	Action	Impression
	Universal Intelligence Innate Intelligence	Transmission from brain cell	Tissue cell
	Immaterial		Material
	Brain cell	Nerve fiber	Tissue cell
1913	Force	Matter	Time
1916	Matter	Mind	Time

1920s: The Impact of B.J. Palmer's Triune Model on Chiropractic

All of these various triune models are available to students and alumni at the Palmer School of Chiropractic (PSC) in the 1920s, which means the entire profession is impacted. An historical viewpoint is useful to interpret this impact. According to Keating's (1997) biography of B.J., the PSC shaped the early profession.[1] Keating writes,

> The spectacular growth of the chiropractic profession during the period of B.J. Palmer's ascendancy (1913-1924) cannot be separated from the phenomenal expansion of his educational institution during this same time frame. ... In that era and for decades to come the Developer accurately proclaimed that this Fountain Head, the PSC, had graduated 75% of all chiropractors in the world. In the years

[1] All of Keating's work should be critically assessed for scholarship and bias qualities based on recent critiques of his most influential papers on chiropractic identity (Senzon, 2022).

> immediately following World War I, when federal educational support for veterans became available and the PSC enrollment approached 3,000 students, B.J. truthfully claimed that this was the largest vocational institution in the nation, probably the world. (p. 139)

Thus, B.J.'s thoughts on the triune influence the thriving student body and alumni in the early 1920s through the latest editions of his books, as well as the many articles and pamphlets he and his students will write. Furthermore, it isn't just the philosophical theory that impacts the profession and the chiropractic literature, but a type of reverence and deep appreciation for profound truths that the philosophy points to. This is exemplified in B.J.'s prayer, "Our Supplication."

"Our Supplication" (Figure 6) is first published in the January/February 1909 issue of *The Chiropractor* (B.J. Palmer, 1909a) and will be republished three times in the 1920s (B.J. Palmer, 1924, 1925, 1926), and in Volume 23 (B.J. Palmer, 1950b). In this entreaty, B.J. includes the triune relations in regard to the Universal, bestowing depth to the culture of chiropractic.

Figure 6

"Our Supplication" by B.J. Palmer

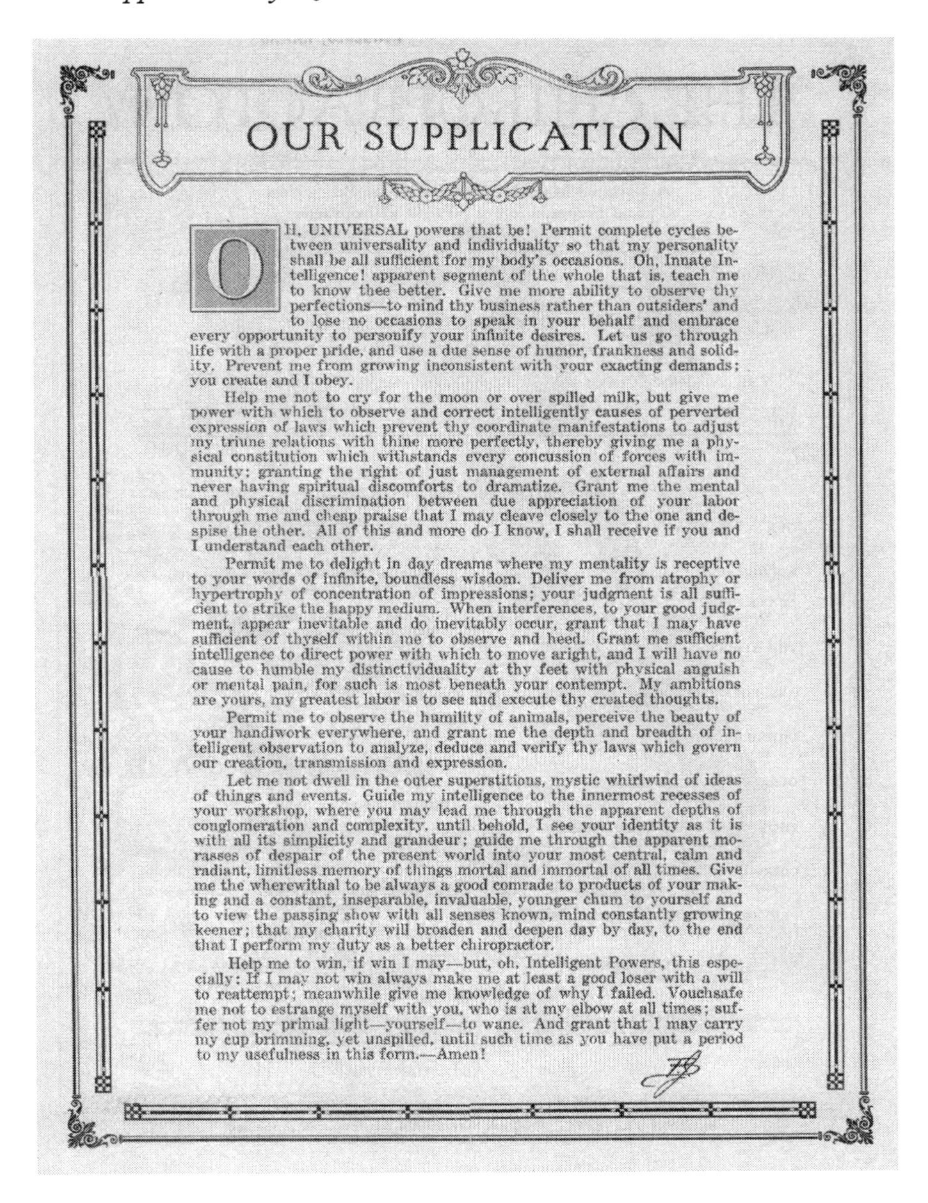

OUR SUPPLICATION

OH, UNIVERSAL powers that be! Permit complete cycles between universality and individuality so that my personality shall be all sufficient for my body's occasions. Oh, Innate Intelligence! apparent segment of the whole that is, teach me to know thee better. Give me more ability to observe thy perfections—to mind thy business rather than outsiders' and to lose no occasions to speak in your behalf and embrace every opportunity to personify your infinite desires. Let us go through life with a proper pride, and use a due sense of humor, frankness and solidity. Prevent me from growing inconsistent with your exacting demands; you create and I obey.

Help me not to cry for the moon or over spilled milk, but give me power with which to observe and correct intelligently causes of perverted expression of laws which prevent thy coordinate manifestations to adjust my triune relations with thine more perfectly, thereby giving me a physical constitution which withstands every concussion of forces with immunity; granting the right of just management of external affairs and never having spiritual discomforts to dramatize. Grant me the mental and physical discrimination between due appreciation of your labor through me and cheap praise that I may cleave closely to the one and despise the other. All of this and more do I know, I shall receive if you and I understand each other.

Permit me to delight in day dreams where my mentality is receptive to your words of infinite, boundless wisdom. Deliver me from atrophy or hypertrophy of concentration of impressions; your judgment is all sufficient to strike the happy medium. When interferences, to your good judgment, appear inevitable and do inevitably occur, grant that I may have sufficient of thyself within me to observe and heed. Grant me sufficient intelligence to direct power with which to move aright, and I will have no cause to humble my distinctividuality at thy feet with physical anguish or mental pain, for such is most beneath your contempt. My ambitions are yours, my greatest labor is to see and execute thy created thoughts.

Permit me to observe the humility of animals, perceive the beauty of your handiwork everywhere, and grant me the depth and breadth of intelligent observation to analyze, deduce and verify thy laws which govern our creation, transmission and expression.

Let me not dwell in the outer superstitions, mystic whirlwind of ideas of things and events. Guide my intelligence to the innermost recesses of your workshop, where you may lead me through the apparent depths of conglomeration and complexity, until behold, I see your identity as it is with all its simplicity and grandeur; guide me through the apparent morasses of despair of the present world into your most central, calm and radiant, limitless memory of things mortal and immortal of all times. Give me the wherewithal to be always a good comrade to products of your making and a constant, inseparable, invaluable, younger chum to yourself and to view the passing show with all senses known, mind constantly growing keener; that my charity will broaden and deepen day by day, to the end that I perform my duty as a better chiropractor.

Help me to win, if win I may—but, oh, Intelligent Powers, this especially: If I may not win always make me at least a good loser with a will to reattempt; meanwhile give me knowledge of why I failed. Vouchsafe me not to estrange myself with you, who is at my elbow at all times; suffer not my primal light—yourself—to wane. And grant that I may carry my cup brimming, yet unspilled, until such time as you have put a period to my usefulness in this form.—Amen!

BJP

Note. This text was published in *The Chiropractor* in 1909, 1924, 1925, and 1926.

1922–1963: The Chiropractic Triune

By first exploring how the triune as a concept evolved in the 1920s, we connect to what later generations will view as the North Star of the philosophy of chiropractic. The emergence of the triune is especially evident at the PSC because it impacts students and alumni, some of whom will go on to start other schools and publish and teach about the triune. Reggie Gold is the ultimate example because his 1963 PhC thesis topic is the triune. Reggie will later help to start two chiropractic schools, an international professional association, and impact thousands of chiropractors worldwide.

The Triune and the Doctor of Chiropractic Philosophy Degree

Reggie Gold continues a long history of Palmer graduates who completed their Doctor of Chiropractic Philosophy degree (PhC) and published articles referring to the triune (Table 4). The PhC degree was granted to Palmer graduates after completing a post-graduate thesis on a topic regarding the philosophy of chiropractic (Stephenson, 1927a). The degree was granted between 1908 and 1968, with the first PhC bestowed upon B.J. Palmer and the last one on Bernard Cirullo (Stout, 1988). It is unknown how many PhC theses were written on the topic of the triune.

Table 4

PhC Recipients Mentioning the Triune in The Chiropractor

Year	Author	Title	*Vol*(Issue)
1922	E. A. Arestad, DC, PhC	From Inside Out	*18*(9)
1923	J. A. Leeka, D.C., PhC	The Soul of Chiropractic	*19*(10)
1924	H. L. Poole, DC, PhC	Health and Disease	*20*(8)
1924	R. W. Stephenson, DC, PhC	Chiropractic Fundamentals	*20*(10)
1926	M. C. Burchfield, DC, PhC	Chiropractic Philosophy	*22*(8)
1929	J. H. Stoke, DC, PhC	What Is Life?	*11*(9)

1929	M. W. Williamson, DC, PhC	Intellectual Adaptation	*25*(4)
1933	E. M. Maute, DC, PhC	What Lies Between	*29*(3)
1935	G. W. Pepper, DC, PhC	What Constitutes Health?	*31*(12)
1936	C. E. Lawrence, DC, PhC	The Expression of Intelligence Through Matter	*33*(9)
1938	E. R. Schmitz, DC, PhC	Why Chiropractic?	*34*(1)
1942	G. K. Frisbie, DC, PhC	Chiropractic at the Crossroads	*38*(7)
1946	F. M. Grossmith, DC, PhC	Autocratic Innate Intelligence	*42*(1)
1952	G. C. Paulk, DC, PhC	Innate-Impetus of Man	*48*(9)
1956	J. H. Stoke, DC, PhC	What's Your Inspiration?	*52*(11)

Early 1920s: Triune Models Put Forward by PhCs

Beginning in 1922, alumni who had completed their PhC degrees at the PSC began to publish editorials and philosophical discourses in *The Chiropractor* using the term triune. These publications may have had a significant impact on the evolution of triune definitions in the 1920s. For example, in September 1922 in an article by Elmer A. Arestad, DC, PhC, the triune of man is described as "intelligent force, matter, and time" (p. 19). This definition is an innovation on B.J.'s momentum triune because it appended "intelligent" to "force," a linguistic distinction that would be integrated by Stephenson (1927a). In 1923, in an article by J.A. Leeka, DC, PhC, the "Chiropractic trinity" is described in three ways: science, art, and philosophy; spirit, mind, and body; and "the soul, the mentality, and the physical expression" (p. 24). In his later years, B.J. Palmer (1966b) would include science, art, and philosophy as part of the triune. Another example is from August 1924: H.L. Poole, DC, PhC, writes that the health formula is unity of "100% of force, 100% of matter, in 100% of time" (p. 25). This way of explaining the triune, by percentages, derives from B.J. Palmer and is congruent with Stephenson's approach. The triune models in this era are still integrating B.J.'s various approaches.

Beginning in the mid-1920s, PhC theses must be viewed in the context of influence from R.W. Stephenson, who joined the philosophy department soon after completing his PhC in 1923 (Faulkner et al., 2018). Some of the descriptions of the triune during this time period are similar to the triune model he developed.

1923–1924: The Emergence of Stephenson's Triune of Life

The development of Stephenson's triune of life model begins with his 1923 PhC thesis and his 1924 article titled "Chiropractic Fundamentals." Since a recent chapter in this Chiropractic White Book Series traces the development of Stephenson's life and work (Senzon, 2018c), the following sections primarily present Stephenson's own words, without significant commentary.

The publication of R.W. Stephenson's PhC thesis represents the first combination in the chiropractic literature of intelligence, force, and matter. Stephenson's (1923) thesis mentions triunity twice; the first instance here including an unpublished quote from B.J. Palmer:

> From these facts we deduce, that is, we can prove that life is a triunity—100% of Intelligence: 100% of Force: 100% of Matter. Also we can see that the Creator does not neglect His creations but cares for them constantly with an infinite precision and calculation. Therefore we say that Life is intelligent and governs all matter. Do we say *all* matter? Yes, to quote Dr. B.J. Palmer, "life is vibration according to degree of vibration." The infinite Intelligence is everywhere, it is Universal, common to every locality, and does not deny attention to the smallest molecule or atom. Our study of physics show us that there is energy everywhere, throughout the Universe. It also shows us that energy is in many forms but is after all *one* energy. What does that signify? Any of these forms of energy can be transformed into another, and every moment we see it being done all around us. In its radiant forms there is no corner of the Universe it does not reach, and consequently every bit of matter receives some energy. (p. 4)

Stephenson concludes the thesis:

> In conclusion the writer wishes to state that this paper has covered most of the salient points of Chiropractic. With the exception of Universal and Innate Intelligence all of the topics have been covered *briefly*; it had to be briefly because the scope of this paper does not allow a lengthy discussion. Many more interesting things could have been said about each and many more interesting phases could have been introduced, but the writer believes that a pretty fair exposition of the philosophy of Chiropractic has been given wherein the fundamental principles have been introduced. Technique has been avoided, tho the technique has been discussed philosophically. The fact that Life is intelligent, that the expression of that life depends upon a triunity of perfection, the combining of that intelligence with matter, the manner of its combination, the interference with that combination, and what happens when there is such interference, and how it may be remedied by man has been the theme of this thesis. The writer has tried to make a professional article of it; at the same time making it simplified so that it can be understood by the casual reader – the layman. (p. 21)

In 1924, in his classic article on "Chiropractic Fundamentals," Stephenson articulates the model further:

> We state the Chiropractic idea of life by saying that life is a triunity; the combination of three important factors; intelligence, force and matter. Matter moves—it gives us evidence of force. Can you conceive a force unless matter shows it to you? Where does this force come from? By its precision, we know it must come from some power intelligent enough to make it precise in its movements. This is usually called Law or Natural Law. Then Law must be Intelligence itself. (p. 37)

1926: Stephenson's Triune Reflected in His Students' Writing

The impact of Stephenson's triune teaching doesn't fully emerge in the literature until 1926. One statement from M. Chapman Burchfield (1926), DC, PhC, captures Stephenson's triune model:

> Life is intelligent. The universe and everything therein was created and is being maintained by a universal power. Life is a triunity, having three necessary united factors, Intelligence, Force and Matter, and in order to have 100% life, there must be 100% intelligence, 100% force and 100% matter. (p. 23)

Stephenson's influence is also found in an article by Agnes Davidson, DC, PhC (1926b), which may be the first published use of the phrase "triune of life" (p. 6). Davidson was a 1925 PSC graduate from Chicago. Documentation that she completed a PhC has been located but no actual thesis has been found (personal communication from R. Riess on August 21, 2021). However, Davidson's two-part article is about 15,000 words (1926a, 1926b), which was the required wordcount for a PhC thesis (Stephenson, 1927b). Davidson doesn't cite Stephenson's textbook; until additional documentation or notes from Stephenson's classroom emerge, Davidson should be given credit for coining the phrase.

1927: Stephenson's Text

Stephenson (1927a) mentions triune four times and triunity 11 times in his textbook; he cites B.J.'s Volume 5, 63 times. Part of Stephenson's genius is his ability to explain B.J. Palmer's most difficult theories in a logical manner organized around 31 steps of the Normal Complete Cycle and his 33 principles. Ultimately, triune becomes a cornerstone of the philosophy of chiropractic because of Principles 4 and 5:

> **No. 4. The Triune of Life.**
> Life is a triunity having three necessary united factors, namely, Intelligence, Force and Matter.
> **No. 4. The Perfection of the Triune.**
> In order to have 100% Life, there must be 100% Intelligence, 100% Force, 100% Matter.

No. 4. The Principle of Time
There is no process that does not require time. (p. xxxi)

By integrating time as the logical step following the triune, Stephenson highlights the various triunes developed by his mentor. He expands on the triune in Article 344 of his textbook:

Art. 344. THE NORMALITY OF INNATE INTELLIGENCE.

Principle No. 27.
Innate Intelligence is always normal and its function is always normal.
This is a principle from the Triune of Life (Prin. 4) for more specific application. Intelligence is always perfect – always one hundred per cent. The forces which it assembles are always correct. They are not correct when they reach Tissue Cell if there is interference with transmission, but that is not because of imperfection in Innate's work, but because of the limitations of matter (Prin. 24). It is because the conducting tissue is imperfect or the receiving tissue (Tissue Cell) is imperfect. Both the conducting tissue and the receiving tissues are matter which is the third factor of the Triune of Life, and the only member of it which can be imperfect. The imperfection, of course, is in structure. The molecules of a wrecked locomotive are just as good as those in a locomotive in running order, but the wrecked locomotive is imperfect in structure and therefore is not a good organ to express man's wishes. (p. 269)

Chiropractic Literature Adopts Stephenson's Triune of Life

It may have taken a few years for Stephenson's model of the triune to become the dominant view about the triune. A 1926 article still defines the triune as force, matter, and time (Rafferty, 1926); Stephenson's triune is quoted for the first time, in a 1929 article by Stoke, DC, PhC. The triune of life is also mentioned in that same year, without attribution, by Maydene W. Williamson, DC, PhC. It is then used in the new classic form a few times in the 1930s and 1940s (Marrs, 1945; Frisbie, 1942), including Livingstone's (1934) article called "The

Reciprocal Link in Life and Health Principles and Practice," which quotes the triune along with the 33 principles.

By late 1927, B.J. Palmer has not yet adopted Stephenson's new terminology and definition. B.J. reuses a sentence from the second edition of Volume 5 (B.J. Palmer & Craven, 1916), where he writes of "our triune state originally with matter, mind, and time; generation, transmission, and expression" (B.J. Palmer, 1927, p. 5). However, at Lyceum 1932, B.J. Palmer's talk, "Crowding the Hour," quotes Stephenson's 33 principles and expands them based on a historical style to 75 principles (B.J. Palmer, 1951). In 1934, he presents excerpts from that talk as part of a radio address, while naming but not numbering the 75 principles (B.J. Palmer, 1934). This could indicate that B.J. Palmer is not attached to the logical structure of the argument. However, Stephenson's (1927a) integration of the time triunes and the force/matter/intelligence triunes is now quoted by B.J. Palmer, who would go on to expand on the triune models in his writings.

After Stephenson's Text: Further Developments of the Triune

Stephenson's (1927a) text became the triune paradigm: it will be the core philosophy textbook for all students at the PSC for decades and will be adopted by other schools started by PSC graduates. Other authors in the profession—some of whom were trained by D.D. or B.J. Palmer, studied their works, or were trained by their students—go on to write triune-like chiropractic theories. For example, Ratledge chiropractic is concerned with the universal laws of matter as they apply to the body, which are comprised of three qualities of "density, chemical composition, and temperature" (Ratledge, 1949, p. 3). Those qualities activate the body, disturbing it from its normalcy, to which the body responds intelligently using the same three qualities of matter, guided by the nervous system. Another example is Drain's (1949) textbook, *Man Tomorrow*. The second part of the book is titled "Triune Relationship," and describes B.J. Palmer's process of intellectual adaptation as an integration of the mental, physical, and spiritual. Two of Drain's students also describe triunes: Fleet, who emphasizes the body, mind, and soul (Keating & Fleet, 1997), and Harper (1964), who studies D.D. Palmer's writings and then develops his theory of internal and external irritations to the nervous system based on the three principles of mechanical, chemical, and psychic irritations, leading to subluxations. Harper (1974) finds that the subluxated state forces the organism to be out of step with time. He writes, "Disease is function out of time with need; and this is D.D. Palmer's abnormal function" (p. 31). All of these triune models have roots in the writings and teachings of the Palmers.

B.J. Palmer continues to develop his models and dominates the discourse about the triune, through teaching and publishing textbooks, especially for PSC students and alumni. For example, B.J. Palmer's talk at Lyceum 1942 includes a section titled "The Triune Conflict," later republished in Volume 24 (B.J. Palmer, 1950a). The conflict involves the triune of Universal Intelligence, Innate Intelligence, and Educated Intelligence, or three intellectualities. To overcome the conflict, man's ego, which stems from Educated Intelligence, needs to expand to more ultimate perspectives. B.J. writes:

> It is proper and befitting that Educated man should look, study, and investigate beyond himself, into space surrounding, to try to know why HE is here, what HE is here to do, how HE fits into the scheme of things, how HE forms a part of the whole, and how HE can better personify its ultimate objectives. (p. 24–25)

In 1950, B.J. writes of restoration as a process, with the triune being of man as mechanics, chemics, and psychics (B.J. Palmer, 1950b, p. 43). He also writes variously of the Spiritualist definition of the triune phase of man as spiritual, mental, and physical (B.J. Palmer, 1949, 1955). However, his next influential transformation of the triune concept is in his final writings, completed the year of his death, the year Reggie Gold is writing his PhC thesis.

In 1961, B.J. Palmer completes Vols. 38 and 39, both published posthumously in 1966. In these works, B.J. proposes that vertebral subluxation at the "occipito-atlantal-axial area, is THE PLACE where matter can distort matter to where it distorts the triune relationship" (Palmer, 1966a, p. 15). He expands on this in his final textbook, Volume 39:

> No other living person has lived as long in years, researched so many ways, always on the *living triune unity* of abstract with concrete, never either one alone, con-

> sequently *the modern today* average chiropractor thinks and believes our position today is questionable, unscientific, subject to serious criticism, needing reformation. (B.J. Palmer, 1966b, p. 10)

He also states that the research conducted at the B.J. Palmer Research Clinic is the only triune research in the profession. The instrumentation he had custom-made, the *electroencephaloneuromentimpograph* or *timpograph* for short, was designed to locate the mental impulse with modified, early EEG technology in shielded, grounded booths (Senzon, 2008). The concept of the research design was to study all three factors of the triune as one unity. B.J. refers to this as the "triune living factors – *Innate* in brain, *Innate* flowing through nerves, *Innate* reaching periphery" (B.J. Palmer, 1966b, p. 34). This is the evolution of his cycle of life, originally developed in 1907. Finally, B.J. seems to associate the triad of philosophy, science, and art to his triune, linking the abstract and the physical:

> By checking our case, from week to week, we could tell HIM whether he was or was not getting better when function was restored. In this way we lined [sic] into one *continuous* study the Innate, mental, philosophy, WITH adjusting technic of vertebral subluxation, *with* the science of living proof offered of one unit of the triune relationships to the abstract AND concrete physical properties. (p. 36)

1963: Reggie Gold's The Triune of Life

This historical timeline is the backdrop for Reggie Gold's (1963) *The Triune of Life*. Reggie helps to reinvigorate the philosophy of chiropractic for thousands of chiropractors by pointing out that the triune of life is the cornerstone of the philosophy. It stands alone as a viable theory and principle of chiropractic. In the text, he cites several textbooks on anatomy and physiology, Volume 5 and Stephenson, as well as two textbooks that transformed subluxation theory: Seyle (1954) and Speransky (1943) (Senzon, 2018a). Reggie's triune also incorporates the essence of time in relation to the triune, whereby interference to transmission of the innate forces carrying the message of the mental impulse, could cause the organism to not be in sync with the needs of the moment, leading to dis-ease. He emphasizes that the transmitted force is the link that is central to chiropractic.

After teaching and leading segments of the profession for a decade, Reggie updates the triune in 1987, appending the term Innate to each of the three elements. He suggests that life is the expression of Innate Intelligence by way of innate force through innate matter. Reggie proposes that this makes the elements of the triune more specific to the living system. This also grounds the chiropractic terminology by differentiating Innate Intelligence to only define the living organism and divorcing it from any spiritual definitions. Life is defined according to the definition found in Stephenson's (1927a) text. This linguistic differentiation is central to Reggie's move to focus the definition of subluxation on the expression of the living organization, the expression of life, which becomes the cornerstone of his chiropractic movement (Senzon, 2018b).

1963–Present: Triune Studies After Gold's Thesis

There is a great deal of chiropractic literature on the triune of life since Reggie published his work in 1963. There are several streams of discourse on the triune from students of Reggie, colleagues of Reggie and their students, and other chiropractic literature citing the triune for a wide range of purposes such as dismissivism, elucidation, and philosophical development.

Several of the most advanced discussions of the topic are from Reggie's students. For example, Joe Strauss, who authors one of two biographies of Reggie (Gold & Nogrady, 2014; Strauss, 1997), first teaches about the triune as part of his first-year philosophy course at Pennsylvania College of Straight Chiropractic (Strauss, 1988). Joe's teaching notes are transformed into his first textbook on philosophy, where he emphasizes, "The triune of life clearly demonstrates the objective of the chiropractor. ... Chiropractic is concerned with only one thing, making sure that there is an unbroken link between the three components of the triune: intelligence, force, and matter" (Strauss, 1991, p. 57). Strauss discusses aspects of the triune in at least 11 of his textbooks. Another influential student of Reggie is David Koch, who publishes the second edition of Reggie's *Triune of Life* (Gold, 1998), which is the version reproduced in this book. Koch's (2008) innovative textbook is perhaps the only critical approach to the triune within the chiropractic literature. Koch writes:

> I wish to give acknowledgement to those many chiropractors, and especially to Drs. Reggie Gold, Thom Gelardi and Fred Barge, who all encouraged me to be bold enough to insist that chiropractic's basic concepts could be updated without necessarily destroying them, in spite of any dogmatic brittleness they may have acquired over the years. (p. 5)

In the text, Koch proposes that Stephenson's triune of life be renamed as the triune of organization, because the term *organization* is more specific to living systems. The linguistic change also distinguishes biological life from universal life. Koch also proposes a reorganization of Stephenson's 33 principles based on argument analysis, moving the principles associated with the triune and time to more logically defensible positions within the argument structure. The third chiropractic textbook author, Claude Lessard (2017), refers to the triune of life as "existence (universal life)" (p. 18). Lessard dedicates the book to his mentor, Reggie Gold.

Other streams of triune writings include Reggie's contemporary, Fred Barge, DC, PhC (1987), who builds upon B.J. Palmer's later philosophy by coining "The Triune of Intelligence" (p. 29) as Universal Intelligence, Innate Intelligence, and Educated Intelligence. Barge captures this aspect of the triune philosophy:

> Knowing the truth of the principles of the Triune of intelligences, as taught through chiropractic philosophy, destroys the barriers of educated prejudices allowing Innate to express itself in man, and Innate as an extension of Universal Intelligence, having communication from above down, is then allowed to express itself form within out. This expression of life force provides for the bearer of this truth the radiant health, poise, and confidence only present in those who live a life without fear. (p. 107)

Several of Barge's students will go on to write about the triune through textbooks and in the tradition of the PhC, the Legion of Chiropractic Philosopher theses (Brown, 2004; Glas, 2003; Sinnott, 2009; Watt, 2003).

There exists other chiropractic literature describing the triune (Faulkner et al., 2018; Hughes, 2002; Mirtz, 2001; Owens et al., 1999; Romano, 2017; Strauss, 2017; Sullivan, 2017; Tsamoutalidis, 2017), citing historical definitions using the term (Bak-Jensen, 2004; Griffin, 1991; Haldeman, 2004; Jolliot, 2012; Leach, 1981; Quigley, 1981; Vernon, 1990; Wardwell, 1993; Winterstein, 1991), citing Reggie's thesis (Donahue, 1992; Haldeman, 2004; Jacelone, 1989; Keating, 2003; Kleynhans, 1999), citing Barge's triune (Kleynhans, 1990), and applying the triune concept to patient care (Serio, 2017; Strauss, 1994). However, besides Koch's (2008) important work, there are virtually no critical writings about the triune. Thus, future works exploring the history of ideas in chiropractic should include critical methodologies to explore triune studies further.

Conclusions

Triune studies are one of the richest and most rewarding areas for chiropractic philosophers to explore. After all, Reggie Gold (1963) wrote, "The Triune of Life, then, should be an area of concentrated study, for it embodies the heart and soul of Chiropractic philosophy" (p. 10). And yet, as the history of the chiropractic triune reveals, there are many theoretical discourses about the triune originating in writings going back 150 years. The challenge for academic chiropractors, scholars, and the profession as a whole is that the literature cited in this short history has yet to be subject to critical analysis using tools of philosophy, critical theory, and social science. This is the next step for triune studies, to become critically self-reflective just like the living systems the triune attempts to define.

The chiropractic literature is filled with arguments about identity as well as arguments for and against subluxation and philosophy. It is the role of any academic chiropractor to critically analyze such discourse and determine whether the arguments are factually based and logically presented. A critical discourse about the triune in chiropractic, one that critiques the original theories and analyzes the secondary literature, is key.

One systematic place for the profession to begin such a critical project is to apply the new methods developed to analyze the chiropractic identity literature (Senzon, 2022). In this way, objective criteria could be followed to understand the strengths and weaknesses of each argument. The strength of the profession is contingent on the quality and cogency of its literature; it is time for the profession to learn from the past and develop rigorous academic strategies to move into the future. This chapter and this book act as a factual and historical foundation, a source for future triune studies, and a wellspring for the philosophy of chiropractic.

References

Aerstad, E. (1922). From the inside out. *The Chiropractor, 18*(9), 19–20.

Albanese, C. (2007). *A republic of mind and spirit: A cultural history of American metaphysical religion.* Yale University Press.

Babbitt, E. D. (1871). Letter from Brooklyn, New York. *Religio-Philosophical Journal, 12*(17), 6.

Babbitt, E.D. (1872). New York magnetic cure. *Religio-Philosophical Journal, 13*(14), 8.

Babbitt, E.D. (1874). *Vital magnetism the life-fountain. Being an answer to Dr. Brown-Sequard's lectures on nerve force: The magnetic theory defended, and a better philosophy of cure explained.*

Bak-Jensen, S.T. (2004). *Manipulative exclusivity: The legitimation strategies of early Danish chiropractors, 1920-1943.* Københavns Universitet.

Barge, F. (1987). *Life without fear: Chiropractic's major philosophical tenets* (Vol. V). Bawden Brothers.

Britten, E. (1871). On the spirit-circle and the laws of mediumship: A lecture delivered at Cleveland Hall, London, on Sunday Evening, July 2nd, 1871. *Religio-Philosophical Journal, 10*(25), 2.

Brown, S. (2004). *Subluxation and chaos theory.* International Chiropractic Association Philosophy Conference.

Burchfield, M. (1926). Chiropractic philosophy. *The Chiropractor, 22*(8), 23–24.

Child, H. (1871a). Light, heat, and electricity. *Religio-Philosophical Journal, 11*(23), 3.

Child, H. (1871b). Re-incarnation, etc. *Religio-Philosophical Journal, 11*(12), 5.

Child, H. (1871c). Soul freedom. *Religio-Philosophical Journal, 10*(17), 5.

Child, H. (1871d). Soul life, past, present and future. *Religio-Philosophical Journal, 10*(22), 5.

Child, H. (1871e). Statuvoluence. *Religio-Philosophical Journal, 10*(26), 5.

Davidson, A. (1926a). Questions of a layman answered: Part I. *The Chiropractor, 22*(10), 30-38.

Davidson, A. (1926b). Questions of a layman answered: Part II. *The Chiropractor, 22*(11), 34-48.

Donahue, J. (1992). The trouble with Innate and the trouble that causes. *Philosophical Constructs for the Chiropractic Profession, 2*, 21–25. https://doi.org/10.1016/S2214-9163(13)60014-7

Drain, J. (1927). *Chiropractic thoughts.* Standard Print Company.

Drain, J.R. (1946). *Chiropractic thoughts* (2nd ed.). Standard Print Company.

Drain, J. (1949). *Man tomorrow.* Standard Print Company.

Edwards, L. (1913). What the boys are saying. *The Chiropractor, 9*(4), 74.

Evans, W.F. (1886). *Esoteric Christianity and mental therapeutics*. H. H. Carter & Karrick.
Faulkner, T., Foley, J., & Senzon, S. (2018). *Palmer chiropractic Green Books: The definitive guide*. The Institute Chiropractic.
Foley, J. (2016). *The chiropractor* 1914: Revealed. *Chiropractic History, 36*(1), 72–86.
FHN. (1920). Chiropractors bill is passed. Fountain Head News, 9(29), 6.
Frisbie, G. (1942). Chiropractic at the crossroads. *The Chiropractor, 38*(7), 17–18.
Fuller, R. (1989). *Alternative medicine and American religious life*. Oxford University Press.
Gebser, J. (1985). *The ever-present origin* (N. Barstand & A. Mickunas, Trans.). Ohio University Press. (Original work published 1949)
Glas, B. (2003). Chiropractic: The force between the mind and the body. In Barge, F. & Callender, A *Philosophical Contemplations: Viewpoints on Chiropractic Philosophy: Vol. 3*. Palmer College of Chiropractic.
Gold, I., & Nogrady, J. (2014). *Gold: A lifetime of love in chiropractic*.
Gold, R. (1963). *Triune of life* [PhC thesis]. Palmer School of Chiropractic.
Gold, R. (1987). The triune chiropractic lecture [Audio track]. On *Reggie's latest tapes: Reggie Gold speaks on chiropractic. Album 1: The Philosophy*. Chiro Products. https://youtu.be/PkDfcAIiE8I
Gold, R. (1998). *Triune of life* (2nd ed.). Sherman College of Straight Chiropractic.
Griffin, L. (1991). D.D. Palmer vs. B.J. Palmer. *ACA Journal of Chiropractic, 28*(4), 25–28.
Grossmith, F.M. (1946). Autocratic Innate intelligence. *The Chiropractor, 42*(1), 14-15.
Haldeman, S. (Ed.). (2004). *Principles and practice of chiropractic* (3rd ed.). McGraw-Hill.
Harper, W. (1964). *Anything can cause anything: A correlation of Dr. Daniel David Palmer's principles of chiropractic*. Texas Chiropractic College. http://books.google.com/books
Harper, W. (1974). *Anything can cause anything: A correlation of Dr. Daniel David Palmer's principles of chiropractic* (3rd ed.). Texas Chiropractic College.
Hart, J. (1997). Did D.D. Palmer visit A.T. Still in Kirksville? *Chiropractic History, 17*(2), 49–55.
Hughes, J. (2002). Chiropractic comes of age: A reflection on the thirty-three principles of chiropractic as a foundation for a contemporary philosophy. *Annals of Vertebral Subluxation Research, 4*(4), 111–113.
Jacelone, P. (1989). The ancient philosophic roots of chiropractic literature. *Chiropractic History, 9*(2), 45–49.
Jolliot, C. (2012). Holism in health care: A powerful notion or an elusive endeavour? *Chiropractic Journal of Australia, 42*(2), 43.
Jones, S. (1871). Personal and local. *Religio-Philosophical Journal, 10*(17), 5.
Keating, J. (1997). *B.J. of Davenport: The early years of chiropractic*. Association for the History of Chiropractic.
Keating, J. (2003). Ain't got enough philosophy. *Dynamic Chiropractic, 21*(13). https://www.dynamicchiropractic.com/mpacms/dc/article.php?id=9252
Keating, J., & Fleet, G. (1997). Thurman Fleet, DC, and the early years of the Concept-Therapy Institute. *Chiropractic History, 17*, 57-66.
Kleynhans, A. (1990). Where chiropractic and philosophy meet. *Journal of the Australian Chiropractors' Association, 20*(4), 129–134.
Kleynhans, A. (1999). A chiropractic conceptual framework. Part 4: Paradigms. *Chiropractic Journal of Australia, 29*, 129–136.
Koch, D. (2008). *Contemporary chiropractic philosophy: An introduction*. Roswell.
Lawrence, C.E. (1936). The expression of intelligence through matter. *The Chiropractor, 33*(9), 20-21.

Leach, R. (1981). The chiropractic theories: Discussion of some important considerations. *ACA Journal of Chiropractic, 15*(S), 19–25.
Leeka, J.A. (1923). The soul of chiropractic. *The Chiropractor, 19*(10), 24.
Lessard, C. (2017). *A new look at chiropractic's basic science*. Lessard Chiropractic.
Livingstone, E. (1934). The reciprocal link in life and health: Principles and practice. *The Chiropractor, 30*(7), 15.
Maute, E.M. (1933). What lies between. *The Chiropractor, 29*(3), 16-19.
Marrs, H. (1945). The subluxation and health. *The Chiropractor, 41*(10), 7-8.
Mirtz, T. (2001). The question of theology for chiropractic: A theological study of chiropractic's prime tenets. *Journal of Chiropractic Humanities, 10*, 48–82. https://doi.org/10.1016/S1556-3499(13)60133-3
Owens, E., Koch, D., & Moore, L. (1999). Hypothesis formulation for scientific investigation of vertebral subluxation. *Journal of Vertebral Subluxation Research, 3*(3), 98–103.
Palmer, A.L. (1871). Letter from Abba Lord Palmer. *Religio-Philosophical Journal, 10*(3), 6.
Palmer, B.J. (1907). *The science of chiropractic: Eleven physiological lectures* (Vol. 2). The Palmer School of Chiropractic.
Palmer, B.J. (1908a). *The philosophy and principles of chiropractic adjustments: A series of twenty-four lectures* (Vol. 3). Palmer School of Chiropractic.
Palmer, B.J. (1908b). *The science of chiropractic: Causes localized* (Vol. 4). Palmer School of Chiropractic.
Palmer, B.J. (1909a). Our supplication. *The Chiropractor, 5*(1–2), 56–57.
Palmer, B.J. (1909b). *Philosophy of chiropractic* (Vol. 5). Palmer School of Chiropractic.
Palmer, B.J. (1909c). Chiropractic. *The Chiropractor, 5*(3), inside-front-cover.
Palmer, B.J. (1911). *The philosophy, science, and art of chiropractic nerve tracing: A book of four sections* (Vol. 6). Palmer School of Chiropractic.
Palmer, B.J. (1913a). Momentum. *The Chiropractor, 9*(4), 45–49.
Palmer, B.J. (1913b). *The science of chiropractic: Containing a series of lectures and other scientific material discovered or developed and delivered* (Vol. 2, 2nd ed.). Palmer School of Chiropractic.
Palmer, B.J. (1913c). Chiropractic: From Encyclopedia Britannica. *The Chiropractor, 9*(7), 27.
Palmer, B.J. (1922). The hot box. *The Chiropractor, 18*(11), s4.
Palmer, B.J. (1923). The chemical analysis of man. *The Chiropractor and Clinical Journal, 18*(11), 5–10, 62–64.
Palmer, B.J. (1924). Our supplication. *The Chiropractor, 20*(1), 2.
Palmer, B.J. (1925). Our supplication. *The Chiropractor, 21*(5), 57, 59.
Palmer, B.J. (1926). Our supplication. *The Chiropractor, 22*(12), 5.
Palmer, B.J. (1927). Are you at ease? *The Chiropractor and Clinical Journal, 23*(10), 5–8, 39–58.
Palmer, B.J. (1934). An explanation of chiropractic: Radio address by Dr. B.J. Palmer, January 14, 1934 (Delivered over WOC-WHO). *The Chiropractor, 30*(1), 5–6, 25–28
Palmer, B.J. (1942). *The law of cause and cure of dis-ease or the law of production and reduction of vertebral subluxation* Lyceum.
Palmer, B.J. (1949). *The bigness of the fellow within* (Vol. 22). Palmer College.
Palmer, B.J. (1950a). *Fight to climb* (Vol. 24). Palmer College.
Palmer, B.J. (1950b). *Up from below the bottom* (Vol. 23). Palmer College.
Palmer, B.J. (1951). *Clinical controlled chiropractic research* (Vol. 25). Palmer School of Chiropractic.

Palmer, B.J. (1955). *Chiropractic philosophy, science, and art: What it does, how it does it, and why it does it* (Vol. 32). Palmer School of Chiropractic Press.
Palmer, B.J. (1966a). *The great divide* (Vol. 38). Palmer College.
Palmer, B.J. (1966b). *Our masterpiece* (Vol. 39). Palmer College.
Palmer, B.J., & Craven, J. H. (1916). *The philosophy of chiropractic* (Vol. 5, 2nd ed.). Palmer School of Chiropractic.
Palmer, D.D. (1872, July 6). Letter to the editor. *Religio-Philosophical Journal, 12*(16), 6.
Palmer, D.D. (1909a). Chiropractic defined. *The Chiropractor Adjuster, 1*(3), 63.
Palmer, D.D. (1909b). Monstrosities. *The Chiropractor Adjuster, 1*(6), 30–32.
Palmer, D.D. (1909c). Response to correspondence between J. F. Petritsch and J. A. Quintal. *The Chiropractor Adjuster, 1*(2), 20.
Palmer, D.D. (1910). *The science, art, and philosophy of chiropractic.* Portland Printing House.
Palmer, D.D. (1914). The moral and religious duties of a chiropractor. In *The chiropractor* (pp. 1–12). Press of Beacon Light Printing Company.
Palmer, D.D., & Palmer, B.J. (1906). *The science of chiropractic.* The Palmer School of Chiropractic.
Paulk, G.C. (1952) Innate-Impetus of Man. *The Chiropractor, 48*(9), 5-6.
Pepper, G.W. (1935). What constitutes health? *The Chiropractor, 31*(12), 13-14.
Plato. (1972). *Phaedrus* (R. Hackforth, Ed.). Cambridge University Press. (Original work written c. 370 BCE)
Poole, H. (1924). Health and disease. *The Chiropractor, 20*(8), 25–27.
Quigley, W. (1981). Chiropractic's monocausal theory of disease: Its origin, current status and implications for the future. *ACA Journal of Chiropractic, 18*(6), 52–60. https://archive.org/details/sim_american-chiropractic-association-the-aca-journal_1981-06_18_6/
Rafferty, W. (1926). A principle and a major. *The Chiropractor, 22*(10), 27–29.
Ratledge, T.F. (1949). *The philosophy of chiropractic.*
Romano, M. (2017). Principle 4: The triune of life. In D. Serio (Ed.), *33* (pp. 21–26).
Santrac, A.S. (2013). Three I know not what: The influence of Greek philosophy on the doctrine of Trinity. *die Skriflig, 47*(1), 1–7. https://doi.org/10.4102/ids.v47i1.719
Schmitz, E.R. (1938). Why chiropractic? *The Chiropractor, 34*(1), 15-17.
Senzon, S. (1994). *Superbikeman, Plato, and the Body/Mind/Soul.* [Master's thesis] Goddard College.
Senzon, S. (2008). Chiropractic and energy medicine: A shared history. *Journal of Chiropractic Humanities, 15*, 27–54. https://doi.org/10.1016/S1556-3499(13)60167-9
Senzon, S. (2011). Constructing a philosophy of chiropractic: Evolving worldviews and premodern roots. *Journal of Chiropractic Humanities, 18*(1), 10–23. https://doi.org/10.1016/j.echu.2011.10.001
Senzon, S. (2014). *D.D. Palmer's traveling library.* The Institute Chiropractic.
Senzon, S. (2018a). The chiropractic vertebral subluxation Part 7: Technics and models from 1962 to 1980. *Journal of Chiropractic Humanities, 25*, 99–113. https://doi.org/10.1016/j.echu.2018.10.005
Senzon, S. (2018b). The chiropractic vertebral subluxation Part 8: Terminology, definitions, and historicity from 1966 to 1980. *Journal of Chiropractic Humanities, 25*, 114–129. https://doi.org/10.1016/j.echu.2018.10.006
Senzon, S. (2018c). Chapter 9: The life and work of R. W. Stephenson. In T. Faulkner, J. Foley, & S. Senzon (Eds.), *Palmer chiropractic Green Books: The definitive guide* (pp. 191-228). The Institute Chiropractic.

Senzon, S. (2019). *D.D. Palmer: A biography of the first chiropractor.* The Institute Chiropractic.

Senzon, S. (2022). *Truth, lies, and chiropractic* [Unpublished doctoral dissertation]. Southern Cross University, Melbourne, Australia.

Senzon, S., & Myers, S. (2019). The Morikubo trial: Content analysis of a landmark chiropractic legal case. *Chiropractic History, 39*(1), 42–116.

Serio, D. (Ed.). (2017). *33.*

Sinnott, R. (2009). *Sinnott's textbook of chiropractic philosophy.*

Stephenson, R.W. (1923). Chiropractic. [PhC thesis]. Palmer School of Chiropractic.

Stephenson, R.W. (1924). Chiropractic fundamentals. *The Chiropractor, 20*(10), 37–38.

Stephenson, R.W. (1927a). *Chiropractic textbook* (Vol. 14, 1948 ed.) Palmer School of Chiropractic.

Stephenson, R. W. (1927b). The PhC. In *Chiropractic textbook* (Vol. 14, 1948 ed., pp. 349–384). Palmer School of Chiropractic.

Still, A.T. (1892). *The philosophy and mechanical principles of osteopathy.* Hudson-Kimberly.

Stoke, J.H. (1929). What is life? *The Chiropractor, 25*(11), 9.

Stoke, J.H. (1956). What's your inspiration? *The Chiropractor, 52*(11).

Stout, R. (1988). The Ph.C. degree: An affirmation of chiropractic philosophy, 1908–1968. *Chiropractic History, 8*(1), 11–12.

Strauss, J. (1988). *Freshman philosophy.*

Strauss, J. (1991). *Chiropractic philosophy.* Foundation for the Advancement of Chiropractic Education.

Strauss, J. (1994). *Case management for straight chiropractors* (2nd ed.). Foundation for the Advancement of Chiropractic Education.

Strauss, J. (1997). *Reggie: Making the message simple.* Foundation for the Advancement of Chiropractic Education.

Strauss, J. (2017). Principle 16: Intelligence in both organic and inorganic matter. In D. Serio (Ed.), *33* (pp. 100–108).

Sullivan, D. (2017). Principle 29: Interference with the transmission of innate forces. In D. Serio (Ed.), *33* (pp. 186–190).

Tsamoutalidis, S. (2017). Principle 4: The triune of life. In D. Serio (Ed.), *33* (pp. 21–26).

Vernon, H. (1990). Toward a clinical philosophy within the discipline of chiropractic. *The Journal of the Canadian Chiropractic Association, 34*(4), 187.

Wardwell, W. (1993). Chiropractic "philosophy." *Journal of Chiropractic Humanities, 3*, 3–8. https://doi.org/10.1016/S1556-3499(13)60013-3

Waters, T. (2013). *Chasing D.D.: D.D. Palmer in the news 1886–1913.* Lulu.

Watt, B. (2003). The intelligence triune. In Barge, F. & Callender, A *Philosophical Contemplations: Viewpoints on Chiropractic Philosophy: Vol. 3.* Palmer College of Chiropractic.

Williamson, M. (1929). Intellectual adaptation. *The Chiropractor, 25*(4), 17.

Winterstein, J. (1991). Philosophical questions for the chiropractic profession. *Philosophical Constructs for the Chiropractic Profession, 1*, 3–5. https://doi.org/10.1016/S2214-9163(13)60001-9

A Teacher Affects Eternity
Arno Burnier

In early September 1973, at around 11:00 p.m., as I was waiting in the now empty Spartanburg-Greenville Airport, an unknown man with sideburns, rhinestone jewelry, and flamboyant clothing walked toward me: "You must be Arno … I am Reggie."

Yes, Dr. Reginald Gold, a world-famous Chiropractor, had come to pick me up in his Citroen Maserati, an exotic French sports car. I knew right then that I was in good hands, especially when he managed to fishtail the car on the access ramp to Interstate 85 North.

What I did not know at that time was that this man would change and transform my life, thinking, decisions, and consciousness about Life, Health, Healing, and Wellbeing.

He was to become my Chiropractic mentor, philosophy teacher, and, yes, tormentor of my intellect. Reggie was a brilliant teacher with a quick mind and keen intellect. His charisma and presence caused one to either dislike or love him, depending on one's ego. What was for sure was that no one would be unaffected by his presence or his teachings.

Reggie had the uncanny ability to present a specific building block of chiropractic principles and philosophy giving everyone a clear understanding. Then, a few days later, he questioned the class on the subject. We were eager students happy to raise our hands with answers, only to, more often than not, crush us with a powerful rebuttal. This process went on throughout all my philosophy classes. It was painful and frequently humiliating, yet it caused us students to deeply ponder the subject matter. We had to get to the very bottom of the issues at hand until it became an unarguable truth.

It is out of this process that I personally grew a strong foundation in chiropractic philosophy and principles. Over time, I realized that Reggie did not actually teach us anything; he uncovered an immutable truth within by removing layers of false beliefs acquired through socialization and the prevalent medical culture.

For me, the impact was life-changing. It gave me an internal GPS to navigate life, health, and healing issues, and a rock-solid framework to build a successful chiropractic practice. Consequently, it rippled into affecting, influencing, and touching the lives of tens of thousands of people who either came to my practice or were exposed to my teachings, seminars, and public speaking engagements.

Reggie imparted to us the awesome and exciting professional responsibility of teaching chiropractic philosophy and science as part of the practice of chiropractic. Without it, the impact of the art of chiropractic via the adjustment was nothing more to the public than a "natural drug, aspirin or pain killer."

Only through practicing all aspects of chiropractic, the philosophy, science, and art would we be able to seed and birth a new paradigm and consciousness about Life, Health, Healing, and Wellbeing. That is a game and a world changer.

It is said that a teacher affects eternity. I believe that to be true. The ongoing ripple effects will move on as long as humanity exists. That is the power of one to impact the world. To this day, some 48 years later, Reggie's words and teachings are cause for my daily gratitude towards him.

Everything I Am & Have I Owe to Chiropractic
Shawn Powers

Long before I met him, Reggie, unknowingly, had already been an influence. In my first quarter of chiropractic school, I received a gift that would change my life; a book with an intriguing title, *The Triune of Life*. Long before coffee table books were in style, the gift sat center stage on my coffee table. At the time, I did not know the value it contained. I was a student paying for my education, money for decorating wasn't available, and it looked good.

To pay for school, I worked as a critical nurse. Between long shifts at the hospital, chiropractic classes, and squeezing in time to study, I began picking up the book. Medicine was all I knew, and the concepts presented in his book were thought-provoking and exciting.

After graduation, my mission was to learn to be a better chiropractor and communicator. To that end, I purchased a box of cassette tapes of Reggie answering questions. I learned so much, especially metaphors and analogies, to improve my understanding and ability to communicate chiropractic. The message in "The Valley of the Blind" is powerful beyond measure, one of the most inspirational talks in chiropractic, and I still love listening to the message today.

After years of listening and learning from Reggie, I finally met him when we spoke at the same event. We shared a meal and had a spirited conversation about the role of x-rays in chiropractic. He was funny, direct, intelligent, and kind.

There is an African proverb, "The one who asks questions will not lose their way." Reggie asked and answered in a way that made me the chiropractor and coach I am today.

His dedication, spirit, boldness, passion, quest for knowledge, love for chiropractic, and willingness to speak his truth are traits I admire. At his 70th birthday party, the love for him was palpable; it was a blast to be there and celebrate him.

He said, "Everything I am and have I owe to chiropractic." A large part of everything I am and have in chiropractic I owe to Reggie. I am forever grateful for his influence and impact on me and chiropractic.

Dr. Gold is My Wife, I'm Reggie
Bill Decken

Dr. Reggie Gold graduated from Palmer College of Chiropractic, where he also earned the PhC for writing a thesis on the triune of life. When others referred to him as Dr. Gold, he corrected them by saying, "Dr. Gold is my wife, I'm Reggie." It is also ironic to note that Reggie spent a portion of his professional life embroiled in the politics of the profession without ever holding a specific position in a political group. His involvement with Sherman College provided plenty of political angst. Reggie was particularly concerned about the future of the chiropractic profession under the reign of the Council for Chiropractic Education (CCE). It would be the CCE that forbade Palmer College from continuing to grant the PhC, stating it was too close to PhD in appearance and not worthy of consideration at that level.

When the CCE was recognized by the Department of Education as the accrediting agency for the chiropractic profession Reggie was upset with the International Chiropractic Association's decision to support it. He and a few others relocated to a different hotel in Davenport, Iowa, and chartered the Federation of Straight Chiropractic Organizations (FSCO). It was Reggie's hope that state groups would emerge in many of the states to become the FSCO.

It was not until many years after meeting Reggie and Irene Gold, Dr. Gold, that I learned of their practice in Spring Valley, New York, a mere 3-4 miles from where I grew up. In fact, in 1983, when my father was seeking chiropractic care, he ended up in the office of Dr. Ernie Landi, who had taken over Reggie and Irene's practice. My father relayed to Dr. Landi that I was considering a career change to chiropractic, and he recommended I investigate Sherman College in South Carolina. So, indirectly, Reggie is responsible for my attending Sherman College, where I make a concerted effort to teach the principles and objective of chiropractic that I learned from him to more generations of chiropractors.

Reggie was not on the faculty at Sherman College during the years I was a student, but he was on campus a lot and always gave all-school assemblies to discuss the profession he loved and wanted to protect and grow. I was able to score a few cassette tapes of his presentations and listened to them on long car rides back home to New York. Of course, his "Layman Lecture" was a big one and probably formed the foundation for many health talks given around the world in chiropractic offices. I learned how to develop my health talk in Dr. Dick Plummer's class. Dick was another referral of Reggie's to Sherman College, and he was teaching the "baseball" talk. Innate intelligence was first base, health was second base, vertebral subluxation was third, and the chiropractic adjustment was the homerun. Right after I graduated, he produced the "N" talk, "The Chemistry of Life" talk, which became another popular approach.

Years into my own chiropractic career, I became involved in the Academy of Chiropractors Philosophers (ACP), a one-year post-graduate program developed at Sherman College that also serves as the first year of a three-year Philosophy Diplomate offered by the Center for Chiropractic Progress. It had been many years since Reggie "retired," but when I contacted him to be a presenter in the ACP program, he did not hesitate. He was always ready and willing to talk about the principles and objective of chiropractic. We did have many good conversations at Lyceums and on the Sherman campus in general.

He took exception to the popular quote, "The power that made the body heals the body." He didn't think it was a correct statement and thought chiropractors repeating that was not helpful to the profession. He said, "The power that made the body doesn't heal the body." I pointed out that the statement didn't claim that exactly, but he said it was inferred.

Reggie is known for his speaking and for keeping the chiropractic message simple. He was not known for his writing. He didn't write much. One article he did write is "The Third Paradigm," which was published in *Dynamic Chiropractic*. This article was a quick reference to how Reggie saw the profession evolve from curing all diseases to curing some conditions before settling on being a profession focused on the correction of vertebral subluxation, whether the person has a symptom/disease/condition or not. He was a huge proponent of removing camouflage and using simplicity to gain clarity of the message.

Starting in Spring Valley, New York, Reggie Gold went on to influence chiropractors around the world. Reggie took time to show interest in everyone, including non-chiropractors. Kathy Plummer Maddaloni, daughter of Dr. Dick Plummer, remembers seeing Reggie a lot. While she never had conversations with him about chiropractic related things, he was always at big picnics and other functions where others gathered around to listen to him speak. She recalls as a child and adult, Reggie always took time to talk to her, to be kind, and ask how everything was going in *her* life, even though she was not interested in the greatest passion he had in *his* life or what he was all about. She spent several Thanksgivings with Irene and Reggie in Pennsylvania and can remember how students would get envious and think it was the coolest thing to have had a meal with Reggie Gold. He was a family friend that always took the time to make her comfortable in having conversations even though they weren't chiropractic based.

It is healthy for all chiropractors in every generation to remain in contact with like-minded docs. To share chiropractic and to learn and grow together. Reggie modeled this in his home in Spring Valley, New York, where chiropractors regularly drove 2 and 3 hours from New York, New Jersey, and Pennsylvania, to attend one of his philosophy sessions. The house was sometimes overflowing, with people having to sit on the steps, maybe not being able to see Reggie, but always hearing him speak, and always hearing his message.

Let's do the same; let's keep it simple. Let's keep it clear.

The Big Idea
Donald Francis

If ever we see more clearly, it is because we stand on the shoulders of giants like Reginald Gold.

Dr. Reggie Gold was probably an excellent chiropractor. In this, he is amongst many, but he clearly stands out from the crowd, for he possessed a gift for being able to tell a story and do so with conviction, humor, simplicity, and eloquence. I never heard his gift in person when I was at Palmer College, but it has endured mercifully through his PhC thesis, *The Triune of Life*, and those clever people who saw fit to make recordings of some of his great talks. Had I heard his famous "Layman Lecture" earlier, it most likely would have energized my chiropractic journey. Still, for many years of that journey, I wasn't ready to accept those principles that make this profession unique.

Chiropractic philosophy is often compared to religion, which is regrettable in that both require the individual to accept the concept of an intangible intelligence, something greater than the mind of a human but without which we could have no form or function. Extending this similarity, I used to make some strong assumptions about our world that could quite easily have been described as atheist. I certainly rejected all forms of intelligence. When you have a strong conviction, it often takes something special to shift them, for before you do, you have to admit you may have been wrong. Mercifully I have conceded I was wrong and accepted certain intangible truths, and I now live my life in full acceptance of and congruence with our first principle and the next 32, but it wasn't always thus.

One day I rejected religious faith of any kind in 2004 as I considered the motives of a young man who killed himself in a catastrophic act of self-harm. He had driven an old Ford pickup truck, loaded with explosives, into the gate of a British Army camp in a town called Az Zubayr in Southern Iraq during the summer of 2004. The act's tragedy was its futility; his death caused no casualties except for himself, but it did wise us up a lot, and it made me think about why someone would kill themselves for a cause. It was an epiphany that sent my soul into the depths of the spiritual sewer for almost a decade. As the product of church schools and a Christian upbringing, I immediately rejected that philosophical basis upon which I had lived the first 30 years of my life and embraced a solid atheist agenda for a decade or more. What motivated a young man to end his life in such a violent manner, and for what cause? It takes enormous courage to kill yourself, along with serious motivation. He had been brought up as a Shia Moslem to Arab Moslem parents in a predominantly Islamic country, and I had been brought up as a Christian child in a Christian society. He was a Moslem, and me a Christian, and I concluded that the biggest difference between him and I was what we understood to be normal and therefore right; had I been born he and he been born me, how easily we could have been in other's shoes. His "Moslem-ness" was the product of his upbringing and environment, as my "Christian-ness" was the result of mine. I concluded at that moment (for we both could not be right we must be wrong) that our beliefs were the product of our circumstances and upbringing and that all religion was, therefore, bunkum. Our beliefs, race, culture, and more are so much a product of our environment and family and so varied upon the earth that religions must all be wrong. Reggie might not have appreciated this paragraph about religion, but it may illustrate why, upon arriving at Palmer College, I struggled so much with accepting chiropractic philosophy at that time. I could not accept an intangible and actively closed my mind to the possibility of it.

I never read *The Triune of Life* at chiropractic college, but I wish I had. It's hard to have a small practice if you get "the big idea," and for too long, my practice was a lot harder than it needed to be. If I had understood and accepted the fourth of our 33 principles, the first few years of struggle could have been shortened significantly and the pain reduced by so much. Sadly despite sitting in the same halls that Reggie had at Palmer College, I didn't know *The Triune of Life* existed as less emphasis had been placed on the study and, more importantly, the understanding of our philosophy than it had once upon a time. We were at least exposed to the 33 principles. But here's the rub; while at chiropractic college, I was not ready for it, so I would have read it with a preconceived notion of rejection. My military experience in Iraq had left indelible marks on my mind. When I arrived at Palmer College for the spring intake of 2006, I was horrified at the principle and notion of chiropractic philosophy. Because of my conservatively formed character, I rejected our philosophy for its difference and strangeness. So, I knuckled down and thought I would get through as fast as possible, and then I could get on with "fixing" people when I left.

Hitherto I had spent many years as an on-off chiropractic patient, always a disciple and always a fan; I had, however, never considered a care plan or thought about the wisdom of my own body. I had instead marveled at the ability of the chiropractor to remove my back pain so quickly or how my chilblains had been "cured" by my chiropractor in only one visit. The day I attended my maiden lecture at Palmer College, 28 years had passed since my first chiropractic adjustment, and I had never heard the chiropractic story. Thus, I held my chiropractors in awe, and chiropractic, well, I had barely given it a moment's notice, especially as to its uniqueness and its potential contribution towards the health of mankind. Forward 15 years, the lens through which I see the world is different, and *The Triune of Life* is venerably "dog-eared" as one of the most simple and admired chiropractic texts I possess. Once I eventually devoured Reggie's 1963 thesis, I was immediately in total agreement, for my mind was opening and ready to accept its "simple" brilliance.

Reggie's most admirable quality as a chiropractic thought leader was to distill the key principles of chiropractic into a logical and easily comprehensible vignette, either in this notable thesis or through his lay lectures which are available to hear for all on YouTube. His telling of "The Valley of the Blind" is the one lecture above most others that hardens the backbones of chiropractors to retain our separateness as a distinct profession. I am immeasurably grateful for this recording, as are chiropractors worldwide. Many would forgo so much of our uniqueness for the "coveted" warm acceptance by our cousins in orthodox medicine. But whenever they try, they often find themselves being treated as a lower form of therapist with a limited remit. I would rather swim alone upstream as a mighty salmon, knowing I'm going in the right direction, than be a guppy with all the other tiddlers in a pond full of bigger fish.

Reggie candidly observed that "to inject one's philosophy into a closed mind is a hopelessly frustrating experience." My journey from a hard-hearted and active atheist, denying the participation of any form of intelligent complicity within universal space, to actively embracing and extolling our philosophical guiding principles was not an epiphany as my Iraq experience had been, but a slow and gradual realization. And thus, it is often with those who seek our care.

Reggie could no doubt have called the birds from the trees with his charismatic charm and eloquent approach. But he also possessed an extraordinary capacity for reasoning and logical delivery, which are very hard to argue against, and heaven knows many tried. This ability to explain the big idea simply but also to defend it logically and systematically has helped so many people struggling with its uniqueness and the vastness of it. So compelling is Reggie's logical argument in his thesis that it was, in fact, his explanation of principle number four that helped me to fully accept principle number one, our overarching principle - a sort of reverse acceptance. Our first principle states that: The Major premise of chiropractic is that *there is a Universal Intelligence in all matter, constantly giving to it all of its properties and activities, thus maintaining it in existence*. I initially had so much trouble with this concept because I had actively closed my mind to its possibility of being true. But it was examining our fourth principle; *Life is a triunity having three necessary united factors, namely: intelligence, force, and matter* and Reggie's simple exploration, that precluded my final rejection of my atheistic stance, the acceptance of our first principle, and of Universal Intelligence. You can imagine what happened to my practice?

When discussing chiropractic philosophy, we must always ensure we are discussing the same thing. There is so much diversity within our profession, and often this diversity finds itself so emotionally expressed as to create division. One of the biggest reasons for this is that we must understand and articulate whether we are talking about the same things, albeit the natural or the supernatural. There is little doubt that Sir Isaac Newton and Albert Einstein were highly intelligent people, and their work shaped the thinking and, therefore, the course of humanity. As a former Officer of Artillery, I never doubted that energy could move matter and deliver lethality at an extraordinary distance. Using Newtonian mathematics, we could calculate how to drop a 100lb shell within 100m square at a range of 40km. The laws are that precise. Einstein said that's all true, but when we break our matter apart, we discover that the energy used to propel that shell and the shell are made of the same fundamental building blocks, and so we have the birth of the quantum understanding of our universe. Energy is matter, and matter is energy; their relationship is relative.

As a former Christian turned atheist, I now find myself deeply spiritual. In this spiritual mind, I could accept that universal intelligence is a supernatural order, and for me, this is okay, but I don't think we have to. Within the quantum model of reality, we understand that there is an intelligent organization that is natural; if everything is energy organized differently and vibrating at different frequencies, there is, therefore, an intelligence within this energy, giving it its properties and, therefore, activities. I hold some of our earlier chiropractic philosophers in very high regard for their recognition of this and their incredible understanding. Their appreciation and articulation of such an enormous topic, Stephenson's careful description in 1927 of the 33 principles, and Reggie's exalted examination of the fourth principle are examples. And D.D.? His visionary understanding is almost extraordinary as to have been divinely inspired.

Max Plank, the father of quantum physics, expressed that "all matter originates and exists only by virtue of a force which brings the particle of an atom to vibration and holds this minute solar system together. We must assume behind this force the conscious and intelligent mind. This mind is the matrix of all matter." (The Nature of Matter, 1944) Am I the only person that finds this similar to our guiding principle and the fourth principle combined?

Stephenson wrote, and I repeat here for ease:

> The Major premise of chiropractic is that there is a Universal Intelligence in all matter, constantly giving to it all of its properties and activities, thus maintaining it in existence, and Life is a triunity having three necessary united factors, namely: intelligence, force and matter.

Reggie's use of deductive reasoning in the *Triune* that "Organization is the prime manifestation of Intelligence, and intelligence the sole cause of organization," is so simple because it is true and concise. There is a level of intelligence within the universe that keeps our world afloat within the solar system, the milky way, and countless galaxies. The more scientists understand the workings and manifestation of this intelligent order, the more they can predict from it. Intelligence, therefore, can be both natural and perhaps supernatural, but before arguing this point, both parties must decide which concept of intelligence they are arguing about. Much of the division pervasive throughout chiropractic's existence has been because opposing views are arguing but have not agreed on exactly what they are arguing about.

As we celebrate the 60th year of *The Triune of Life*, chiropractic finds itself a larger profession with its people distributed across the globe. Divisions exist because of the diversity of our profession and relative and mutual intolerance of this diversity. Before I fell into step with the "big idea," I had some success with patients and grew a small practice. Once I accepted that there are three necessary distinguishable and yet wholly integrated elements needed for the expression of life; force, matter, and intelligence, and that through the mechanism of the chiropractic adjustment, we can affect the level of that expression, causing an infinite ability to change the course of a person's existence, my practice exploded. In this acceptance of the major premise, I had become a ChiropracTOR, whereas before, I just did chiropractic. As I *am* a ChiropracTOR, I *do* ChiropracTIC, and therefore I *have* a wonderful life of service and abundance. Reggie was so full of "certainty" and "purpose" that he had no fee and suggested his patrons spend as much as they perceived to be equal to the value they received. A wooden box existed on the wall in his reception, into which these monies could be inserted. His faith was rewarded, as his office was probably the largest of its time. When you get the "big idea," it's impossible to have a small practice. In gratitude and appreciation for Dr. Reginald Gold for helping us all to stand on his shoulders and, therefore, to see more clearly.

One of a Kind
Armand Rossi

Two Brief Personal Stories about Reggie Gold:

In 1971, at twenty years of age, I had just ended my two years of pre-chiropractic education at Rutgers University and matriculated into Columbia Institute of Chiropractic in Manhattan, New York, to begin my chiropractic education. I had been a chiropractic patient regularly since five years of age. I loved chiropractic care and could see myself in this profession as a doctor/physician, creating healthy lifestyles for my patients and bringing the medical profession and chiropractic together under one roof.

Then during that first palpation class I had at Columbia, I was paired up with a woman in the class named Irene Gold. Little did I know how much that pairing would change my life. Irene would talk to me, push me, and cajole me to a better and deeper understanding of chiropractic philosophy. I learned that she was married to Reggie, who was in his early stages as a chiropractic icon. I visited their home in Spring Valley, New York, which was my first in-depth exposure to the chiropractic philosophy that would forever change me into a "chiropractic radical."

Every time I heard Reggie speak (too many to count), I gained a greater depth of the knowledge behind chiropractic. Interestingly enough, I don't think Reggie's words changed at all. I just listened with different ears each time.

To this day, Irene and I have remained good friends and share a common wish for the unadulterated purity of the chiropractic profession as a separate and distinct expression of the correction of vertebral subluxation. I have had no intention of amalgamating chiropractic as a part of any other profession.

In 2009, I was honored to be included in a book by David Scheiner, DC, called *Chiropractic Revealed, One on One with the Great Masters of a Misunderstood Profession.* I was one of 20 interviews with many renowned chiropractors conversing on different aspects of the profession. Of course, Reggie was one of the group.

After the publication, Dr. Scheiner organized a presentation by many of us held at Life University. Topics were given to us. My topic was "Optimum Abundance" and how it relates to chiropractic. When

I put together my presentation and got ready to present it, I noticed that Reggie was right there in the audience. I immediately started to sweat. Reggie was steadfast on the philosophy of chiropractic, and I've seen him call out other people regarding it. The last thing I wanted was to be "called out" by him. So my nerves were exploding during my talk.

After I finished and walked off the stage, Reggie beckoned me over to him. Now I was really shaken, thinking that he was going to give me a piece of his mind. Well, he looked at me and said, "One of the best talks on chiropractic philosophy I've heard in 30 years!" It was an amazing moment for me. To hear that from one of the most respected philosophers in chiropractic truly made my day, week, month, year, and possibly my life.

He was one of a kind, an original, and one of the mentally strongest people I have ever known.

A Turning Point in Chiropractic
Felicia Stewart

Reggie Gold was a turning point in chiropracTIC. Between the publication of *The Triune of Life* and his writings which put forward the construct for "The Third Paradigm" of chiropractic, he was a pivotal point in the evolution of vitalistic chiropractic. Reggie was a leap forward in communicating chiropractic philosophy with elegant succinctness. Historically, the elemental diagram of the triune often makes chiropractic philosophy difficult to grasp. Surely nothing so straightforward could be so profound or have such far-reaching implications for humankind. In B.J.'s letter of approval to Stephenson for his *Chiropractic Textbook*, B.J. praises Stephenson distilling the principles of chiropractic into a book "simple enuf for the layman, deep enuf for the savant" (p. vii). In Reggie's *The Triune of Life*, he is well remembered for making the same contribution. It is a masterpiece of focus on force, the "missing link." The connection between the immaterial and the material, intelligence, and matter. The function of intelligence is to create force, and the function of matter is to express force. Force unites intelligence and matter.

That is our access point in the triune. We assist in removing the interference to the forces created by innate intelligence so that the matter of the body can fully express the intentions of innate intelligence that are contained in the messages sent as the mental impulse. The simplicity of the relationship between the points of the triune makes clear our purpose as chiropractors. It is not our innate intelligence creating the forces which keep the body of the person we are caring for in active organization; it is their innate intelligence. We are not trying to control or reorganize the matter of their body either, the matter of their body responds to the directives of their innate intelligence. Our only access point in the triune is the recognition that the forces created by innate, mental impulses, must be transmitted. In many living organisms, they are transmitted by a nervous system. Being a physical pathway, the transmission of those forces can suffer interference via subluxation. Hence, our reason for being chiropractors is to correct subluxations. In his "The Third Paradigm," Reggie again distills chiropractic down to its essential nature, saying, "Chiropractic holds that a vertebral subluxation, by its very existence, inhibits the body's ability to fully express its inherent potential." And that "In short, people with vertebral subluxations would be better off without them."

It is one thing for chiropractors to grasp the essential nature of chiropractic and quite another for those we are caring for to grasp it. Reggie was as clear and direct in his teachings concerning communicating with the public as he was about communicating chiropractic philosophy to chiropractors. Many have heard Reggie describe what transpired in his office during an initial visit. He often described how he would get out a piece of paper and dutifully record the person's symptoms and illnesses. Once completed, he would crumple up the paper and toss it aside, saying that he did not treat any of those things, and would then proceed to tell them what chiropractic was about. Demonstrative and to the point, to be sure, but even if the listening student or chiropractor chose a slightly less dramatic tactic, Reggie's message was clear; be bold, be fearless. Chiropractic deserves no less. Those who come to us for care deserve no less. People have all kinds of beliefs about what chiropractic is, and Reggie reminded us that it is up to us to educate them on what chiropractic is and is not.

Chiropractic is about correcting subluxations, and that act alone has profound and far-reaching implications for humankind. As it says eleven times in the Green Books, "We never know how far-reaching something we may think, say or do today will affect the lives of millions tomorrow." Reggie shared a personal story that speaks to the heart of this. He spoke of a man who came in to see him seeking back pain relief. Reggie educated him on the nature of chiropractic, and he got under Reggie's care. After a while, he brought in the rest of his family. After a month or two of the family being under regular care, Reggie said he asked one of the children what she liked best about being under chiropractic care. "My daddy doesn't beat me anymore," was her startling response. To this day, I cannot relate this story without tears streaming down my cheeks. How can we possibly know the totality of the life-altering impact on those we free from the devastating consequences of vertebral subluxation? It is too immense to comprehend. However restoration of ease plays out in each individual, it is out of our hands; but we can be sure that across the whole of humanity, it results in greater wholeness of being.

A truly wonderful thing about chiropractic is that excepting the chiropractor's obligation to meet the responsibilities of practice, foremost being educating people and correcting subluxations, chiropractic isn't really about the chiropractor, it is about those receiving care. It's about their expression of life. Another story Reggie told puts this into perspective and is most relevant to the times we live in at the moment. Reggie spoke of a thought experiment that had gone around in chiropractic circles whereby chiropractors were asked to consider someone with a heart transplant. Should they be adjusted or not? The potential issue is that if the body worked better without subluxation, might it not do a better job of rejecting the foreign heart? Chiropractors were divided in their answers, some saying yes, others no. Reggie too had an answer; ask the person with the heart transplant what they would like to do. Was it not, in reality, their decision? This also has stayed with me across the years of practice. It's not about us as chiropractors; it's about them—their expression of life, their choices. Clearly educate, we must, but we can only make decisions about ourselves and respect the sovereignty of others to choose their path.

To love chiropractic philosophy is easy. It is rational, logical, and applicable to all life, inorganic and organic. The organization of matter is the manifestation of the forces created by intelligence. The organization is the same whether we consider a planetary system or a table, a human being, or a living tree whose innate intelligence is doing the same job as our innate intelligence, keeping the matter of the organism in active organization. It is fundamental to how the natural world works.

It can be challenging to wrap one's head around this philosophy as the universal principle and then bring it down to the ins and outs, ups and downs, of running a practice. Yet, Reggie spoke to both with ease and clarity. He made the philosophy accessible to the student, putting it into context with their classwork, and to the chiropractor caring for people in their office. He was a master of making chiropractic relevant to our daily lives. Reggie said the triune describes the heart and soul of chiropractic philosophy, and he shall be remembered similarly. He shared himself with the chiropractic profession, giving his all from the heart and soul of his love for chiropractic. We are still in awe of Reggie and forever grateful for this.

ChiropracTIC
Graham Dobson

I'm honored to be asked to write this tribute for the 60th anniversary republication of Reggie Gold's *The Triune of Life*. I am enormously grateful for Reggie Gold's influence on my life, but I'm not sure I ever thanked him for that. When I was a student at Palmer College from 1968 to 1971, he often held philosophy talks on campus, but it wasn't until after I graduated in 1971 that I really heard what he was saying. Reggie did a public lay lecture in a large auditorium in my home city, Auckland, New Zealand, in late 1971. Local chiropractors filled that venue with busloads of their patients. Reggie was courageous, dynamic, so logical, and charismatic and made a huge impression on me and everyone else. He was always held in high esteem over the years by most New Zealand chiropractors.

In 1972 Reggie held a weekend seminar in Sydney, Australia, and I was there, hanging on to every word. I bought his LP record "The Golden Facts of Life and Health" and played it endlessly, absorbing every story and every one-liner. The record gave me the ammunition and confidence to explain chiropractic enthusiastically in my own way. I eventually developed the courage to hold regular "lay lectures" and grew a large family practice based largely on Reggie's inspiration.

As my vision to reach more people with the chiropractic story grew, I realized that, like Reggie, I could have a greater worldwide influence by teaching chiropracTIC. I was accepted for a faculty position at Sherman College in 1979. This is where I first read his wonderful *The Triune of Life*, and I have owned and given away many copies over the years.

We eventually returned to New Zealand for family reasons, and in the late 1980s, Reggie would stay in our house at Orewa Beach for two weeks in December each year. He came to rest up after a busy year of traveling and lecturing before traveling to Queensland, Australia, to meet Irene, where they would spend an extended southern hemisphere summer vacation. It was a privilege to host Reggie in our home. We were able to give him the space to have quiet time, take long walks, rest, and read novels. He also would chat with our kids about their lives, but mostly they remember him at that time as being a very quiet man.

My association with Reggie did not end there. In the early 90s, I was inspired to return to teaching and took up a faculty position at Southern California College of Chiropractic, and Reggie often visited there to lecture. In 1998 I joined the faculty of the New Zealand College, where we have enjoyed a long association with Reggie and Irene. They have both contributed their time and talents to students and faculty in the classrooms and at the NZCC Lyceum, as well as financial support.

In my years of teaching which often involved chiropractic technique, I endeavored to include the philosophic "why?" The triunity of intelligence, force, and matter is so relevant in that context because it is at the heart of what we do in practice. Reggie taught technique seminars which were based on the concept that the body is smart; "Innate is always aware of every physiological need and will therefore employ the intrinsic and intersegmental spinal muscles to strive to correct subluxation." He taught muscle palpation as a means of reading what innate intelligence is trying to do with subluxations. He also taught "adjusting into ease" instead of fighting with fixations. It works because the body certainly is smart and will use the force to bring about the correction of subluxations. Being adjusted by Reggie was an enlightening experience in more ways than one. It was so smooth, easy, and masterful.

Being in the TIC headspace is so important in keeping me on purpose in practice. There is nothing better than the concepts of the triune of life to provide that higher purpose headspace of turning on life in people rather than focusing so much on the small stuff.

I am grateful to have spent time with the great Reggie Gold, with his amazing intellect and ability to bring the philosophy of chiropractic to life. Although we mourned his loss in 2012, we also celebrated his contribution to the profession he so dearly loved. He lived a courageous and inspirational chiropracTIC life.

It's About the Music
Patrick Sim

Reggie sat at a table by himself, watching the crowd dance. The New Zealand College of Chiropractic Lyceum party was in full swing, yet he kept to the side, content to be witness to the fun. I seized the moment and pulled up a chair next to him. My arrival seemed to bring him back from his thoughts, and he gave a blink, turned to look at me, and gave a small smile.

I opened with something weak like, "Are you having a good time?" He replied, "Oh, this really is not my thing."

I tried to be funny by saying, "I bet you'd rather be defending chiropractic on TV!" but that got absolutely nothing. I clearly felt Reggie didn't want to make small talk.

I tried to engage him on spinology and chiropractic politics, but that only gained a little interest. Left in that awkward position where you don't know what to say next and don't know how to make a graceful exit, I sat there with Reggie Gold for what felt like years in awkward silence. The revelers were jiving to some 70's classic like *Blame It on the Boogie* or *Nutbush*, miming the lyrics with body gyrations. Feeling the beat of that music in my body stimulated a question, so I asked, "What kind of music do you like, Reggie?"

His face changed, and it seemed he became more animated, "I like jazz," he said, turning to look straight at me.

"I don't know much about Jazz," I admitted. "Just some of the names like Ella Fitzgerald and Miles Davis, but I couldn't tell you any of their songs. What do you like about jazz?"

"Yes, that's them, all of those guys. Oh, it's not about the songs; it's about the music. The way each instrument works independently and yet works off each other; how one instrument can seem to go off on a tangent and yet come back to the rhythm; how it can all seem so chaotic and yet still in perfect harmony; how each musician can take the lead at different times, and the music is better for it. That's why I like jazz."

Reggie looked at me.

Strangely, I can't remember leaving that chair beside Reggie. I don't remember anything else from that night. I don't even know if the way I remember the conversation was how it really went. But I know how what he said to me felt.

I'd like to think I am still chatting with him, sitting next to him at that table. Perhaps there are others around that table, other chiropractors and teachers who are no longer on this earth but counsel and inspire me nonetheless.

I have tried to like jazz since then, but it doesn't sound to me as it must have to Reggie, and, of course, that's not the point. The point is that for a few minutes, in a loud, dark, post-seminar celebratory dinner, I chatted with Reggie Gold, and he spoke to me. From the heart. And I met his intelligence.

Chiropractic is About Life
Neil Cohen

Reggie Gold changed my chiropractic life.

Now I know that is not unusual for some of you to hear because Reggie (and Irene) changed and influenced many lives by pouring into various audiences and individuals for decades in an "always developing" chiropractic profession. As this profession developed, one thing was for sure, Reggie was anchored, and he knew what he knew. This came with an incredible desire to impart logical and significant meaning to the philosophical constructs that make chiropractic separate, distinct, and distinguished from anything else offered to humankind.

For me, as a newly married twenty-five-year-old, it was deciding to go to Life Chiropractic College in 1983 that became the backdrop and where my "Reggie" story begins. It's curious sometimes how and why we make certain decisions. It was 1980 when I received my first chiropractic adjustment, and at that moment that day, I chose to be a chiropractor.

In those days, Dr. Sid Williams was at Life College, and I swallowed subluxation-centered chiropractic hook, line, and sinker. In those years at Life, a philosophical seed was planted deep within my chiropractic soul. I believed chiropractic was the answer to a misinformed and fallen world that idolized unnatural and pernicious choices that only the most medically educated minds could offer. I was thoroughly unaware of objective straight chiropractic at the time. The only thing I was certain of was that the world needed what chiropractic had to offer.

My first seven years in practice were spent as an associate delivering subluxation-centered chiropractic adjustments absent of any teaching of Reggie Gold. Frankly, I did not know or feel I was missing anything. I was happy to deliver chiropractic in this model. I opened my first office in late 1993, and after a few months of early success, I decided to hire my first associate, Dr. David Yachter. It's funny how you can always tell the winners from the starting gate. David was the passionate young chiropractor to turn me on to the brilliance of Reggie Gold. We listened in my car to the same cassette tape over and over again. In this one message, Reggie Gold gave me a brand new and deeper perspective of chiropractic philosophy and decision-making as it pertained to practice, life, and the intimate connection and profound presence (or absence) of vertebral subluxation. I don't know exactly how I missed this message at Life College, but I did. Chiropractic is about life and the best expression of ourselves in this life. Health just happens to be one of those expressions among many.

Reggie used to ask rhetorically on the first visit, "If I can correct all your subluxations and not even one of your symptoms gets any better, would you like me to put your subluxations back where I found them?" He knew and understood that it was more than just getting sick people well and keeping the well from getting sick. He apprehended and declared without any hyperbole what it would mean if every policeman, politician, airline pilot, barber, and garbage man lived unsubluxated lives. His mission was to change the world, even if he had to do it one family at a time. He certainly deepened my understanding, and in turn, he made me a better communicator and a better chiropractor.

It wasn't long before I was introduced to the "Chemistry of Life," the letter "N." This logical, insightful, and cohesive explanation from a physiological perspective gave me the confidence and certainty to take my practice to another level. It reinvigorated and fed the early love I was supernaturally given for chiropractic and its inherent simplicity.

Keep in mind I did not meet Reggie Gold until around 2011. It was the first and only time I was able to hear him live. I was not disappointed. He spoke no differently than any other time I'd ever heard him, but you see, that was the brilliance of Reggie Gold. His message always remained the same; it never changed. He just knew how to say the same thing fifty different ways. Here's what happened when you listened to Reggie; if you were ready, his message changed you!

The following week after his live presentation at the Southern Chiropractic Association's Saturday Night Live, I was compelled to do whatever it took to locate and dive into Reggie's *The Triune of Life*. Ironically the only place I was able to find and purchase *The Triune of Life* was the Sherman College of Chiropractic bookstore. This was the first time Sherman College had ever come across my chiropractic radar. I mean, I heard of Sherman but had at no time had an inkling that someday (March 2014), I would be the Executive Vice President of Sherman College of Chiropractic.

The Triune of Life is 55 pages of pure chiropractic scholarship. I voraciously unpacked, digested, and swallowed it hook, line and sinker. Once again, Reggie Gold changed my chiropractic life. It's been 60 years since its publication as Reggie Gold's thesis for his PhC, and I am honored to have had access to the wisdom therein.

As fate would have it, after twenty-eight years of practice, I was called into leadership where chiropractic currently lives, Sherman College. I have, like Reggie, adopted Sherman College of Chiropractic, and although I only met Reggie that one time in 2011, Irene Gold has become a close family friend to my wife Randi, Dr. Sarah, my daughter, and Dr. Michael, my son. They are both chiropractors and Sherman College of Chiropractic graduates.

Thank you, Drs. Reggie and Irene Gold, for your hard work, dedication, philanthropy, and commitment, and all you have displayed, and you, Irene continue to demonstrate as the Gold legacy continues. Your myriad contributions have blessed our profession. There are many lives you have changed and many lives you have yet to change.

The "Gold"en Years
Patti Giuliano

The first time I met Reggie Gold, I was being interviewed by his wife, Irene, for the position of becoming the wife of Peter Kevorkian, chiropractor. Irene was Peter's "Chiro Mom," and he wanted her blessing.

I remember Reggie firing questions to me (over dinner in Sheepshead Bay, New York) about my philosophy of life and chiropractic. I felt very intimidated by him, and I don't think I was able to eat much. After all, Reggie was a legend, and I was a new graduate sitting here having dinner with him and his wife, the infamous Dr. Irene Gold. Needless to say, I got the seal of approval from Irene, and thankfully, I passed Reggie's inquisition. Peter and I have been happily married for over 38 years to date.

Fast forward a year or so to Scottsdale, Arizona, and the "ADIO" seminars hosted by Drs. Terry Rondberg and Gary Dunn. I got to hear Reggie speak from the stage for the first time. WOW!!! I could listen to that English accent all day!! I was blown away at how he was able to relay the essence of chiropractic, the impact of the subluxation, and how correcting a subluxation allowed the body to adapt better to the environment. It wasn't about "getting sick people well," as I was previously taught. It was more than that. Using logic and deductive reasoning, Reggie was able to get me to see the bigger picture and get the concept that everyone with a spine who was alive was a chiropractic candidate.

Reggie rocked my world with that talk, and Peter and I went back to our practice and "tweaked" our procedures and communications, and our practice grew in quantity and quality as a result. Many of our patients could see the benefits of staying under care for a lifetime – because it was the best thing they could do for their bodies whether they had symptoms or not. Many of those patients are still in our practice 30 + years later.

Reggie taught me the "pie chart" (the pie representing all the people in my community), in which he explained that if you are going to treat conditions, you will get a certain percentage of people (a slice of the pie) that will come to you, as a chiropractor, for that condition. And he would ask, "If their pain goes away, what will they do? And if their pain doesn't go away, what will they do?" And the obvious answer to either question was that the patient would leave because their objective was met.

He ingrained in me over the 30 or so years of listening to him give the same talk, "If you are taking care of vertebral subluxations, you have the entire pie to draw from." And if you could "get people to see the benefit of correcting subluxations because they are an abomination to their physiology, then they would most likely stay and bring their children." Hearing that was an aha moment for me (even after the 50th time I heard him say it).

Reggie had a tremendous impact on my life as a chiropractor. I credit him for being one of the most influential mentors, to me, in my success. He brought out in me the essence of what I already valued in life and knew chiropractic could be. That has allowed me, along with my husband Peter, to transform the lives of hundreds of thousands of people in our 38 years of practice.

Reggie was a great man, and I would be remiss if I did not acknowledge the significant contribution his wife, Dr. Irene Gold, has made to chiropractic and to me personally. She was Reggie's life partner and his greatest supporter. Irene is "golden" through and through. Most of all, I am proud to call her my friend.

I was blessed to be at Reggie's 80th birthday gala in Pennsylvania, and I am honored to be a contributor to this historic document celebrating what would have been Reggie's 97th birthday.

Setting Me on My Path
David Koch

What can I possibly say about Reggie, the person who single-handedly set me on the deeply fulfilling philosophical and professional path I have walked for the last forty-seven years of my life? My high school chiropractor, Dr. Ed Rahuba, made me watch a 16mm film strip of Reggie in his office. Since that first moment when I heard Reggie speak, I have tried my best to do the only thing Reggie ever actually demanded of me: "Think, dammit, think!"

It was in that same moment he gave me my first exposure to the simple but very subtle ideas that underly, define, and validate the chiropractic that I received, learned to deliver, and delivered. I've had the privilege of helping many others embrace what I learned as the foundation of their philosophical and professional lives. Reggie, thanks for the shoulder up!

I had the privilege of writing the preface to the second edition of Reggie's *The Triune of Life* in 1998. In it, I wrote:

> Reggie Gold's *The Triune of Life* stands as one of the classic interpretations of the philosophy of B. J. Palmer as developed in R. W. Stephenson's *Chiropractic Text Book.*
>
> This reprint is the outcome of my experiences as a straight chiropractor and a chiropractic philosophy professor. In both capacities, I have been asked many times if there was some book or article that would give the interested party a deeper insight into chiropractic philosophy. Whereas as a philosophy instructor, I have always been quick to refer to Stephenson's, the classic chiropractic philosophy text, I have also known that most people are not going to take the time to dig into such a thick, expansive tome. I have, therefore, always been pleased to have Dr. Gold's *The Triune of Life* as a more accessible alternative recommendation.
>
> (Abridged from p. 5)

Thank you, Reggie, for the philosophic legacy you created for us.

Making the Message Empowering
Adrian B. Wenban

Dr. Reginald Gold was a giant in the chiropractic profession. His ideas inspired a generation of practicing chiropractors and will likely influence generations to come. Gold's simple and clear chiropractic message helped shift the direction of many in the profession towards non-therapeutic objectives. However, even with the passing of 60 years since the publication of *The Triune of Life*, many of the questions and much of the potential of Gold's writings remain academically unexplored.

When asked to consider the influence of his ideas and how they have impacted the world, I am immediately drawn to the question, *How have I most obviously used Gold's words and concepts as a practicing chiropractor?* The answer is that I have used the related clinical metaphors as heuristic devices with which to frame patients' thinking in order to better empower patients to make health-related decisions and take positive action in their lives.

In this brief commentary, I suggest there may be value in comparing and contrasting the metaphors that dominate communication driven by biomedical theory and chiropractic core metaphors. Furthermore, I suggest that the utility of Gold's ideas and the profession's core metaphors deserve at least preliminary testing in relation to concepts like growth mindset, self-efficacy, and health-enhancing behaviours. Finally, I posit a set of hypotheses for testing, which might provide more answers to the questions: What is the lasting influence of Gold's ideas, and how might they further impact the world?

Communications about health and disease often employ metaphors, which can help people understand complex issues. Metaphors lie at the heart of our everyday communications and our practice as chiropractors. The purpose of a metaphor is to take something we know and use it to explain something we don't know. The word has roots in the Greek *metapherein*, meaning to transfer or carry. Metaphors influence how individuals think about and frame a particular topic—that is, they establish a mindset (Lakoff & Johnson, 1980). Research on conceptual metaphor theory shows that metaphors shape how we think and impact our emotions, motivation, and, very importantly, our behavioral intentions (Landau et al., 2018; Wallis & Nerlich, 2005).

The metaphors of "Killer Bugs" and "War" are often used to discuss biomedically related topics ranging from cancer, acute infectious disease, and epidemics/pandemics. Such disease-related metaphors emphasizing threat-from-outside, draw on shared knowledge to grab attention and express a sense of urgency, thereby creating a call to emergency action (Flusberg et al., 2018). However, when such "threat-from-outside" language is used to describe diseases, it comes at a cost. For example, metaphors focusing on "disease-from-outside" can move the locus of control beyond the individual's grasp and fail to build self-efficacy and empower health-enhancing action (Hauser & Schwarz, 2015; Hauser & Schwarz, 2020). This is currently of heightened importance because the very actions needed by those who find themselves in COVID-19 high-risk groups (obesity, hypertension, diabetes, asthma, Chronic Obstructive Pulmonary Disease) are lifestyle-related (Ko et al., 2021).

In contrast to "disease-from-outside" focused rhetoric, "health-from-within" metaphors that evoke attainable proactive health-enhancing behaviours, like those that might benefit the health-related challenges accompanying the current COVID-19 pandemic, may be more likely to foster growth mindsets and self-efficacy (Landau et al., 2018). Metaphors drawn from Gold's *Triune of Life* together build a health-from-within narrative. Metaphors like "dis-ease," "adaptability," and "intelligence," when woven together, help move one's focus and the locus of health-related control within, as seen in this quote:

> The ability to change function instantly in response to need is a tangible demonstration of the difference between the living and the non-living. A living body, when cut, moves instantly to initiate repair processes well as the many other responses needed to adapt to the new situation. Every single change in internal or external environment demands a corresponding adaptive change by the living organism... Since the internal environment changes in thousands of ways everysecond of life, adaptive response must also be as constant and as rapid. By this method, and only by this method can the intelligence of the body fulfill its purpose of maintaining coordinated function, with each part doing its job for the benefit of the whole unit (Gold, 1963).

Just as scientists advance theories to explain the world, people also develop implicit theories, often referred to as a mindset, to help them to understand the nature of reality and human attributes (Dweck, 1999). Growth mindsets are built on the assumption that humans and their characteristics can change due to growth, life experience, education, and maturation. In contrast, individuals with fixed mindsets believe human characteristics are relatively fixed and unchangeable across time. These individuals think of attributes as "carved in stone" (Dweck, 2006). As a result, mindsets are typically assessed along a continuum from fixed to growth and, despite their location on the continuum, can be moved by way of metaphor and/or explicit messaging.

Research generally supports the idea that mindsets create cognitive frameworks that drive the meaning assigned to events, especially when individuals try to cope with stressful or threatening situations. Individuals with growth mindsets tend to react more adaptively than those with fixed mindsets (Compas et al., 2001). Furthermore, evidence links growth mindsets, reduced psychological distress, and active coping (Burnette et al., 2020).

Self-efficacy is the belief in the ability to plan and strategize ways to progress toward desired end states (Bandura, 1977). A growing body of literature now links growth mindsets to greater self-efficacy (Burnette et al., 2013), such that individuals with growth mindsets view challenges as part of human development and thus acquire a more resilient sense of self-efficacy throughout life. Furthermore, growth mindset interventions lead to greater self-efficacy (Burnette et al., 2020).

I posit that Gold's core metaphors deserve attention in relation to their potential as enhancers of a growth mindset, self-efficacy, and boosters of behaviours that can bring about positive change in health status. Evidence exists that experimental interventions designed to increase self-efficacy also improve targeted health behaviors (Sheeran et al., 2016).

Given the above commentary, I offer the following hypotheses for testing:

1. Patients reading a biomedical "killer bug-war" metaphor laden message, compared to a chiropractic "innate-adaptive" laden message, will report weaker growth mindsets.
2. Patients reading a biomedical "killer bug-war" metaphor laden

message, compared to a chiropractic "innate-adaptive" metaphor laden message, will report weaker self-efficacy.
3. A growth mindset and greater self-efficacy will relate positively to greater psychological well-being, marked by lower levels of anxiety and higher levels of global well-being, and positively to intentions to engage in health-related behaviors aimed towards COVID-19 related risk factors.

Having posited each of the above hypotheses and having selected the target population, sampling frame, sampling technique, and an appropriate set of self-administered questionnaires with favourable psychometric properties, I now move into the early phase of data collection.

In summary, the writings of Dr. Reginald Gold have clearly been of great importance to many practicing chiropractors. However, even with the passing of 60 years, those writings have received very little attention in academic and investigative circles. The utility of Gold's ideas and the profession's core metaphors deserve at least preliminary testing in relation to concepts like growth mindset, self-efficacy, and health behaviour change. Finally, such testing might provide fertile soil for adding to and answering the questions: What is the lasting influence of Gold's ideas, and how might they further impact the world?

References

Bandura, A. (1977). Self-efficacy: Toward a unifying theory of behavioral change. *Psychological Review, 84*(2),191-215.

Burnette, J., O'Boyle, E., VanEpps, E., Pollack, J., Finkel, E. (2013). Mind-sets matter: A meta-analytic review of implicit theories and self-regulation. *Psychological Bulletin, 139*(3), 655-701.

Burnette, J., Babij, A., Oddo, L., Knouse, E. (2020). Self-regulation mindsets: Relationship to coping, executive functioning, and ADHD. *Journal of Social and Clinical Psychology, 39*(2), 101-116.

Compas, B., Connor-Smith, J., Saltzman, H., Thomsen, A., Wadsworth, M. (2001). Coping with stress during childhood and adolescence: Problems, progress, and potential in theory and research. *Psychological Bulletin, 127*(1), 87-127.

Dweck, C. (1999). *Self-theories: their role in motivation, personality, and development*. Psychology Press.

Dweck, C. (2006). *Mindset: The new psychology of success*. Random House.

Flusberg, S., Matlock, T., Thibodeau, P. (2018). War metaphors in public discourse. *Metaphor and Symbol, 33*(1), 1-18.

Gold, R. (1998). *The triune of life (Second ed.).* Sherman College of Straight Chiropractic.

Hauser, D., Schwarz, N. (2015). The war on prevention: Bellicose cancer metaphors hurt (some) prevention intentions. *Personality and Social Psychology Bulletin, 41*(1), 66-77.

Hauser, D., Schwarz, N. (2020). The war on prevention II: Battle metaphors undermine cancer treatment and prevention and do not increase vigilance. *Health Communication, 25*(13), 1698-1704.

Ko, J., Danielson M., Town, M., Derado, G., Greenlund, K., Kirley, P., et al. (2021). Risk factors for Coronavirus disease 2019 (COVID-19)-associated hospitalization: COVID-19-associated hospitalization surveillance network and behavioral risk factor surveillance system. *Clinical Infectious Diseases, 72*(11), e695-e703.

Lackoff, G., Johnson, M. (1980). *Metaphors we live by.* University of Chicago Press.

Landau, M., Arndt, J., Cameron, L. (2018). Do metaphors in health messages work? Exploring emotional and cognitive factors. *Journal of Experimental Social Psychology, 74*, 135-149.

Sheeran, P., Maki, A., Montanaro, E., Avishai-Yitshak, A., Bryan, A., Klein, W., et al. (2016). The impact of changing attitudes, norms, and self-efficacy on health-related intentions and behavior: A meta-analysis. *Health Psychology, 35*(11), 1178-1188.

Wallis, P., Nerlich, B. (2003). Disease metaphors in new epidemics: the UK media framing of the 2003 SARS epidemic. *Social Science & Medicine, 60*(11), 2629-2639.

THE VALLEY OF THE BLIND

Palmer College of Chiropractic
Davenport, Iowa - 1972

The Valley of the Blind
Reggie Gold

So what if D.D. Palmer was a fish peddler?

Jesus Christ was a carpenter, and that didn't denigrate what he had to teach.

It's kind of nice to be one of the early speakers on your program. Last night, I circulated around in the lobby of the Blackhawk Hotel and talked with all of the other speakers. In fact, we swapped funny stories, so I can get up now and tell all their best material, and they have to follow me.

Last graduation, or the graduation before, I had the privilege of being commencement speaker. At that time, I told a story which I think bears repeating today. It's a story written by H.G. Wells called the *Valley of the Blind.* And it's interesting how, even though H. G. Wells knew nothing of chiropractic, he wrote about chiropractic thinking in this story.

Somehow, whatever I read seems to remind me of chiropractic. That's like the fellow who went to a psychiatrist because he had a problem, and the psychiatrist gave him a Rorschach test. He made these ink blots and showed the man the inkblot and said, "What is it?" And the man looked at the inkblot, and he said, "Well, that's easy. That's a man and woman making love." And the psychiatrist looked at the inkblot, and he couldn't quite understand the analysis, so he put it down and he took another one. And he showed that to the man, and he says, "What's that?" And without a second's hesitation, the man said, "Aha, that's a man and woman making love." And the psychiatrist thought, there's something weird going on here. He then took a plain piece of paper and drew on it a single line, and said, "What's that?" The man said, "Well, that's a man and woman making love." And finally, he took a last piece of paper and put in a tiny little dot. And he said to the man, "What's that?" And the man said, "That's easy. That's a man and woman making love." And the psychiatrist said, "I can see your problem; you're a sex maniac." And the man said, "Me, you're the one who keeps drawing the dirty pictures." Apparently, whatever he looked at reminded him of only one thing. Well, whatever I look at reminds me of chiropractic.

So here was I reading a story that had nothing to do with chiropractic, but I think you should hear about it. It's a story about a remote village hidden in the Andes Mountains in Columbia, South America. Thousands and thousands of years ago, thousands of generations ago, there was a genetic weakness among some of the people living in this remote village; and as a result of it, they all tended to have weak eyes. But as new blood came in from neighboring villages and they intermarried, that weak gene remained a recessive one, and there was never any real problem. But one day, due to a cataclysm of nature, a tremendous earthquake deposited millions of tons of rock on the only pathway into and out of the village, and the village became totally shut off from all of society. And as a result, with no more new people coming in, the people living in this village began to intermarry. And as they intermarried and intermarried, the recessive gene became dominant, and little by little, eyesight was lost until after several generations every man, woman, and child in that valley was totally blind.

As more and more generations went by, not only was eyesight gone but now even memory and understanding of what eyesight was had disappeared. People didn't even have a word for eyesight. Through the physiological law of use or lose, because they weren't using their eyes, even those organs became vestigial and disappeared. And the people in this remote village just had plain smooth places in their faces where you and I have eyes. Eyebrows and eyelashes were no longer known, and it was indeed the valley of the blind.

One day in fairly modern times, a mountain climbing expedition going through that area was headed by a man called Bogota, from the city of Bogota in Columbia. And as they were trying to find their way around the mountain, Bogota got separated from the rest of the group; he fell over a cliff, was severely injured, and was given up by his companions for dead. They turned and made their way back to civilization, leaving him in this remote little cleft in the hillside, given up for dead. But he wasn't dead, and he recovered from his wounds. And he began to live off the land; he was, after all, an experienced mountain climber. He knew which berries to eat and how to trap small game, and he survived, and he grew stronger, and he started to try and find his way out. But because he was wedged so far into this crevice in the rock, there was no way he could climb back up the sheer precipice to the pathway back to civilization.

So he went the other way instead, and he wandered for days, lost and alone. And the days turned into weeks and the weeks into months. And then, one day, quite by chance, he went through a small cave through an opening on the other side and came out upon a beautiful lush green valley. And there, down at the bottom of the valley, he saw signs of habitation. There was indeed a village. Unbeknownst to him, Bogota had stumbled upon the valley of the blind. Of course, he didn't know they were blind in the beginning. And as he moved down into this community, he thought, at last, he had a chance to get back with people. He'd been alone for so long he welcomed the sight of his fellow man.

But as he got closer and closer, he realized there was something strange about these people. They tended to walk with their hands in front of them, and there were ropes set up from building to building that the people were holding onto as guidelines and cables. And as he got even closer, he realized that every man, woman, and child in that village was indeed totally blind.

Now somewhere, Bogota had heard that in the valley of the blind, the one-eyed man is king, and he felt here was his golden opportunity to serve his fellow man. He could go down into the valley of the blind and allow them to use his eyes. He could be their passport to sight. And he went down there, radiant with joy at the opportunity to help and to be among fellow human beings.

And in the beginning, they welcomed him with open arms, until he tried to explain to them about his eyesight. Remember, in their language, they had no word for eyesight. They had no knowledge, no understanding of what he was trying to communicate. Can you imagine, for example, trying to explain the taste of chocolate to somebody who has never tasted chocolate? How do you explain what it tastes like? You have nothing to compare it to. And here he was trying to explain eyesight to people who had no knowledge, no history of knowledge of eyesight.

And like most people faced with something they can't understand, they labeled him as being a bit weird; and they were a little afraid of him. And Bogota was determined; he said, "No, you don't understand." He said, "Through these openings in my face, I can actually see pictures." And they said, "What are pictures?" And he said, "Well, for example, if you were to cast your face upward, overhead, you'll see the clouds and the sun in the sky."

And now they knew there was something strange about him because their history taught them that over their head was a broad stone covering that ended through all eternity, and everybody knew that's what was up there, a smooth stone roof. What's this nonsense about sky and fleecy clouds and sunshine? So they began to realize that this man was not only weird, but perhaps he was dangerous. This was no person to expose to their children, and they segregated him. They wouldn't allow him to mix with the children in case he contaminated them with his weird ideas.

And again, in an effort to explain, he said, "Look, let me demonstrate to you." and he took the hands of the headman of the village and put the man's fingers up against his own face so the man could feel his eyes, and the man was revolted by these horrible soft spots in somebody's hard face. Can you imagine touching somebody on top of the head and your fingers sink into soft squishy brain? Well, this is how that headman felt when his fingers sunk into the face of this Bogota; and now they were really bothered by him, and they drove him out of the village in fear. And he turned back, and he begged with him to be allowed to stay, and they said, "All right, we'll allow you to stay provided you don't fill our children with your wild ideas ... provided you learn to conform."

For quite a while, he was okay hanging around the village; he was tolerated. But as he began to make friends more and more with the people, there was one particular gal there that he became interested in, and she became interested in him. And after a while, these two decided they'd like to get married; and now Bogota was faced with going to the girl's father and asking for her hand in marriage. Now at first, the father was absolutely adamant there was no way he was going to let his daughter marry this freak, except they began to think, "Well, this chick is not such a good looker anyway." As a matter of fact, the other guys in the village didn't particularly dig her because where pretty girls had plain smooth faces, this one had vestigial eyebrows and eyelashes, so she was quite revolting to the rest of the guys around. And perhaps Bogota was going to be the last chance she would have to get married.

So the old man got a little interested. But before doing anything, he decided to consult with the headman and the wise man of the village, and they had a conference one night, and the next morning the father came to Bogota and said, "We've solved your problem. I'm going to allow you to marry my daughter on one condition. The wise men of the village have decided that the thing that makes you crazy is these soft spots on your face. We have a surgeon who will remove those soft spots, and then you'll be just like the rest of us; you won't be crazy anymore, and I'll allow you to marry my daughter." And as you read this story, your blood begins to run cold; you can see where H.G. Wells is going. You can see the turn of mind of Bogota, who is faced with the alternative of either giving up his eyesight to be tolerated in the valley of the blind or keeping his eyesight and being turned out into the world at large friendless, to roam for all time, perhaps without ever again contacting another human being.

And there goes the debate in Bogota's mind, as you see him vacillating back and forth on which way to go. And you begin to realize that he's giving up, that as the pages are turned, one by one, he's getting closer and closer to the fatal surgery that will make him as blind as everybody else. And on the night before the ceremony is to be performed, Bogota leaves the circle of the village fire for the last time to go out and look at those things that he can still see because, in the morning, he'll be blind. And as he walks away from the village, he turns back and looks at all the beauty that nature has provided, and he begins to walk a little bit up the hillside; and the farther he got away from the village and the closer he got to nature, the more he questioned the wisdom of his judgment, the better things began to look to him and the worse the girl began to seem.

And then, as the story ends, Bogota makes his decision. He forsakes all human companionship. He leaves the girl. He keeps his eyes. And he wanders friendless and alone for the rest of his life, lost in a wilderness, but at least keeping his God-given eyesight, rather than giving up that gift in order to be tolerated in the valley of the blind.

Why is this a chiropractic story? Because that's exactly the decision that you are being asked to make. You are being asked to give up not your eyesight, but your vision. Millions are born without much vision, and that's unfortunate. But to be born with vision, or to be exposed to vision, and then to give it up because we don't have the courage to go it alone, that's not unfortunate, that's tragic. You are being asked, and you will be asked to give up your God-given wisdom, your vision, your understanding in order to be tolerated out there in the valley of the blind.

B.J. quoted the Bible one time; he said, "Where there is no vision, the people perish." There are millions who have the eyesight of a hawk and the vision of a clam. You are going out into a society and a community that has the eyesight of a hawk and the vision of a clam. And they will fight against your vision because they lack understanding. I don't want you to believe that the path you have chosen in chiropractic is an easy path. It is not the line of least resistance. Following that line of least resistance, as B.J. said, that makes rivers and men crooked. If we follow that line, we know where they're going to end up.

Chiropractic is something so different from what society now knows, now understands, and now accepts that you will, of necessity, be an outcast as long as you stick to radical new ideas. If you want to be accepted, then give up your new ideas, pluck out your eyes and be as blind as the rest of society then, and only then, will they tolerate you.

In order to be accepted by a sick society, you must become as sick as they are. If chiropractic is to be accepted in a sick and misunderstanding society, chiropractic must give up its wisdom, its understanding, and the things that make it different from that society.

Now your choice is clear-cut. Do you change chiropractic to conform to a sick society? Or do you change that sick society until it's ready to understand your chiropractic principle? This is your decision.

All right, what is the difference between the chiropractic way and the other way? Is there that much difference?

I did a radio show in Detroit, Michigan. I did a television show, as a matter of fact, in Detroit, Michigan, not too long ago, and the interviewer was very much interested in the subject of acupuncture. Because since President Nixon's trip to the Orient, acupuncture has leaked into the forefront of American health thinking. And the interviewer asked me, "Isn't acupuncture very close to chiropractic?" He said, "After all, they're both drugless. Don't you and they have a lot in common?" And the way I explain the difference is the way I explain the difference between chiropractic and anything else.

Many people tend to think that the healing arts can be divided in two, with the drug professions on one side and the drug-less on the other. Many chiropractors try to live by that distinction, saying as long as we are drug-less, we are non-medical, and therefore we're in our own little ballpark. The distinction, however, doesn't lie there. If we divide the healing arts in two, we don't find medical doctors on one side and all the rest on the other. What we find is chiropractors on one side and all the rest on the other. There is a philosophical difference between chiropractic and everything else relating to healing and the healing arts.

We over here are the DCs. Now you may think DC is Doctor of Chiropractic, and I suppose it is. But DC is also a doctor of cause. We are the doctors of cause; we are also the doctors of correction, of course. Maybe we should be DCCs.

And over here, on the other side, we have the DTs. A DT is a doctor of therapy; he treats disease. Chiropractors do not treat disease. Chiropractic is based upon the premise that this human body has built into it the ability to heal itself; that this body is created by all of the wisdom of the universe. Scientists tell us the body is capable of living for 120 to 150 years. Now, I can't believe for one moment that a wisdom which was smart enough to create this body to live for 120 to 150 years was so stupid as to put into it a gallbladder which is only good for 40 or 50 years. I must assume, therefore, that the entire body is meant to last us as long as we live.

The body, in fact, replaces itself as we go along. There is no such thing as curing disease. When the cells of your body get sick, even nature can't cure them. Sick cells can never be healed; they will die. But that's nothing to be concerned about because even the healthy cells die after a few weeks or a few months, only to be replaced by new cells so that that which we call healing is, in fact, the creation of new life. If I brush my hand, I brush off millions of dead cells. As you sit here right now, the cells of your heart are dying, but don't worry about it because as one dies, nature makes a new one to replace it.

A heart cell lasts approximately 90 days. If you have a sick heart cell right now, 90 days from now, that sick cell will be dead and be replaced by a new one. Now, of course, if the new cell comes in just as sick as the old one, the disease will go on forever until it kills you. But if that sick cell dies and is replaced by a strong, healthy cell, the disease has gone. Who cured it? Doctors of Chiropractic can't cure disease. Life cures disease by creating new cells to replace old ones. All of healing is a creation of life. And before we go around telling people that we can cure disease, we better ask ourselves if we can create life. Only that wisdom which created the body can recreate it, and that recreation daily is what we call healing.

So chiropractors don't try to treat, cure or heal disease. What does a chiropractor do? One thing, and one thing only; he restores and maintains the mechanical integrity of the nervous system based upon the fact that in order to be healthy, every human body needs a good nerve supply to every organ, every gland, every part, and every cell. If there is no good nerve supply, if any single part of this body is deprived of proper neurological function, there is no way on God's earth that that body will ever function properly again, and all the pills, powders, potions, acupuncture needles, physical therapy treatments, voodoo, witchcraft, prayers, or anything else is ever going to make it work again until somebody restores the flow of life from brain to tissue cell over those nerves, and that can only be done by a specific scientifically applied chiropractic adjustment.

Chiropractors don't treat disease, and they don't help nature. I just love to see chiropractors trying to help nature. All of the wisdom of the universe, and you're going to help it?

All right, let's talk to the seniors for a moment; all the smart ones. You're all ready for your state boards; you passed your national boards. You all remember your Spinology. Let's go back into the liver for a moment, okay? Think about your own liver, don't worry about the state board's liver; think about your own liver. Pick out one little cell in your liver, and you tell me what chemical change it needs at this moment to function better. Well, before we start helping nature, don't you think we should know the answer to that question?

And yet all of the practice of the other healing arts is based upon a person getting sick, going to a doctor, talking to the doctor for 15 minutes, and then the doctor tells him what changes his liver needs. He doesn't know his own liver needs. You can't help nature. And yet all of the things that are done in the name of chiropractic but outside the realm of chiropractic are done "to help nature." Let's burn one thought into our minds; in order to heal, nature needs no help. Let's remember that we can never help nature because nature needs no help. No help from medical doctors, no help from acupuncturists, no help from osteopaths, chemists, therapists, or chiropractors. In order to heal, nature needs no help from anyone, just no interference.

Now your job and mine is very simple, get the interference out of the way. We don't have to cure; nature knows how to cure by creating new life. Until you can teach nature how to make new cells better, you do much better staying the heck out of the way and let nature do her job. Leave that to the expert. In order to heal, nature needs no help for anybody, just no interference. Don't you think we have a big enough job to do getting the interference out of the way? If only we did just that, then we would have all of the wisdom of the universe, once again expressing within that body, creating living tissue the way it was meant to, and restoring total life to a body which was hitherto deprived of life energy by a vertebral subluxation.

So over on one side of the fence, we have of the doctor of cause and the doctor of correction of cause, and on the other side, the doctor of therapy, the man who treats diseases. Now, it doesn't matter about your methodology of treating; there are some people that think chiropractic is different because it relates to spinal adjusting and the others don't. That's not true; there are other healing arts that relate to spinal adjusting, including physical medicine. There's an organization now called the North American Academy of Manipulative Medicine. Medical doctors called physiatrists, who meet together on weekends and teach each other crude procedures in spinal manipulation for the treatment of backaches, stiff necks, headaches, orthopedic problems, all of the things on which some of our chiropractic friends would like to hang their hats.

There is a movement in chiropractic to limit this practice to people who manifest symptoms of backaches and headaches, saying that if we hold it right there, we can be accepted. We'll give up our vision for the sake of acceptance in the valley of the blind. Unfortunately, of course, that part of our practice has already been taken over by the physical therapists, by the osteopaths, and by the physiatrists. If chiropractic is nothing more than spinal manipulation, they've already stolen that; they've written books about it. The one thing they can't take from you is your chiropractic philosophy that the body cures itself. Because if they were to take that from you, they'd have to give up all the quackery that they've been practicing for lo these 200 years and all of the millions of dollars that's going into their pockets from this fraudulent quackery practice.

The only thing you have, the only reason for surviving, is your philosophy. The fact that we don't treat or cure disease, but that this body has inherent within it the ability to heal itself from every disease known to man without exception. There's no such thing as an incurable disease; well, there are incurable patients. There are some patients who've gone so far that nothing can save them now. They've gone beyond the limitations of matter, beyond the limitations of time. But for every disease from which somebody dies, somebody else recovers.

I had a discussion with a medical doctor about cancer, half of our chiropractors are afraid to talk about cancer because that's a radical thing to talk about. Wow, you'll be labeled as a radical if you think you can help a cancer patient. I know this, if I had cancer, I'd want to make darn sure I had no nerve interference, wouldn't you?

So I talked with a medical doctor about cancer, and he said, "Yeah, but you can't claim any chiropractic cures for cancer, you know. There are thousands of cancer patients who get well every year all by themselves without chemotherapy, without drugs, that is, without surgery, without x-ray treatment; they just get well. So that if one of your patients were to get well, you can't say chiropractic cured him, he may have got well anyway." I said, "That's great. I don't want to say chiropractic cured him. I never claimed that chiropractic cures cancer. I just got through telling you chiropractic doesn't cure anything." But listen to what the doctor said; when this body is working right, it has the ability to recover, even from cancer. Hey, you know something? If the body were working right, maybe it wouldn't get cancer in the first place. How does that hit you?

People ask what can chiropractic do for cancer. I'll tell you what it can do; how about prevention? This seems to be, to me, the only intelligent approach to health, the one approach that chiropractic has missed all of these years and that our medical friends and our other non-chiropractic friends can never get, the maintenance of the integrity of the nervous system for the prevention of dis-ease. And while I'm on the subject of this word, disease, let's rub that one in a little bit because it, more than anything else I can think of, explains the big difference between chiropractic and therapy. And under therapy, I include anything and everything that is done to treat disease, including chemotherapy, surgery, acupuncture, physical therapy, psychotherapy, concept therapy, prayer therapy, manipulative therapy, anything you do to treat or cure disease, vitamin therapy, they all belong over here.

What is the one common underlying factor which every sick person has? Their body wasn't working right in the first place. If their body were working right, there's no way in God's earth they would get sick. Why do you think people get sick? You heard Dave ask the question a few minutes ago, speaking of his grandfather, why is it two people sitting at the same table, eating the same food, working at the same bench, doing the same thing with the same genetic factors, all of their life, twin brothers, one gets gallstones, and the other doesn't, why? Is it bad luck? Come on, let's be logical; we're supposed to be scientists. Is it logical to you that luck rules whether a person gets healthy or not? That's like you going out in practice, and you do everything in a sloppy, disorganized, backhanded way and expect good fortune to make you a successful chiropractor. And we see the guy who is successful, and we say, "Boy, he sure hit it lucky." Work has nothing to do with it; there are laws of cause and effect. We establish certain causes, and the effects must follow as inevitably as night follows day.

Why do people get sick? Not through bad luck but because something in their body is not working right. When their body is not working right, we call that condition dis-ease, lack of ease, or lack of function. Here's another way to explain it, dis-order. What is health? All of your patients now are coming to you to find health. Can you give it to them? No, because it was theirs in the first place. What do you mean? What is health? Health is a state of harmony in which the 25 to 30 quadrillion cells of their body are doing their job. If every one of those cells were doing its job in harmony in response to a single control, then the person would live a full, normal life.

I believe life should be like a candle that burns brightly from the beginning all the way down to the very end, then stutters once or twice, and goes out. Sickness and disease are not normal, you know. In spite of the ads you hear on radio and television, selling pills for ordinary morning headaches. They're not really ordinary. You're not supposed to get headaches every morning, and you're not supposed to get cramps every month. You're not supposed to have a gallbladder go bad on you at age 35 or 40. Sickness and disease are not normal; they are the result of a dis-order in the body, dis-organization. Health is harmony; it is order. For your body to function in health, you have 25 to 30 quadrillion working parts, each one with a highly specialized job to do. If every cell in your body were doing its job, there's no way on God's earth you'd ever get sick. Life, as I said, would be like a candle burning brightly from the beginning all the way down to the very end, then sputter once or twice and go out.

Health is your God-given birthright. You have a body that is supposed to maintain you in health. If it's not doing its job, blame that body. The cause of sickness is a body which is malfunctioning; that malfunction we label as dis-ease, dys-function, or dis-order. This universe functions in beautiful harmony. Anything which works harmoniously is well organized and healthy. If you belong to a Toastmasters club or any other kind of club or organization where things work in harmony, all responding to a single control, you have order; you have a tightly knit group that is healthy. But if everybody's going off in different directions doing his own thing, with no coordination, you have dis-order, dis-harmony, dis-organization, and a sick group, which won't last very long.

A healthy body, then, is one which is in order, control, controlled by the wisdom of the universe. And a sick body is one which is in a state of dis-order. And you know what our medical friends do? They say, "Ah, yes, but we've got to specialize. It's not just disorder; he's got a stomach disorder, kidney disorder, mental disorder, rectal disorder." And they try and separate all the parts because it's convenient for study. That's like you studying where the central nervous system ends, and the peripheral nervous system begins, you know the true answer to that? Nowhere. The body doesn't have two nervous systems, it only has one. Ask your body. You didn't think of that, did you?

Order is when all of the parts are working together, and in chiropractic, we try to express that the only reason you get sick is because there's a breakdown of communication between the central control and the rest of the body. There is dis-order resulting – dis-ease. To the medical professions, and I mention those because they're the biggest group in this camp of therapists, there are others who follow along in the therapy camp, but the medical groups seem to be the thought leaders of that group, and all the others trail along and follow. The medical profession says that disease is the enemy. It's an entity to be rooted out and destroyed. Cancer makes you sick. The chiropractor says, "Nonsense, cancer doesn't make you sick. You get cancer because you're sick." Cancer is not a disease which comes into the body and makes you sick. Cancer is the end result of years of dis-ease, of malfunction. Diabetes doesn't make you sick; sickness makes you diabetic. Influenza doesn't make you sick; sickness allows influenza to develop.

And so it is through every single disease you can mention. There's no such thing as a disease entity lurking out there in the environment, and some healthy character goes walking by, and the disease jumps on him and makes him sick. And yet all therapy is based upon this supposition that healthy people get sick because they happen to trip over a disease somewhere. God, you wonder where LBJ got sick. Do you remember a few years ago, LBJ had gallstones? All the specialists came in from all over the country to diagnose him and incidentally to treat him illegally in a jurisdiction where they weren't licensed. They examined him, and they said, "Well, he's got gallstones. Cut out his gallbladder; that'll make him healthy."

The thing that bugs me is when all of these experts came in, don't you think one of them might wonder why did he get sick? I mean, forget about his politics for a minute; why do you think he got sick? Where do you think LBJ got his gallstones from? Do you think he caught them from Hubert? What, did Lady Bird put them in his chicken soup instead of matzah balls? No. Why? And yet all of our medical friends don't ask. They go, "he's sick; bad luck, cut him open." Gallstones didn't make him sick; sickness allowed gallstones to develop. So the enemy is not sickness; it's not disease. It is that dis-ease, that dis-order, that dis-harmony, which allows these states of malfunction to develop to the point where they present symptoms.

And all of your life, you've been lied to. You've been led to believe that if you have no symptoms, that means you're healthy. And so we found Gil Hodges for 17 years taking pills to suppress symptoms of circulatory damage. For 17 years of his life, he took pills which totally eradicated his symptoms of circulatory damage. He had no symptoms at all on that beautiful day a couple of months ago when he went out and played 36 holes of golf. And then this fine strapping young man came off the golf course and dropped dead of a heart attack, totally asymptomatic. You want me to believe that he was healthy? The fact that he had no symptoms doesn't mean that he's healthy, and yet you and I have been trained to reserve our chiropractic for just those people who have symptoms.

By what right do we hold chiropractic back and only give it to people who are so sick that symptoms have developed. I hear statements like, "Chiropractic gets sick people well." Well, if it does, it's a rotten shame that we let him get sick in the first place. It seems to be the only intelligent approach to help is the restoration and maintenance of the integrity of the nervous system before people get sick, not after. What the hell are we doing?

We've got practices and fee systems and office procedure systems based upon allowing mankind to get sick. Even your Medicaid and Medicare insurance programs are all based upon the fact that you don't get any help until you're sick. What do we mean by sick? Presenting symptoms. On the insurance form, you're asked to list the symptoms. If there are no symptoms, the insurance companies won't pay. In other words, the insurance programs are owned and operated by the same medical thinking that owns and operates the therapies. They are not geared towards chiropractic thinking. What we need is a total revolution in health thinking. You see, your problem is you're trying to promote chiropractic in a medically oriented world, and it can't be done. You've got to first dis-orient the world. You've got to turn them around.

Now, if it sounds as though I'm laying out a blueprint for a revolution, that's exactly what we're going to have to do if we want to turn this world around. And before you go out there and buy a gun, let me explain; I'm not talking about bloody revolution. I'm talking about revolving the thinking of mankind, turning it around, but you can't turn them around by thinking and acting the way they do.

I see chiropractors trying to conform to the pattern set up by a medical thinking society. The more you act, talk and think the way the medically oriented society does, the less chance there will ever be of them turning around to your way of thinking. Your job is leadership to change the world. And I'm constantly accused of this, "Reggie, what do you want to do, change the world?" You're damn right I do.

I don't like this world the way it is. Right now, there's never been a better time in the history of man for the development and growth of the chiropractic principle. There's a revolution going on our college campuses all over this country. A turning around of thinking, a very serious attempt to end the pollution of our environment. And we are in the heart of this battle to clean up the pollution of the internal environment that is perpetrated by the leaders of the therapeutic professions, meaning the chemical industry and their pushers, the medical profession. You and I are in a position to start in leadership here. Most of us have been followers all of our life, get in front and lead, or get in line and follow or get out of the way because chiropractic's coming through.

We talk about electing leaders, you are going out into your community, and you are going to be a thought leader. But you don't lead people by standing where they are. People are like wet spaghetti; they can be pulled but not pushed. Think about it. If you want to move people, you've got to move out in front of where they are. You can't stand squarely in the middle and say follow me. Squarely in the middle, there's nowhere to follow you. Take a position and stand by it. They'll follow you, don't worry. And then don't move back to meet them halfway; take another step. And as they take a step towards you, you take two steps farther on. Keep moving ahead; that's leadership.

What we normally think of as leadership is, in fact, following. We elect national leaders; they're not leaders at all, they're followers. We take the guy who represents the majority viewpoint, and we give him an office. But he got that office because he represented the majority. In other words, he follows where everybody else is going. He's not a leader, he's a follower. Followers get elected, and leaders get out in front and lead. And don't worry if the others are lagging their feet behind you. If you are right, just go do it. What do you need applause? You need people around you to tell you you're right. Dammit, don't you know you're right? Then what are you waiting for? Take a position and stand on it.

Get in front and lead, or get in line and follow. Or, as we said earlier, get out of the way because this chiropractic is not going to stop. We're on the march now, and we are moving. But we need you; we need leaders in your community. And you can't lead as long as you think the way the rest of the community does. If you're not prepared to stand up and be counted, you're not going anywhere. You're asking society to tolerate you instead of you changing society.

For years now, chiropractic has been giving up its vision in order to be tolerated in the valley of the blind. It's time we change. It's time we change society's thinking. You see, we've been led to believe that if your principle is right, it will survive. If you live the good life, and you love motherhood and the flag, and you go to church on Sunday, everything will come out, and it'll be all right in the end. Well, that's just where you're going to get it, right in the end.

Don't you know that your entire society was raised medically? You think you can go to an American court of justice, and the chiropractic cause will be heard, and justice will be rendered. Let me tell you, first of all; there are no courts of justice in the United States of America. This is not mentally an inflammatory or revolutionary statement. It is a statement of fact.

In this country, we have courts of law, not courts of justice. The job of a courtroom is to decide what the law says. It is a court of law. It is not the court's job to determine what is equitable or what is just, merely what is legal. So, you have no courts of justice. And if you did, in order to get justice, the first thing you need is an unbiased jury.

Now, where in the world are you going to find 12 good men and true, who are raised without the medical brainwashing? Where can you find 12 chiropractors who are not second or third-generation chiropractors who are not raised without medical brainwashing?

Look at the people who sit on either side of you in class. Look at the guys you talk with in the cafeteria; how were they raised? The same way you and I were, with a medical brainwashing. The public at large is raised to think medically. How in the world do you expect them to understand chiropractic while they think medically? You turn to science, and you ask the departments of government and the scientists to give a fair, unbiased look at chiropractic, and they do within the limits of their medical understanding. They take your scientific research, and they scrutinize it under the microscope of medical thinking, and they come up with a conclusion that they think is honest and fair, and unbiased. But how can it be when the mind that examines it is biased to start with?

We've got to realize that in chiropractic, we are a minority group. We are behaving as though we were the majority. We're not; we are a minority group. Can't we learn a lesson from other minority groups? Haven't you seen what happens to minority groups in this country who keep quiet? For 200 years, the black man kept quiet. And for 200 years, he rode at the back of the bus. And every time some revolutionary black came forward and said, "We've got to move this thing. We've got to change this country." The other blacks were the ones who turned on him. It wasn't whitey who put him down, it was the other black man who said, "Hey, look man, everything's all right in this town, just leave things alone. It could be a lot worse, you know, we haven't had a lynching in this town for seven years now. You start making waves, and we get lynchings again." It was the other blacks, the Uncle Toms, that put him down.

Don't you find the same thing in chiropractic? Some chiropractic revolutionary or visionary gets up and shows you the path to freedom, and all the other chiropractors say, "Hey, cool it, man. They're allowing us to live. They're giving us Medicaid. If we don't blot our copybooks, they'll carve up the dirty medical pie with us. They'll give us some of their money if we play their dirty games."

All right, it's these Uncle Toms in chiropractic that are going to put us down too. And yet we have to move this thing off dead center, and we can't do it without moving ourselves. You can't make omelets without breaking eggs. Some people are going to be very unhappy with what we do. But chiropractic is going to do one of two things, it's either going to move forward, or it's going to stay where it is. And if you stay with the people who want it to stay where it is, then you are not a part of the solution, are you? Then you're part of the problem.

We must start changing minds, and we do that by standing up and being counted. By becoming leaders in our own right and telling that chiropractic story, though 10,000 other chiropractors tell us we shouldn't do it. There's a tremendous movement afoot for acceptance, for tolerance. When you leave here when you graduate, and even when you leave here today to go back to your apartments and to your places of employment, pressures will be put upon you to be reasonable, so we can accept you. "You're not one of those radicals who want to take cancer patients, are you?"

You know, there was a time when a chiropractor couldn't join a country club. Now they welcome you with open arms, "Come on in. We want your kind; we need chiropractors around here. You're not one of those Reg Gold fanatics who wants to take cancer patients are you?" And pretty soon, "Well, no, I like it here. It's nice with your arm around me." "I'll shell out; how much do I get?"

The pressures that will be brought upon you today are very subtle pressures. There will be pressures for you to give up your heritage, give up your principle, and be accepted in the valley of the blind. To use medical terminology, to try and limit chiropractic to the treatment of certain diseases, and refer others to therapists. In actual fact, we shouldn't be treating any diseases. The treatment of disease is a fool's game. The purpose of chiropractic is the restoration and maintenance of the integrity of the nervous system in all people 20-30 years before the disease is identifiable.

All of this so-called medical science is based upon diagnosis. Nothing can be recognized until the pathology is so far advanced that classic symptoms present themselves. And by then, it's very often too late. You are going to offer a new thought in healthcare, prevention. And when it comes to prevention, you have no opposition. You have no competition. Nobody on this earth can offer healthcare. Everybody else is offering disease treatment. So chiropractic does have a reason for existing as a separate and distinct healing art. Now that may mean changing some of our thinking about Medicare and Medicaid and insurance programs. It may mean changing some of our thinking about fitting into a medically oriented society, but it's that self-same society which has led the world to the sorry state that it's in today with regard to health and emotional health.

I don't think you begin to realize the potential of your chiropractic. Do you know what you can do with those two hands? With those ten fingers? My God, you are the answer to all of the health problems of mankind, physical and mental. Emotional dis-order is caused by an imbalance in body chemistry. Look at the kids who drop acid. They take a little LSD, their body chemistry changes, and all of a sudden, their emotions are out in left field. And that's no different from mom with her martinis. I love to see a mother with a cigarette in one hand and a martini in the other saying, "Boy, I hope my kids never turn on the grass." They make a big distinction, but that martini changes body chemistry enough that she's ready to go out and do the Boogaloo. The emotions change with a change in body chemistry.

Don't you think by restoring nerve supply to the organs which balanced body chemicals in restoring homeostasis, you'd be contributing largely to the emotional health of the world? Don't you think that might bring about some political change in the world? I wonder how many stupid wars in the history of man were caused because somebody was emotionally disturbed because of a hormone malfunction caused by vertebral subluxation. My God, I'd love to get out there in Washington, DC, and start adjusting a few subluxations.

Where I think chiropractic should go, and how and the root, I think, is clearly known to you. I was thinking about it the other day on a long plane ride back from San Antonio, Texas, where I've been giving a seminar and talking with some chiropractors there. And the thought developed as to where would chiropractic be 50 years from now. And I thought, "Well, that depends on which one of two paths it takes. It could be everywhere or nowhere." Now I'm essentially an optimist, and I projected chiropractic into its rightful and proper place in my mind, the place where it's going if you'll take it there. Get in front and lead.

But then I thought, it could go the other way if we follow some other kind of leadership. If we are prepared to give up our principle for acceptance, if we will give up our vision in order to be tolerated in the valley of the blind, we could one day see this article in a newspaper, an article datelined Spring Valley, New York, August 16th in the year 2022.

Headline

The Last Practicing Chiropractor Dies at Age 97

Today in Spring Valley, New York. Dr. Reginald R. Gold, chiropractor, passed away at age 97. He is survived by a wife who is also a chiropractor and who retired from active practice several years ago. Thus ends an era in American history. Chiropractic started in Davenport, Iowa, in 1895, and there followed a long and bitter struggle for survival against the combined might of organized medicine and the pharmaceutical industry.

In the beginning, it seemed as if the dedication and devotion of the chiropractors and the logic of their cause would be enough for them to overcome their monumental foe and to replace it as the world's number one healing art. But sometime during the 1960s and 1970s, the tide gradually turned against the chiropractors. More and more chiropractors realized the hopelessness of their self-appointed task of saving the world. One by one, they crumbled under the pressures of society and gave up fighting for their lost principle. They took instead the easier path of working for their personal acceptance and for status in the community. One by one, their radical leaders died off or were deserted by their followers. And with each successive move away from their radical and unacceptable theories, the chiropractors became more and more a part of the established health team.

Seven years ago, in September of the year 2015, just 120 years after its birth, chiropractic officially died, as almost all of its remaining few practitioners were formed into a paramedical group to aid doctors of physical medicine in manipulation. A few who failed to qualify continued to practice illegally under their defunct chiropractic licenses. The last of these, Dr. Reginald R. Gold, passed away last Monday. The funeral was unattended.

Sacred Trust
Jim Dubel

Reggie Gold, DC, PhC

Friend, Colleague, Mentor.

I first heard about a philosophical chiropractor named Reggie Gold back in the late 1970s while at Palmer College of Chiropractic. Numerous Palmer students had heard him speak and told me he was a must to hear in person.

At the time, I couldn't attend a philosophy talk by Reggie, but I was able to get a copy of his talk "Valley of the Blind" on a cassette tape.

This story intrigued me and left me wanting more of the incredible philosophy and profession of chiropractic. I listened to the tape so many times it wore out in my cassette player. Now I needed more! I begged, borrowed, and purchased everything Reggie did.

I was enamored with Reggie and his message. He had a unique way of explaining chiropractic in a story-like manner, and that, plus the message, made me sit on the edge of my seat whenever I heard him speak.

After graduating from chiropractic school, I searched out his philosophy talks whenever I could and listened to his wisdom. I was fortunate that Reggie was close by in Pennsylvania and had actually practiced in New York.

Over the years, we became friends and as a mentor of mine helped me build a very successful philosophical practice. He was very approachable and would talk to me on the telephone whenever I called for advice or support.

One story that comes to mind that I would like to share is having Reggie speak here in Red Bank, New Jersey.

I asked Reggie if he would come to speak to a group of local chiropractors that needed some *spizz* and philosophy to get their practices back on track.

He, of course, accepted the invitation. We set things up for a Saturday afternoon at a local Elks Club. Reg had few requirements: a bar chair, microphone, and easel. I got everything organized and met Reggie on the day of the event. We met up at the Elks and made sure everything was in place for his presentation about an hour before he was to speak. He made himself comfortable and said he would start at two and speak for two hours, then answer any questions the docs had.

As I sat at the entrance of the hall waiting for Chiropractors to arrive, Reg reminded me he always starts on time! I told him everyone was told that and not to worry. As two o'clock approached and only one person was in the room (me), I began to worry!

I looked over at five minutes before Reggie was to begin and realized Reg was going to start at exactly 2:00 p.m. as he said. With or without anyone in the room.

It was at this point that I figured I might be the only person to hear his incredible philosophy that day. I took a deep breath and decided to pull up a chair and get dipped in his philosophy. At that exact moment, the first two chiropractors arrived to hear him, followed by five, ten, twenty, and many more, all scurrying into the room to listen.

Reggie did start at exactly 2:00 p.m., as he said.

By the time he took his first drink of water at 2:30 p.m. to clear his throat, the room was packed to capacity with over 150 people in attendance and overflowing the room.

His talk captivated every person in attendance; everyone wanted more and asked that I bring him back to the Jersey shore as often as I could. For the next 30-plus years, he did come HOME to share and fellowship with Chiropractors who wanted his words of wisdom. To this end, he never failed to have a packed room.

This was the start of our multiyear philosophy meetings, which have continued for the past 30 years and are known today as "New Beginnings for a New Future" Chiropractic Philosophy Weekends.

The persistence and on-purpose message that Reggie shared time after time attracted hundreds of chiropractors to New Beginnings. He alone enabled thousands of chiropractors to become successful and understand the philosophy and principles of chiropractic.

His legacy will remain as a guiding light for our New Beginnings movement. He left us with a sacred trust, one that he asked us to guard and share with generations yet to come.

To My Friend Reggie,

I love you, respect you, miss you, and will Honor you forever!

All My Love, Loyalty, and Friendship.

We All Stand on the Shoulders
Donny Epstein

Dr. Reggie Gold was among the most important influencers in my career as a chiropractor. The principles and philosophy he articulated have inspired the development of my methods, impacting countless lives. I anticipate even more profound change as the greater humanity gains further awareness of the model I now call EpiEnergetics.

I enrolled in the Columbia Institute of Chiropractic (CIC) in 1974 – shortly after Reggie had left to join Thom Gelardi in creating and launching Sherman College of Straight Chiropractic.

Despite the curriculum shifts after Reg's departure to South Carolina, the *field* of chiropractic consciousness he pioneered was still profoundly evident.

When I was handed my diploma bearing Columbia Institute's re-named identity as New York Chiropractic College, the school had already changed dramatically.

Many remember Reggie through his larger-than-life personality and consistently coherent communication of the principles of chiropractic. I was in awe of his ability to engage, inspire and entertain at his talks while transmitting his passion and love for the organizing wisdom of life and the power of the chiropractic adjustment to potentiate its expression.

My bigger vision of service to humanity and my frankness in communication, or *chutzpah,* in sharing universal truth were ignited both directly and indirectly by the gifts received from this chiropractic great.

His talk on "The Valley of the Blind" was pivotal, inspiring me to keep moving on with a clear vision in a world that was blind. During my first couple of years in practice, I shared his talks with my patients, and later incorporated much of the spirit of what I learned from him in my communications.

Reggie personally took me under his wing, advising me about giving talks, phone and radio interviews, and later about handling questions from politically motivated chiropractic boards that aggressively pursued me. He helped me claim ownership of those critical conversations. To this day, I remember his words, "Donny, it's simple. Just never let the question asked interfere with sharing what you want to say!"

Later Reg started ADIO College to support the chiropractic vision and preserve the right to practice. As an early board member of the Federation of Straight Chiropractic Organizations, I feared the demise of TIC and the way the practice of chiropractic was being directed with the formation of the CCE. Reggie's school of Spinology continued to provide a haven I could refer students to where the principles of chiropractic flourished.

We all stand on the shoulders of those who created paths, served truths, and selflessly sacrificed to make a better world. I am one of the thousands of chiropractors and millions inspired by the torch lit and passed on by those who stood, jumped, stomped, or levitated upon the shoulders of Reginald Gold, DC.

The simple and brilliant description that B.J. Palmer shared was driven home to me and elegantly memorialized in Reggie's PhC thesis, *The Triune of Life*. More than a chiropractic principle, it was modern thermodynamics laced with the understanding of how living systems survive, adapt, grow, and evolve. Central in Reggie's thesis was the dynamic relationship between intelligence, force (energy), and matter defining the expression of the innate organization of life.

Academic research at over a dozen colleges and universities has been spurred by my methods inspired by my studies of Reggie's teachings (especially *The Triune of Life*). I learned and experienced that this simple principle manifests in thermodynamics and quantum realities. The degree to which energy can be made available to innate intelligence is a reflection of the degree to which the self-organizing intelligence of life is fueled, creating, as I see it, in-formation in action.

In chiropractic and all living systems, this principle manifests the magic of creation itself. In the chiropractor's realm, it is the advancement of spinal, neural, and information expression by innate adjusting the vertebral subluxation with our conscious force application.

Every cell form, function, emotion, thought, or conditioning by the educated mind is expressed in relationship to the amount of energy available. The principles amplified within me by Reggie's tenacity have helped create my means of helping individuals, families, societies, and cultures and provide a doorway to the next portal for humanity.

Many have personal stories about their interactions with this larger-than-life articulator and defender of the principles of chiropractic. In the late 1980s, when New York Chiropractic College (NYCC) was put on probation by the CCE, Thom Gelardi, then president of

Sherman College, suggested I arrange a talk with Reggie and Joe Donofrio Sr. to introduce the NYCC students to *real* chiropractic philosophy (in contrast to what they were learning). I was providing care for many students, at the time, and was excited to organize a philosophy night near the school and my practice.

When Reg arrived to a packed standing-room-only audience out in Long Island, I reminded him it was important to seek to create more unity. I suggested he share stories reflecting chiropractic philosophy and mentioned that any good/bad polarity might be a turn-off to attendees as TIC was hardly represented at the school. In addition, 'radicals' such as myself were barely welcome at the campus, so treading lightly seemed wise to allow the 'straight chiropractic' influence to continue to be represented there.

Reg hugged me while thanking me for inviting him, and my suggestions.

After I warmed up the group with my presentation, it was Reggie's turn to speak. I vividly recall him starting with a bang! He said that now that they had heard from Dr. Epstein, they had to realize that as a graduate of their school, I had no more of a clue than they did as to what chiropractic really is. He finished by advising the audience to consider suing the school for promising them a chiropractic education, and instead delivering a substandard medical education.

Then it was time for Reggie to give the microphone back to me. Instead, he told the students that he would share more time with them since, after all, they could always hear from me.

When the crowd dispersed, Reggie thanked me. He asked that I not be upset for his doing things his way, mentioning that he was experienced at inspiring students and, given the urgency of his message, this was not the time for concern about political correctness.

As you may imagine, it created quite a stir and, indeed, did begin a raw and real conversation at the school!

Reggie and his other half, Irene, risked everything over and over as torch holders for what was and is the unique central organizing principle of chiropractic. To this day, I still choose to take the flame he ignited within me and pass it on to add light to the world.

Not even the greatest darkness can extinguish the light of a single candle. We stand on the shoulders of those who have come before us. Because of our chiropractic forefathers commitment, we have this gift to share. Reg, with his huge shoulders, head, heart, and *whatever it takes approach*, gave his full commitment to that which chiropractic serves.

In his unparalleled, entertaining, charismatic, brilliant, novel, coherent, and loving way - Reggie's light continues to burn through the lives he has touched, and whose lives they continue to touch.

Thank you, Reggie, for making the choice to set an unreasonable standard for an extraordinary future world illuminated through chiropractic and its principles.

Chiropractic with a Big C
Greg Venning

Wellness chiropractic was where I got lost. Lifestyle factors like nutrition started to matter more to me than the process of locating, analyzing, and correcting vertebral subluxation did.

I was doing chiropractic with a small "c." I accepted the role the spine and nervous system play in health (to a point), and I understood that the mind-body always works toward homeostasis. Still, whenever I wanted to help someone, my focus was very divided. I was torn between focusing on improving spinal and neural function or broadening my focus to counsel people early on about how they ate, moved, and thought.

Despite going to lots of seminars and extensive coaching, the result was that my message was unclear, and people's follow-through under my care was fuzzy. Few people stuck to their adjustment schedule beyond symptomatic relief and a low level of maintenance. A handful came to some of my monthly health talks and changed their lifestyle meaningfully. It was the worst of both worlds.

The problem wasn't that the fundamental truth of wellness was wrong; the problem was that my philosophical stance on my role as a chiropractor was unclear.

I was feeling uninspired and felt like I could do better for my community by focusing on lifestyle factors. I felt chiropractic was too small and that I had outgrown it.

Then came Reggie. I knew of him and had listened to a few audio recordings of him back when students traded tapes, CDs, or even mp3 files illegally.

I recall watching a video of Reggie talking about "The Chemistry of Life" and relating it to the spine and nervous system and, ultimately, to innate intelligence. The way he spoke seemed to fill in the little gaps left open by the experiences I'd had and create clarity where there was confusion.

What I took away from that moment did not deny or belittle the wellness learning and experience I'd had. What I took away was a greater perspective.

He gave me the perspective I needed to begin to talk about innate intelligence confidently. My university education had programmed me to the idea that innate was a kooky thing that did not belong in clinical practice. The wellness message helped me claim the idea but in a very limited way. Now I had an order of priority: subluxation first.

That was the one domino that, as a Chiropractor, I could knock over that other professionals in my community couldn't. This was the highest point of leverage I had to help people to reclaim their human potential.

Reconnecting man the physical with man the spiritual became a meaningful task to which I could devote my life's energy.

I still get a kick out of helping people with their relationship to nutrition, movement, and their mental state. Now I find it much easier to help them get more meaningful change because they are better adjusted first.

Our Most Amazing Philosophy
Jay Komarek

Chiropractic, chiropractic philosophy, and patients were always a topic of discussion in our home. My dad and his two brothers were chiropractors. So around our table at dinner, there were often discussions about "health."

My mother was a fan of Dr. Reggie Gold and had a recording of "The Valley of the Blind" produced in 1972. She played it repetitively!! I was in my mid-teens and was taken to programs and seminars and, at an early age, had the opportunity to listen to Reggie in person. His gift for explaining the principle and philosophy of chiropractic reached me. In so many ways, he shaped a good part of my philosophy moving forward as I became a chiropractor.

Nearing my graduation from Western States Chiropractic College, Dr. Gold was invited to speak to the students. Surprisingly, the school board would not let him speak on campus. A group of us found a grade school auditorium for him to give his talk. It was then that I realized how controversial his very fundamental and basic message of chiropractic was. Who was in the audience? Many of the administrators who were preventing him from speaking at the school. It was then that I realized there was a division.

After an amazing talk, I was able to take Dr. Gold to dinner and ask a few questions. The first was, what do I do when I get out? He told me two key factors that I attribute to my subsequent success. The first was, learn to speak in public. For me, this was a fate worse than death. However, I overcame my fear and began teaching at a college outside of Philadelphia. The second thing he told me was, make a decision that you're going to see 100 people a day. Little did I know the obstacles I would have to overcome, mostly in my mind, to achieve that goal. It took me about a year.

Down the road, Dr. Gold's path and mine crossed, and to this day, I am forever grateful for the road that he set me on. We are better without a subluxation than we are with it, end of story. Dr. Gold drove this point home, and it became the foundational piece of my practice and education.

I am very grateful to Dr. Irene Gold and Reggie for standing strong amidst so many who tossed slings and arrows at them. I wasn't always in agreement with Dr. Gold and his ideas about chiropractic education, but I admired his fortitude and very special gift at communicating our most amazing philosophy.

You Honor a Person
Steve Tullius

Dr. Reggie Gold was a master. As he stood or sat on stages, he commanded the room's attention like a spiritual guru. You could feel the palpable energy of the crowd leaning forward as they took in his sage wisdom, delivered only by someone who had done the deep work of thoroughly evaluating all of their premises.

Countless chiropractors, myself included, were transformed by his style of communication and deep understanding of our philosophy. He gave the profession tremendous wisdom, insight, knowledge, and ability to communicate our message. He challenged us and, above all else, encouraged us to think. Reggie took a beautiful philosophy handed to him by other great masters, and refined elements to make it more complete; so it could approximate the timeless and perfect principles it seeks to describe.

One of the saddest moments for me as a chiropractor was not his passing, but the last time I heard him speak. He stood on the stage and shared a message contradicting the principles and practices of a large majority of the room. They smiled and nodded in agreement as the message flew past them, and then they went back to their lasers and ultrasound units on Monday morning. To add further injury, many mourned and lit candles for this great chiropractor, and offered up his quotes on social media, even though the next day, their actions flew in the face of those quotes.

You honor a person by honoring their message. Dr. Gold did not want to be loved for the sake of being loved. He was driven by our purpose of ensuring that the world has access to our unique and distinct philosophy and practice. He grasped in full totality the massive ramifications of our *big idea* being actualized. And conversely, he understood the grave consequences of it never coming to fruition. And that is probably one of the greatest gifts he gave to me, and so many chiropractors. The deep awareness of our moral obligation to get pure, unadulterated, and unmixed chiropractic to the masses.

If you haven't yet heard his famous "Valley of the Blind" presentation, I highly recommend you listen to it and do so over and over again. It is arguably one of the greatest chiropractic speeches ever given and one every chiropractor should be intimately familiar with.

Dr. Gold deserves to be honored and remembered both within, and outside the profession for his work and commitment to humanity. For his sake and for that of chiropractic's future, it is imperative that he be honored by both our words and our actions.

When He Walked Into the Room
Danny Knowles

> The non-therapeutic model, as represented by the Chiropractic Trust, is NOT about wellness, is NOT about health, and it is NOT about sickness. It is about the recognition that vertebral subluxation causes more than just a loss of health potential but a loss of every human potential. The nerve system is the coordinating system whereby the countless billions of body cells interact in harmony to express mind, body, spirit, emotion, artistic talent, speed, stamina, coordination, and family relations. Vertebral subluxation is a cause of disharmony to this beautiful thing we call life and all of its expressions. -Reggie

Sometimes, someone shares something with you in passing, and suddenly, it changes your life forever. It could be your spouse, child, healthcare professional, coach, or anyone. They say one thing and your perspective changes. You have a newfound awareness moving forward. For most of us, we can hope to have that impact on just a handful of people in our lifetime - and that's perfectly okay. Reggie Gold impacted hundreds of thousands of souls, if not millions, throughout his lifetime. One of whom was me.

Reggie Gold was one of the greatest orators that the chiropractic profession has ever had. The way he could articulate his teachings and break them down to the simplest message so that every person in the room could connect and comprehend was nothing short of a masterpiece each time he stood in front of a crowd.

Whether he was speaking to a lecture hall filled with doctors, young chiropractic students, or a group of people who knew little about the work of chiropractors, you can be sure that they left the room with a new passion. One that they didn't have moments earlier before he began to speak. People like Reggie empowered chiropractors to give all they had to the profession, to make it a mission and a calling rather than a vocation. Equally so, as he spoke with such passion and intelligence, he had the power to show people that the solution they were seeking was chiropractic care. That chiropractic care was the key to optimizing their potential and enhancing their life experience.

At least, that is what happened to me. I can remember so vividly the first time I reluctantly went to visit Sherman College of Straight Chiropractic.

At the time, I had zero intention of becoming a chiropractor. I had been a chiropractic patient as a teenager, yes—but did I want to practice it? No. However, my mother began attending chiropractic school due to its phenomenal impact on my health growing up. Soon after, she started dating Donny Epstein. Later on, they got married, and well, the rest is history!

Like many young adults, the last thing I wanted to do was the same thing as my parents. I had other ideas, big plans in all directions but chiropractic. Hence, attending another talk on chiropractic or visiting Sherman College wasn't high on my priority list. Nonetheless, my parents, Jackie Knowles and Donny Epstein convinced me it might be a fun family trip and a good idea to check it out before proceeding with any other directions I may go in. They were traveling down anyway, so I figured, "What do I have to lose?"

There I was, an undergrad NYU student from The Bronx, sitting in the sweltering heat under a tent that shaded me from the South Carolina sun, not really wanting to be there. That was until the panel started to present. At that moment, the heat didn't matter anymore as I was listening. I mean, *really listening.* That day is still so vivid in my mind that I can even tell you the sequence of presenters. First up, Arno Burnier, next was Donny Epstein, then Joe Donofrio, and last? Reggie Gold, of course.

That day my life changed. What they all shared resonated through and through to my head, heart, and soul. That undergrad, sweating in the southern sun, was thinking, "I am going to be a chiropractor."

You see, Reggie had a way of changing people, impacting them in ways they may not have even understood at the time. He had such a way of stating the obvious that it just got through to you. He made the most complex things simple, concise, clear, and comprehensible. So much so that they smacked you around a little and made you think, "How did I not think of it like that before? Am I stupid?!"

As students, any time one of my classmates or I had the opportunity to hear Reggie speak, we were there. It could have been a presentation, seminar, off-campus, or on-campus—if he was in town, anywhere within driving distance, there were no questions needed. So often, he said very similar things, but every time I'd hear them, it felt like the first time. It felt like I was learning something from a new angle I hadn't thought of before. In fact, I was excited to hear it again and again because when I understood what he was conveying, when he presented, you could feel his purpose. And, rather than self-serving, he was filled with purpose and on a mission.

After graduation, I was opening my first practice, something that I had dreamed of and envisioned for years. Richelle and I were dating then, and she put so much energy into making the event phenomenal. Unsuspecting to either of us Reggie walked in, and it was as if time had stopped. When Reggie walked into a room, he had a presence. All eyes gravitated to him. Everybody remembers their first office opening; however, this made it unforgettable. It was as if royalty had arrived.

The most powerful talk I heard Reggie give was "The Valley of the Blind." The audio cassette lived in my car, and I listened to it over and over. Truly, I am surprised that it never broke. Then I read *The Triune of Life*. With a background in studying philosophy as an undergrad, this read so clearly and concisely. It elegantly expressed the principles of our profession. His simplified message drove the essence of chiropractic principles for me. Yes, you could (and should) read Stephenson's textbook and read plenty of Green Books to deepen your knowledge. However, the essence of the principles of chiropractic are summarized in this short read. So much so that you can read it again and again and get more understanding each time of the depth, breadth, and impact of chiropractic philosophy on every aspect of health, family, and life. That is what makes it so profound.

Much of my life has been impacted by what Reggie taught us. The lessons and principles he shared on stage and within *The Triune of Life* have made me the chiropractor I am today. If you have never read *The Triune of Life* and are reading this, it is time you picked up that text. It is the chiropractic expression of the principles of thermodynamics. Practically all I do today with NetworkSpinal is based on and revolves around *The Triune of Life*. Reggie outlines how 100% health necessitates 100% organization. In the closing passage, he states, "this is the principle of Chiropractic." If you want to understand our principles, read and re-read *The Triune of Life*.

Reggie helped so many chiropractors and chiropractic patients understand that chiropractic is about recognizing that vertebral subluxation impacts more than just a loss of health potential, but a loss of every human potential. The nerve system is the coordinating system whereby the countless billions of body cells interact in harmony to express mind, body, spirit, emotion, artistic talent, speed, stamina, coordination, and family relations. Vertebral subluxation is a cause of disharmony to this beautiful thing we call life in all of its expressions. The adjustment was about so much more than getting rid of something that we didn't like but rather liberating life to have the opportunity to organize towards 100% and human potential being optimized so every man, woman, and child could live life through a healthy spine and nerve system.

I will forever honor his memory for that and the significant impact he had on so many young chiropractors like me. Whether it be the public, my practice members, students, or chiropractors, I intend to be in alignment with what I learned from Dr. Gold. Thank you, Reggie. Your memory will live on in those that you guided in an abundance of different ways. If we can have even a fraction of the impact that you did, congruent with your message, it is a life well lived.

A Master of Words
Peter Kevorkian

Someone handed me an audio cassette of Reggie Gold's lecture, "The Valley of the Blind," when I was a first-quarter student at Palmer College. That lecture molded my trajectory in chiropractic. His passion, logic, simplicity, and powerful communication skills (the British accent didn't hurt) touched me. After that, I watched every video, listened to every audio, and read everything I could find on Reggie Gold. This man not only shaped my understanding of chiropractic but also inspired me to develop my ability to speak and teach. Being an introverted geek, that was a major accomplishment.

While I was a student, I helped sponsor Reggie to speak in Davenport. At that time, Reggie had started Spinology because he felt chiropractic was moving too far away from the fundamental principles of our philosophy. Palmer College would not allow him on campus, so I arranged for him to speak at a venue a few miles away. When I picked him up at the airport, I asked him what he wanted to do before going to speak. He mentioned that he wanted to play racquetball. I had played a few times, but I figured that it would be better to get him on the court with a more seasoned player. A good friend of mine, Rob, was a competitive racquetball player; I called him and asked if he would be Reggie's opponent. We met at the gym. I needed to do some errands before the talk that evening. I hoped that Reggie would be enough competition for my friend. When I returned, about an hour later, to pick them up, I peeked in the court, and my friend said they had been playing for most of the hour, and he (Rob) hadn't scored a point. As they exited, Reggie looked ready for another opponent, and I almost had to pick up my friend off the floor. Reggie's competitive nature and his striving for excellence in *everything* he did was inspirational.

Years later, we (my wife Patti and I) asked Reggie to be a guest speaker at the Massachusetts Alliance for Chiropractic Philosophy. Without a moment's hesitation, Reggie agreed. He would *never* hesitate to do anything to advance chiropractic. He arrived at my home office late on a Friday afternoon and wanted to be adjusted. We were in the process of renovating the office at that time. While working on the lights, an electrician observed several patients getting adjusted. After the last patient left, and Reggie was sitting in the adjusting space, the electrician started asking me about a health issue that he was having. As I explained the chiropractic story to this person, I knew that Reggie, my mentor in patient education, was within earshot. After the electrician made a new person appointment and left, I asked Reggie how I did, hoping that he would find my education process acceptable. He replied, "With what?" I said, "With explaining chiropractic to that electrician." He smiled and said, "You did great, though you used a lot more words than I ever would." Lesson learned, keep it simple. Reggie was indeed a master of words. He would never use more words than necessary in any conversation or lecture.

Of all the mentors and people who have influenced my professional development and skills, I do not think there is anyone that impacted me more than Reggie Gold. That influence was so much more than an understanding and articulation of our philosophy. His consistency, passion, commitment, and seeking excellence were attributes I continually strive for in all that I do and say. I miss him, and his soul and essence are present daily in my office and in everything I do for TIC.

THE LAY LECTURE

Transcribed from Reggie Gold's
Chiropractic Expert Series
1987

The Lay Lecture
Reggie Gold

The more you know about chiropractic, the more benefit you can get from it. The more you know about anything, the more benefit you can get from it.

If you got a new food processor for Christmas, and the only thing you know about it is that it can be used as a mixing machine, well then you can use it and enjoy it and get benefit from it. But after a while, you find out it's also a blender, and you can puree, you can make soups, you can make apple sauce, you can mix cookie dough, you can chop salads, you can grate cheese. You can do all kinds of things with it if you know how to use it. And the more you know, the more benefits you get. Finally, after about a year of this, you read the instruction book, and then you say, "Wow, there's so much this thing can do for me," and you really begin to get your money's worth as you learn more.

Now the same is true in chiropractic. Obviously, you know about chiropractic, or you wouldn't be here tonight. But if you can learn more, then you can get your money's worth more. You gain more benefits from chiropractic as you know more about it. When you first heard about chiropractic, when you first became aware, you probably heard that people with bad backs and stiff necks, and headaches go to chiropractors and get help.

So you finally went to a chiropractor, and as you start in the waiting room, you began to hear other people talk about chiropractic saying things that you hadn't even heard about. For example, somebody will say, "Well, I came because I had high blood pressure, and the chiropractor helped me." And somebody else will say, "Gee, that's funny. What did he do for your high blood pressure? Or what did she do for your high blood pressure?" "Well, the chiropractor just pushed on my back, and strangely enough, the high blood pressure has diminished. It's not as bad now."

And somebody else says, "Gee, that's really strange because I went to the chiropractor because I had low blood pressure, and what the chiropractor did to me was push on my back, and the blood pressure went up to where it belongs." And somebody else said, "Well, I came because I had menstrual cramps, and that was helped." And somebody else said, 'Well, I had arthritis, and I'm not sure if it's any better, but at least it's not getting any worse." And somebody else said, "This recovered and that recovered," and you learn that chiropractic does a whole lot more than backaches.

Now, what I want to tell you tonight is that chiropractic properly used has nothing to do with back aches, and it has nothing to do with any of those disease conditions that I mentioned. Yes, it is true that if you have lots of physical health problems, going to a chiropractor might well help you to recover from those problems. But if you use chiropractic for that purpose only, you're using about 2% of chiropractic, and you're wasting all the rest.

To understand the real value of chiropractic, you have to understand a little bit more about the way the body works. First of all, let me point out that chiropractic deals not with just the health potential of the body, chiropractic deals with every physical activity. Every level of human performance is involved in chiropractic simply because every level of human performance is controlled by body chemistry. It is your body chemistry that determines: how much energy you have in the course of a day, how well you sleep at night, your moods, your attitudes, and how well you get along with other people.

Let's just talk a little bit about the role of chemistry in running your life. Do you know, for example, that you're sitting here right now, and your heart is beating away at a certain rate for you? If you were to get up and run for the bus, you couldn't make it. There's not a person in this room athletic enough to run for a bus and catch it unless they first change their body chemistry. There are little glands in the body called adrenal glands that make adrenaline, and for you to generate the speed and the energy to run, you have to have adrenaline pumped into your bloodstream by those two little glands. And if you don't get enough adrenaline, then you lack the power and the speed and the strength and the ability.

Why do you think athletes change their chemistry? And very often, they kill themselves by changing their chemistry in a desperate effort to get more performance out of the body because the body's performance is controlled by chemicals. Do you remember Len Bias, the basketball player? Maybe the greatest college basketball player this country has seen, certainly in a generation. He went out, and he could run faster and jump higher than any other athlete. He could sustain energy better than any other athlete. He could spend more minutes on the court without becoming exhausted. And one day, he went out and played one of his greatest games ever, a magnificent performance, and then he went home and keeled over and dropped dead. And we found that this excessive performance was brought about by the ingestion of chemicals.

Chemicals in the body change your performance levels and what he did was, in one hour, burn up 30 years of his life. So changing body chemistry controls your performance, but it has many, many broad effects other than the ones some athletes are seeking. The Russian women athletes recently were stripped of their gold medals from the Goodwill games because it was discovered that some of these women athletes had achieved male strength by taking male hormones. So they won the shot put and the discus and the javelin, but they paid a price. They grew mustaches, got deep voices, and their breasts shriveled up as their body became half-male from taking these anabolic steroids.

When you change body chemistry, you change performance. Do you know you can't even go to sleep at night without making a chemical? Some people make borderline quantities of that chemical. They say, "Well, I can sleep most of the time if I don't drink coffee. Coffee keeps me awake." Yes, of course, it does. Coffee is a chemical. And if you're only making borderline amounts of the sleep chemical, and you add the coffee, then you can't sleep. And some people, when they can't make the right chemicals to go to sleep, go to a drug store, buy a chemical, and that makes them sleep. Then they can't wake up in the morning, because to get up in the morning you have to make another chemical.

Everything you do requires that you change your chemistry. You breathe in polluted air. The only way you can survive is by making the right chemicals. There are hundreds of different carcinogens, cancer producing drugs in the food you eat, the air you breathe, and the water you drink. How do you survive? You survive by making the right chemicals. And if you don't make enough of the right chemicals, now you're going to be a victim of some disease, which you could have resisted if your body chemistry had been in the right balance.

To extract nutrients from your food, your body has to make enzymes, which are chemicals. If you make the right enzymes, then the food you eat becomes good nutrition for the body. They say, "Well, you are what you eat." That's not true. You are what your body's able to extract from what you eat. And if your body chemistry is out of balance and you can't utilize the food, eating more doesn't help. I happen to believe the American people probably have more nutrients in their urine than the rest of the world has in its diet. They keep popping more nutrients into their system, more vitamins, more minerals. And that's okay if your body can use them. But if your body chemistry is such that you can't use them, they're just going to waste.

Do you know you can't even laugh without making a chemical? Your sense of humor is controlled by chemistry. Years ago, there was a dentist by the name of Morton who tried to make dentistry painless. And he made it painless by having people breathe in the chemical, a chemical called nitrous oxide. That's laughing gas. And people would breathe in this chemical, and the whole sense of humor would change, and they'd relax. So here comes a dentist with a bloody great drill in one hand and a pair of pliers in the other, and a patient would think, "Oh, that's funny." And they breathe in a little more of this chemical, and they become unconscious. And if they breathe in a lot more, they become dead.

See, changing your body chemistry changes your sense of humor, your degree of relaxation, your energy, changes everything, your moods. Why do you think the police won't let you drive a car when you've been drinking alcohol? Because alcohol, as a chemical in your bloodstream, alters your physical coordination: you can't walk a straight line, you can't talk straight, and you can't think straight. But it also affects your reaction time, your judgment is impaired, you can't see straight, and you can't think straight. You're a menace to yourself and everybody else.

Look what happens to people's moods and personalities with alcohol; not picking on alcohol because there are lots of other chemicals. There are some people who just can't face a social life. They're little wallflowers till they get a couple of belts inside them, and then "yaha," life of the party. Hey, walk into a bar sometime; here's somebody who has had a few drinks, and he wants to beat up the whole bar, beat up everybody in sight. And then somebody else has a few drinks, and it becomes all gabby. And somebody else has a few drinks and becomes all lovey-dovey… can't do anything about it, but he's all lovey-dovey. So changing your body chemistry really changes who you are.

It changes your ability to resist disease. If you breathe in ragweed pollen in the summertime, your body responds by making a chemical called histamine. Now, if you make the right amount of histamine, then you don't even know there's pollen in the air, and it doesn't bother you. The person next to you is making too much histamine, not able to control the production, the histamine causes a runny nose and watery eyes, and coughing and spluttering, and sneezing. And they say, "Boy, the ragweed pollen is making me sick." No, it isn't. If ragweed pollen could make you sick, we'd all be sick. We all breathe in the same pollen.

What makes you sick is the fact that your body is not responding properly chemically. You produce too much of this histamine, and it's the histamine that makes you sneeze and splatter and cough. And lots of people then go to a drugstore, and they buy an antihistamine, and it works. It dries up the membranes and dries up some of the symptoms. Of course, it causes other problems and other symptoms: drowsiness, can't do a decent day's work, can't maintain energy. Then there are things like constipation or diarrhea, intestinal hemorrhage, intestinal bleeding, prostatic cancer in men. And interestingly enough, when you take an antihistamine, guess what your body does? Makes more histamine. So the problem goes on and on. Changing your body chemistry is necessary to life, but when you change it artificially, it creates all kinds of problems.

In order for you to do anything, you need to change your chemistry. To think clearly, just imagine your kids, you send your kids to school, and they're supposed to get an education. How much do you think they learn if they sit in class until break time, then go out on a break and smoke pot and go back to class? Do you think that would affect their learning ability, would affect their IQ, their memory, and their concentration? When body chemistry is out of balance, nothing works right.

Hey, let's talk for a minute about the menstrual cycle. Now we know there are physiological changes, there are physical changes. There's water retention and weight gain, sometimes complexion problems, straggly hair, lackluster eyes, and don't feel like working. These are just the physical things. Are there emotional changes at premenstrual time? Does PMS sometimes be so severe that it leads people to suicide? What is it that turns the perfectly rational human being into this once-a-month witch syndrome? What is it? It's a change in body chemistry, a tiny, tiny change. And boy, when body chemistry changes, it affects moods, attitudes, and capability.

Have you seen Howard Cosell recently? Howard Cosell can't hold a microphone; he shakes so badly. He can't thread a needle because his brain lacks a little chemical called dopamine. And boy, if you don't have dopamine in your brain, then you can't coordinate. He can't do any fine coordination, and they stick a label on you say you have Parkinson's disease. Well, it is a disease, but it really is a chemical imbalance in the body. The lack of a little chemical. Alzheimer's disease is another one. Loss of memory because your brain is denied a certain chemical. For you to perform properly every day, your chemistry has to be in balance. And when the chemistry is out of balance, you'll never again be all that you could be.

Now, for you to perform properly every day, your chemistry has to be in balance. When chemistry is out of balance, you'll never again be all that you could be. Now, what has all of that to do with chiropractic? Just this, I've talked a lot about chemicals from the outside of the body-changing performance; let's talk a little more about chemistry within the body-changing performance.

You have a little gland up in the throat called the thyroid gland. That makes a chemical called thyroxin. If you make the right amount of thyroxin, your life is good. If you make too much thyroxin, they say you're hyperthyroid, and you're nervous and jittery, and you can't sleep, and you can't maintain your weight. Then, somebody else is labeled hypothyroid. That means they're not making enough thyroxin, and too little means they just look at food and they put on weight, and they get tired very easily, and they sleep too much, they can't produce a decent day's work. Imagine what that does to their income-earning capacity. Some of you out there make a living by the use of your energy. Maybe you sell cars, maybe you sell real estate, maybe you work at some other kind of job. If by three o'clock in the afternoon, you're so pooped out that you can't continue working and you lose a sale here and a sale there, what does that do to your life?

What happens when your concentration begins to go because there's a tiny little chemical imbalance? Is there anybody here who would like to go to a dentist at the time that the dentist has a hangover? Why not? "Ziiiiiillp, sorry. Ziiiiiillp, sorry", that's why not. See, when your body chemistry is out of balance when you're being poisoned, and that's what a chemical imbalance does, it poisons you, and it stops you from performing properly.

There are some 70,000 billion cells in your body, and every one of them is a little chemical factory. You make chemicals, not just in the thyroid gland and the adrenal gland, you make all the chemicals necessary to adapt to a change in the environment. You make all the chemicals necessary to adapt to a virus or a bacterium in your environment.

Boy, if your chemistry is in balance, you're strong as a horse. You know people like this. There are times in your life when you can get soaking wet, get on an air-conditioned bus for three hours, have people sneezing in your face all the time, and you couldn't get a cold if you tried. With all the viruses around you, your chemical balance is so good that your resistance is high.

Then there are other times when somebody will sneeze in Boston, and you got the flu in Stroudsberg. Why are you so susceptible? Because sometimes your chemistry is a little out of balance. You're a little rundown, you say, rundown means chemical imbalance. You have 70,000 billion cells that make chemicals. Boy, if they're all making the right chemicals in harmony, you're in perfect chemical balance, and you're all the you that you're going to be. You're the best that you can be when your body chemistry is in perfect harmony. Not only is it not messed up from the outside, but the body itself is making thousands, tens of thousands of different chemicals in the right performance levels all of the time. You make the right quantity, the right quality, the right place, right time.

You eat meat, and your body has to make an enzyme to digest meat. Now, if that enzyme is not there, you have indigestion, then when the meat is gone from your stomach, then you're going to make the enzyme? Then it does you more harm than good, and you have indigestion again. You have a different problem. If your chemistry is not in balance, you're eating yourself up. It is the job of your glands and organs to make the chemicals.

Again, what does that have to do with chiropractic? For you to make the right chemicals, they have to be controlled by a master control system. How do the chemical-producing glands know what other parts of the body need? How does your heart know, at this second, how much activity the legs are doing? Are you sitting down? Are you running for a bus? How does the heart know that? Simply because all parts of the body are constantly feeding a stream of information to the brain. The brain is the central computer. This is why chiropractic is so involved.

This brain is a fascinating organ. A lot of people think the brain is just like a blob sitting up in the head, but it isn't; it's a blob on a stick. See, that's what the brain looks like. I'm fascinated by this organ. Not only does it run everything in the body, it runs the production of every single chemical. It controls all functions in the body, whether you're awake or whether you're asleep.

This brain and spinal cord start out in an amazing way. Let's talk about the creation of a new human being. A new human being is formed by the union of a tiny little female egg cell; this thing is about the size of a dot made by a finely pointed pencil. So small you can barely see it with the naked eye, and it's not even a complete cell; it's missing half its chromosomes. It meets up with a male sperm cell that's even tinier (that may be a little smarter, but okay). It's smaller, and it too, is missing half its chromosomes. So we have two half-cells that unite and form one perfect cell. Now, this one cell gets a little bigger, and it divides into two, and then it divides again, and it becomes 4, 8, 16, 30, and it just keeps multiplying.

After about eight weeks, when this blob of cells looks something like a little mulberry, an amazing thing happens. See, they all started out as one single cell; they should all be the same. After about eight weeks, some of the cells begin to change and form an organ. Guess what the first organ is. It's not the heart. It's not the skeleton. See, if I were drawing a human body, I would probably start with the skeleton. You can see what kind of an artist I am, and I would start with the skeleton and fit in the bits and pieces wherever there's room. Nature doesn't do that.

Nature says the first thing we'll set up is a control system. The first organ to form is the brain and spinal cord. Then after it has formed, before any organs show up, branches develop major nerve trunks from the brain and spinal cord, and those divide and redivide and subdivide and spread out in a network all over the body. After there are nerves, then organs can develop.

So, you get up in the throat, the thyroid gland, and over the kidney, the adrenal gland that makes adrenaline and makes cortisone. I'm fascinated by this thought; our medical friends seem to believe that cortisone is an effective treatment for all forms of arthritis and joint inflammation. If arthritis can be successfully treated with cortisone, do you think it may be possible that at least some cases of arthritis are caused by a lack of cortisone? Maybe if you were making the right amount of cortisone, you wouldn't have arthritis in the first place. You don't go to a chiropractor after 40 years of arthritis and expect to get adjusted twice, and the arthritis will go away. But it's just possible there's a relationship between the function of that gland and whether you will get arthritis or not in later life. The thyroid gland, as we said, controls all of your metabolism.

The ovaries make female hormones. Boy, too much of that stuff is a known cause of breast cancer. You better have just the right amount. You better have just the right amount of every chemical produced by every gland in the body. But before the glands can even exist, they have to have a nerve supply. The thing to remember is that's how everything works. You don't first get glands and then a nerve supply to make them work. If you wanted to grow apples, what do you do? Get a bunch of apples and throw them up in the air, and plant a tree that'll catch the apples when they come down? No, first you plant the tree, it grows a trunk, the trunk gets branches and smaller branches, and the fruit grows at the end of the branches. That's how the body works.

The glands don't exist until they first have a master control system. The brain and spinal cord are the most important organ in the entire body. You might as well know one, they are the first organ ever to develop. Two, it's an organ that seems to have to last you the rest of your life. See an organ like the liver is very important, but you could destroy two-thirds of the liver, and the body will grow it back. You can't do that with the brain and spinal cord. So chiropractors say maybe it'll be a good idea to take care of the brain and spinal cord. They seem to be rather important. They control everything and regulate your body chemistry.

Did you ever wonder what the difference is between a living, breathing, walking, talking human being and a corpse? See, physically, they are the same. The difference between a living person is electrical energy. In fact, you are now legally pronounced dead when all electrical activity in the brain has ceased. As long as your brain is producing electricity, you're alive. That's the difference between life and death. This electrical energy travels through all parts of the body over nerves. At the University of Pennsylvania many years ago, an experiment was done in which they hooked up an electroencephalogram, a thing that measures brain energy. They hooked it up to a living rabbit, and they measured the electricity in the rabbit's brain. Then they went a step further; they harnessed that electricity and used it to run a radio. The radio had no batteries, it wasn't plugged in anywhere, its only power source was the electrical energy from the rabbit's brain, and the radio worked. But because it was drawing the life energy from the rabbit, the rabbit died, and then the radio stopped. So they plugged in another volunteer rabbit, and the radio worked again.

Your body is like that radio, all of the parts of your body need electrical energy to function. They only get it from one place, and that is the brain. Not only do chiropractors believe that the brain and spinal cord are the most important organ of the body, but apparently, nature believes the same thing too. Nature has surrounded the brain and spinal cord with solid bone. Now, up in the head, you've got the skull or rather surrounding the brain, you've got the skull, the cranial vault, and that protects the brain. What about down here? Well, nature says this spinal cord is just as important as the rest of the central nerve system. It too, is surrounded by solid bone.

See, you have a hole in your head. Did you know that? I know it's not very scientific to say you have a hole in your head, but it's true. The brain extends through the bottom of the skull and is protected now inside the bones of the spine by passing through this hole in your head. Now, because it's not very scientific to say you have a hole in your head, science stepped in and gave this the name in Latin to make it scientific. The Latin name is *foramen magnum,* and that's Latin for a large hole. Now the brain extends through that hole and goes down the full length of the body, and that intervals down branches pass out. See, if this were a tube bone the way I've shown it, you'd be protected, but you wouldn't be able to bend or twist or turn. So old mother nature said, "These people need to bend and twist and turn. Let's cut this tube of bone up into 24 movable segments called vertebrae, the bones of the spine." Now, you're flexible.

Let me show you a model here. Here's a fiberglass model of the human spine. This sitting on top, and I hope you can see it from where you are, this is the base of the skull. The brain sits in here. If I tilt this forward, can you see there's a large hole in the bottom, and this yellow thing represents the bottom of the brain and the start of your spinal cord. It runs down inside all of these bones of the spine. In between each pair of bones, there's an opening through which nerve trunks pass. Now, if all of these bones are where they belong, your nerve system is protected, your brain regulates and controls your body chemistry, and you can adapt to every change in your environment up to your peak capacity. Now, that still doesn't mean you're going to be as good as the next guy, but it does mean you are going to be as good as you can be.

Our problem is we take too much for granted. Did you ever stop and think how your fingers just happened to fit in your hand? They wouldn't fit the person next to you. They're custom-made for you. They fit perfectly. Your eyeballs are exactly the right shape and size for the eye socket, which is just as well, otherwise, every time you bent down, you'd lose something. Everything fits.

The bones of the spine fit together so perfectly that the openings totally protect the nerve trunks unless something happens, something that chiropractors are concerned with, something called vertebral subluxation. I'm not going to bother you with a lot of technical terms, but this is one you really need to know.

Vertebral subluxation is what it's called when one of these bones of the spine, instead of being in its proper position protecting the nerves, slips out of place just the tiniest bit, just enough to cause a breakdown in the communications between the central nerve system and the glands that are supposed to be controlled by that central nerve system.

Now, what happens? When you have a vertebral subluxation, all the parts still work, but they don't coordinate quite as harmoniously. So your body is a little slow to change its chemistry, or maybe a little too fast to change its chemistry. If those nerves are irritated, you could get too much of a chemical, just as well as you could get too little. It means the control mechanism is lost.

It's like the control mechanism of your thermostat in the house going wrong, and you can't control the heat. "Oh, I got plenty of heat." You're going to get too damn much some of the time and not enough the rest of the time. That's what happens to the control of these organs when you have a vertebral subluxation.

When you have a vertebral subluxation, your body begins to undergo subtle abnormal chemistry. The thyroid gland here makes a little too much thyroxine. The adrenal gland makes a little too much, or a little too little adrenaline, a little too much, a little too little cortisone, too much, too little of this hormone, that hormone, this enzyme, that enzyme; as a result, the balance of your body chemistry is a little bit off, a little bit slow.

You need to change to adapt to environmental changes. You don't change quite fast enough. You eat foods, and you don't get the best nutrition out of them. You can't think as clearly. We talked about the mood changes of the menstrual cycle. See, this menstrual cycle is just a tiny little hormone change. And if it changes inappropriately because control is lost, then we get all of the problems associated with this, including the suicidal tendencies and the bad tempers, and guys, don't think you're off the hook because you don't have a menstrual cycle. You do have chemical cycles that are all controlled by the brain and the nerve system and don't think your kids don't know when to talk to the old man and when to stay the hell out of his way. For God's sake, don't talk to him before he had his dinner because if his blood sugar is low, that's a chemical, he's going to snap your head off.

When you have a subluxation, yes, you can get sick. It is so stupid to go to a chiropractor when you have a backache and ignore your life-line the rest of the time. I even know people, maybe there are some in this room, who go to a chiropractor to get well and leave their own children home to get sick. "Well, the kids don't have a backache." Chiropractic is not for back aches. The only purpose of chiropractic is to find these vertebral subluxations whenever and wherever they exist in anybody and to help the body to restore these channels to normal to regain control over your chemistry. Because when your chemistry is back in control, you're better off than when the chemistry is not under control. That's the message of chiropractic.

Chiropractic is not for sick people or people with backaches; chiropractic is for everybody. It's funny, I talk about this, and you are watching this, and you're saying, "Boy, I'm glad I don't have one of those subluxations." Yes, you do, and I'll prove it to you right now if you haven't been going to the chiropractor regularly.

Do you ever watch a one-year-old learning to walk, learning to stand, to walk, to run? Does the kid ever fall down? Like 30 times a day? Or 300 times a day? Forget the one-year-old, let's move up to a two-year-old. Were you ever two? Let's watch a day in the life of a two-year-old. The two-year-old gets up in the morning, and the first thing he does is fall out of bed-- whack subluxation. Now he gets back in, and he kicks his brother out – you got two of them subluxated. They come down to breakfast one step at a time on their rear end-- bump, bump, bump. Think that's good for the spine? Okay, the kid's not subluxated yet? Now let him go out and play. He rolls down the hill, he fights, he wrestles, he falls off his scooter, falls off his skates, falls off his skateboard, falls off his bicycle, falls off his tricycle, and falls out of a tree. Just in case he's not subluxated before he sits down to lunch, he dives into the sofa head first a half a dozen times.

This was you growing up. You grew up subluxated all of your life, but you didn't have a backache all of your life. You didn't have headaches. If a little girl aged three falls off her tricycle and gets a subluxation that damages the nerve supply to the ovaries, she's not going to get menstrual cramps at age three or at 13, maybe not at 23 or 33. But at a certain age, maybe she now comes down with breast cancer because a known cause of breast cancer is an excess of that female hormone that's made in the ovaries, and it could have come from that fall.

The fact is anything you do to cause a subluxation sets your body chemistry out of balance, and it messes up your entire life. When you have a subluxation, yes, it will interfere with your health capacity, but it will also interfere with your work capacity, your concentration, your memory, your sense of humor, your digestion, your ability to earn a living, your sex life, your relationships with your kids, your friendships with other people. I had a person tell me the other day she wasn't sure and said, "We've been under chiropractic care for a few months now, and I think something strange is happening. Is it possible that when you get adjusted, food tastes better?" Of course, because the taste buds are controlled chemically. I was talking with a dentist who told me that the chemical content of the saliva is what determines the rate of cavities. That's why they don't want you to eat sweets because it makes saliva acid. Well, supposing you have a subluxation that alters your chemistry and makes your saliva more acid, couldn't that give you more dental cavities?

Well, can you prove that? I don't need to prove it. You have to understand that there's no way on God's earth you can have a subluxation that doesn't mess up your life somehow. I don't have to know how, and if you come to me or any other chiropractor with a certain ache or pain or disease and say, was it caused by subluxation? The only honest answer is I have no idea. But whether that condition is caused by subluxation or not, you don't want to go through life with subluxation.

And the point is every child grows up with subluxations. It really bothers me to see people go to a chiropractor to get well and leave their kids home to get sick. You have to understand one major thing, vertebral subluxation, this deadly killer, this destroyer of happiness, does not have symptoms. Sitting here right now, you don't know if you have a subluxation.

I'm a chiropractor, and I've been one for a long time; I don't know if I have a subluxation. It doesn't hurt. So what I do is regularly, at least once a week, go to my chiropractor and get my spine checked. See, the chiropractor is a trained expert in finding subluxation. I really get frustrated by patients who come in and say, "Boy, I really need it today." What they're saying is, I hurt today, therefore, I think I must need it.

The other side of that is if you don't hurt, maybe you don't need it. Hey, maybe you don't, but the only way to find out is to see an expert who will check your spine.

I wish you had a big red light in the middle of your forehead, and every time you got a subluxation, it would flash. Tilt! And you look in the mirror, and you know you need a chiropractor, but you don't have a red light. How do you know if you need a chiropractor? Answer, you don't. The only way to find out is to go to a chiropractor who's trained in it, who will check your spine, find subluxations and correct them.

Please don't wait until symptoms show up. You understand, of course, that symptoms are the last stage of disease, not the first stage. Pick up today's newspaper, wherever you live, and you've come from far and wide, wherever you live, pick up today's newspaper and read about the person who never had a sick day in his life and then keeled over and dropped dead of a heart attack. He didn't go from perfect health to perfect death. Somewhere in between, there was a cause that was ignored month after month and year after year.

You don't go to a chiropractor when you're sick only or waiting for symptoms to show up. Intelligent people go regularly throughout their life, and I would love to see you get your focus away from the sickness and disease that's caused by subluxation and focus instead on all the other lessening of human potential: the loss of energy, the loss of coordination, the loss of stamina, the loss of everything. When you have vertebral subluxation, it affects your entire life by the slow process of poisoning the body by improper chemical balance. So let's understand chiropractic is not just for sick people.

Virtually everybody got subluxated in childbirth and has been subluxated all of their life, and when you have a subluxation, you have no way of knowing it without having your spine checked by an expert. That's what chiropractic family lifetime maintenance care is all about. If you have a halfway decent car, you don't drive it until the engine seizes up. You have a brain in your head; you get the car serviced regularly. Do the same with your body. If your car engine seizes up, you can throw the damn thing away and buy a new one for money. When your body seizes up because of neglect, it's too late. Don't use chiropractic care as a patch-up, use it intelligently the way you get your car serviced get your body serviced.

Now, I want to get down to my project that I want to invite you to join. Most of you here, I think, are chiropractic patients. And I know a great number of you have your families coming in regularly. But do you realize how many people are in your community that don't know about chiropractic?

There are kids growing up with subluxations, your friends. With knowledge comes responsibility; I want you to tell people about chiropractic. Voltaire said the hottest place in hell is reserved for all the good people who see evil being done and stand idly by. Is that us? Do we see kids growing up unnecessarily limited because of subluxations, never doing as well as they could? Your kids may be sitting in school, and they're coming home with B's and an A-. Hey, they could be getting straight A's if their chemistry wasn't messed up. You can't get decent grades when you're sitting in school smoking pot, and you can't get decent grades when your chemistry is out of balance from subluxation.

And you can't do a decent day's work. Some of you are employers. Let's say you're an employer; you're a construction contractor, and you build houses. How would you like to hire somebody who's so incompetent from subluxation? A carpenter who's pounding nails and bending them because he's not accurate, his coordination is a little off. His subluxations are costing you a lot of money. You're paying a full day's pay for a half a day's work, and then somebody else has got to clean up after. You must realize, please, the damages done by subluxations. Not only aches and pains and days off of work for sickness, I'm talking about incompetence on the job, people arguing on the job because they're out of balance.

When somebody has an emotional disturbance or they're depressed, how do they treat it? They go to a doctor who gives them chemicals. The cause of the problem is usually chemical, and very often, it's a chemical imbalance caused by subluxation. Give yourself, give your family, and give your neighbors a decent chance at balancing body chemistry, so you can be physically, emotionally, mentally, and spiritually in good shape. Everything is controlled by body chemistry, and if you let that chemistry get out of balance, or you let other people's chemistry get out of balance, what a mess it's making of the world!

I live just the other side of Philadelphia, just off the Pennsylvania Turnpike. Two summers ago, there was a story in the newspaper about a drunk driver who ran a police car off the road. Of all the people to run off the road, don't pick on a cop. He runs a cop off the road, and the policeman pulls over, swings around, pulls the car over, and walks over. He doesn't take out his book and start writing a ticket, he takes out his 38 and blows the guy's brains out. Now the driver was drunk, but what about the cop? He wasn't under the influence of anything except his own body chemistry. Did you ever have rotten moods like that where you can snap somebody's head off? It's caused by an imbalance in body chemistry.

You're living in a world in which everybody's subluxated. I flew in the other day from Toronto, and there were 200 other passengers on the plane. The damn pilot was subluxated, that affects his judgment. Two weeks before that, I was on a plane just out of Los Angeles, and an air traffic controller brought in a US Air 727 on top of another small plane that was on the same runway. And he said, "Well, I wasn't feeling too good." I bet he wasn't. See, subluxations cause all kinds of massive problems.

When you leave here tonight, you're going to get in your car and drive home. You might as well know that because this is a Thursday, the alcohol level in the people on the road is not that high. Nevertheless, one out of 10 on a Thursday is under the influence of alcohol. Another one or two out of 10 are under the influence of some other chemical, and all the damn rest are subluxated. It's not safe out there.

What I'm thinking of is making this a safer community. Wouldn't you like to be able to call somebody to fix your roof and know that he's going to give you a decent day's work for a decent day's pay because he's not subluxated? Have you ever felt so irritated, either chemically or for any other reason, that you're going to snap somebody's head off? Hey, down in Washington, DC, you got people making judgments for the whole world, and they're subluxated; that's scary. Do you think the Ayatollah Cockamamie wasn't subluxated or Saddam Hussein? Oh, I'd love to check his body chemistry.

Why do you want to go through life with your body chemistry out of balance, getting by? Please talk to your chiropractor about a lifetime family maintenance fee system. Let's set up a fee so you and your spouse and all the kids can get the chiropractic care you need, not just go when your back hurts or your headaches. In addition to that, won't you join me in a campaign to make this a better neighborhood, a better community, a better country, and maybe a better world? This is what I'm talking about. There are kids out there just growing up subluxated because their parents don't know. With knowledge comes responsibility. Don't you care about these kids? Have you seen the ads on television that friends don't let friends drive drunk? Hey, well, friends don't let friends walk around subluxated either.

I had an experience in my office, and I was talking about this today to a group of people. A new patient walked into the office accompanied by his 12-year-old son, who was asthmatic, and like so many asthmatics, when he started to get adjusted, the asthma cleared up. As he walked in, he saw an old friend sitting in the corner, and he said to the friend, "Oh, how long have you been coming here?" The friend said, "I've been coming for about nine years. How about you?" He said, "I've just been coming for a couple of weeks, no thanks to you." "What did I do? What do you mean no thanks to me?" He said, "What did you do? Every Tuesday night, you come over to my house to play poker. You call yourself my friend. You eat my food, you drink my booze, you hear my kid gasping for air in the next room, and you never said a word about chiropractic. You knew about chiropractic for nine years, and you let that kid suffer? He came in here for a couple of visits, and he's better already. I know twice you were sitting in my house when the ambulance came and dragged this kid off to the hospital because he needed emergency treatment for the asthma. If you had only said one word, this kid could have been better that long ago."

Now I'm asking you to think of your friends and your neighbors who need to know what you know. Come to think of it, the only way you found out about chiropractic in the first place is somebody cared enough for you to tell you about it.

Let me teach you how to share chiropractic with other people; it's very easy. You don't have to get up and give an hour's lecture.

Remember the letter N. This is how we're going to explain chiropractic, five simple steps.

Number one, chiropractic deals with every level of human performance. There's not a thing a human being does that is not in the realm of chiropractic because all of human performance is controlled by body chemistry. When people ask you about chiropractic, you don't start talking about the spine and the nerves, that's too technical, and it's not really what chiropractic is all about. What chiropractic is about is raising the level of human performance, and all performance is controlled by chemistry.

The chemistry is controlled by glands that make chemicals. Tens of thousands of glands, 70,000 billion cells in the body all make chemicals. For them to make the right chemicals for chemical balance and maximum performance, those glands have to be under the control of the central nerve system. That's the system that controls the brain and the spinal cord. When they're in control and all the glands are harmonized, it doesn't matter what age you are. Your body will do the best that it can because the master control mechanism, the brain, is in charge.

That system is controlled and protected, of course, by bone. Now we have the perfect five principles. Every level of human performance is controlled by chemistry. The chemistry imbalance is the result of glands producing the right chemicals because they're harmonized by the nerve system. The nerves, in turn, are protected by bone.

Until vertebral subluxation.

What's that? Vertebral subluxation means the bone has slipped from its proper positioning. Now instead of protecting the nerves, it's actually irritating the nerves. When the nerves are not coordinated properly, the glands lose their control mechanism. The glands still make chemicals, but not in perfect harmony. The result is an imbalance in body chemistry and lowered performance. When that performance is down, it affects every aspect of life. Everything, and it'll stay down there. You will never again be all that you could be if your body chemistry is out of balance because of a subluxation.

This is why we have chiropractic, not to treat your stupid backaches, headaches, and arthritis. When you go to a chiropractor, don't be upset if your arthritis or your backache doesn't go away the way you want it to. I'll tell you a little secret; chiropractic always works 100% of the time.

You can't get rid of a subluxation without your life potential improving. It always works, but it's absolutely impossible to predict in advance what changes you will see. Some of you want to know, don't you? Ask the chiropractor, "You think my sciatic will go away." The honest answer is, how the hell do I know? You're not a walking backache. My job as a chiropractor is to keep all your life channels open. God bless you; I hope your sciatic goes away, but if it doesn't, what are you going to do? Close up the life channels again? Keep the channels open all of your life for yourself and the whole family, that's the message.

So chiropractic exists not to treat conditions but to give an adjustment. What is an adjustment? It's that little shove that allows the bone to go back into place to free up the nerve system, so once again, it can control the glands. When the glands are controlled and interact in harmony, body chemistry now gets back into balance, and your body again performs at its best level for what it has left. The longer you'll leave the subluxation there, the more permanent damage will accrue. Don't believe that if you get adjusted, you'll never have a problem again, or your current disease will go away.

I can promise you one thing. When subluxations, look, I'll promise you two things. I won't promise you, you'll get wealth, but I will promise you if you keep your subluxations, you'll get worse. That's an absolute promise. There's no way you can keep those subluxations there without getting worse, year by year. The damage from vertebral subluxation is cumulative. If you had the subluxation since you were one and you got adjusted a day later, well, that's not so terrible. You get adjusted a month later; that's not so great. You get adjusted 30 years later, don't be surprised that some of the damage is permanent. Don't let your kids and your grandchildren start chiropractic as late as you did.

You know, sometimes people come into me or any other chiropractor, and somebody's had arthritis for 40 years, and they get four or five adjustments, and they say, "It doesn't feel any better yet." What the hell do you expect? The only thing we have to work with is this rotten mess that you bring in with you, that you call your body. What I said is, "Why don't you get in the car and go home and bring in your grandchildren, so 40 years later, they're not in the same rotten mess looking for a miracle."

The job of chiropractic is to correct the subluxation and free up the nerve system so it can once again take control of the glands and bring your chemistry into as much balance as it can so that your performance levels will go back to as high as they can go. If you want to get more results, start your chiropractic care earlier.

Now I want to ask you one more time about this final thing. Won't you please help somebody else as you were helped? I'd like you to do two things now. When you go home, the first thing I would like you to do is call up the person who first told you about chiropractic and say thanks. Tell them how you feel. They send so many people to a chiropractor, and nobody ever bothers to say thank you.

Then the next thing is to sit down and make a little list of some of the people that you are going to tell about chiropractic. If you get home early enough, maybe you can tell them tonight. Let's start the phone calls tonight. Boy, I would love to come back here six months from now and talk to all of your friends and all of your neighbors that got into chiropractic care because of you, and you can sit back and know when that kid does well and gets into a good college, the only reason they get into that college is because I told his parents about chiropractic. Hey, not too shabby.

It's one thing you can do for humanity that doesn't cost you anything. And then you can do what I do, go home at night to sleep, put your head on the pillow and fall asleep with a big old grin on your face because you know you did good stuff that day, and the world's a better place because you took the time and the trouble to care about somebody else.

Thank you, and goodnight.

The Power of One
Judy Nutz Campanale

Henry David Thoreau wrote, "The mass of men live lives of quiet desperation and go to the grave with the song still in them." Reggie Gold was NOT one such man.

Reggie, as he was affectionately known around the world, was a man who lived his life with focused determination, persistence, and passion. Over several decades, changing times and attitudes, and despite the lack of cultural authority and acceptance, Reggie persevered in his quest to grow others' understanding of the chiropractic philosophy for the sake of mankind, leaving an indelible mark on countless people and on the chiropractic profession as a whole.

My path crossed with Reggie's in the late 80s. I was a pre-med student at Carnegie-Mellon University in my early twenties, and Reggie was the keynote speaker at a *Living Principles* seminar in Pittsburgh, Pennsylvania. I knew virtually nothing about chiropractic, and he was the most dynamic, charismatic speaker I had ever heard talk about *anything*. After one two-hour session with Reggie, my life would never be the same.

He had that way about him. He was so polished and easy to listen to that you didn't even realize he was teaching you. His "letter N" presentation remains the most logical and easy-to-understand layman's explanation I have ever heard of chiropractic's true and significant impact. His PhC thesis, *The Triune of Life,* which we celebrate with this 60th anniversary publication, has stood the test of time and remains the definitive work on the topic. It is the North Star by which I and many others run our practices today, as well as how I, as Chairperson of the Board of Trustees, and others make decisions for Sherman College of Chiropractic.

I was blessed to spend considerable time with Reg over the years, as we lived only about 15 miles apart in the suburbs of Philadelphia. Whether it was breakfast at a diner, lunch at a Jewish deli, or dinner at his favorite sushi place (Reggie knew and enjoyed good food), it was always the conversation that stole the show. He could speak knowledgeably about so many topics, wine, of course, but also his passion for art, his and Irene's spectacular travels, history, politics, and my favorite, of course, chiropractic.

Understand, though, Reggie never spoon-fed me (or anyone) chiropractic philosophy (or any philosophy.) When I asked a question, he inevitably responded with another question. He wanted me to think, he wanted all of us to think, and in fact, for decades, he would often be heard passionately issuing from stages around the world one of his most famous edicts, "Think, Dammit. Think!"

And that is precisely the legacy of his thesis, *The Triune of Life.* He calls this one concept "the crux of the entire philosophy," and adds that "Failure to understand the 'Triune of Life' must inevitably result in failure to understand the entire philosophy of which it is a cornerstone." Eerily, these words of his echo through our profession today in various ways. For the most part, the profession has abandoned the fundamental of chiropractic. As with the rest of the world, chiropractic has become whatever an individual wants it to be or has a loud enough voice to suggest that it is. Many schools teach philosophy only from a historical perspective or teach no philosophy at all, and many organizations worldwide deny the very existence of vertebral subluxation.

Yet, Reggie also astutely posits

> A philosophy does not become valued when a great number of people accept it. Nor does it become invalid because a great number of people reject it. Its validity can only be measured in terms of its acceptability in the mind and reason of one individual person. (Gold, 1963)

And so it is for us as we press on in chiropractic.

Principle Number Four, The Triune of Life, states, "Life is a triunity having three necessary united factors, namely, Intelligence, Force and Matter." (Stephenson, 1927, p. xxxi) Without question, the most misunderstood of those components is the first, intelligence. This may be partly due to the fact that it is an immaterial component, yet logic defines it well for us.

Since we cannot see intelligence itself, we must look to other ways to define it or measure it. What is its purpose? The purpose of intelligence is to organize. We can look around the universe and note that surely it is organized. Organization bespeaks intelligence. Reggie puts it, "Organization is the prime manifestation of intelligence and intelligence the sole cause of organization." (Gold, 1963)

So both universal intelligence and innate intelligence (that intelligence manifested in living things) are principles of organization, nothing more, nothing less. They are not some kind of voodoo that talks to us, or worse yet, talks to others. It's not some kind of magic that helps us find a parking spot. It is simply a principle of organization. It does what it does, like gravity, no matter who you are or where you live or whether you're good or bad or big or small, healthy or not.

In practice, the challenge is to raise people's awareness of the fact that they are amazing and that they are organized at such a high level that we can't even understand it all. Your job is to remind people how amazing they are. Too often, people seek out chiropractic for back pain, headaches, or ruptured gumpture of the trash bag (wink wink), not knowing that chiropractic doesn't address what's wrong with the body. Chiropractic works with what's right with the body, that principle of organization that's constantly keeping them in existence.

They don't realize that within them is an intelligence that is constantly adapting them to the countless physical, chemical, and emotional stresses that bombard us all every day in this crazy mixed-up world. Your job consists of teaching people the principles by which the body works so they can think for themselves, the principles of the triune of life.

In vertebrates, that intelligence uses the nerve system to communicate the information (known as force) developed by the intelligence and expressed through matter. That nerve system, and hence that communication, can be disrupted by vertebral subluxation, and when that happens, the living thing is not what it was intended to be. Chiropractors assist in the restoration of the amazing principle of organization. It's not a big thing, but it doesn't have to be to have an enormous impact. Ecologist Bill Mollison said, "Though the problems of the world are increasingly complex, the solutions remain embarrassingly simple." I think that may hold true for our bodies as well.

I was honored to be able to visit Reggie several times in the weeks before he passed. He always had me check his spine when I was there, which is genuinely one of our greatest gifts. On one of those visits, I also checked another visitor that was there and laughed out loud when he literally critiqued my technique. "Watch that rotation, Jude." As it happened, I was with Reggie and Irene just hours before Reggie's passing. They were both courageous and calm, and as I held his hand and loved on him for the last time, I reminded him of all of you, his students, the countless number of people who admire him, have learned from him, owe much of their lives to him, and love him. You were all there. Make his life matter by making your own matter.

2 Ellish Parkway
Eric Plasker

2 Ellish Parkway in Spring Valley, New York, is one of the most famous addresses in chiropractic history. It's right up there with Brady Street in Davenport, Iowa, and Barclay Circle in Marietta, Georgia. This is where I received my first chiropractic adjustment in 1976.

At the time, I had no idea of the relevance this home office was going to have in chiropractic history. I wish our profession had the foresight to buy that property and turn it into a museum.

Ernie Landi had merged his practice with Reggie's, and the volume of adjustments was legendary. So was the healing. Ernie gave me my first adjustment, and it changed the course of my life instantly. Reggie's presence was palpable in the building and in the always overflowing parking lot.

I would drive to the office to get adjusted after school and take a number, the same way you would when you went to Pakula's Bakery Shop down the road for a black and white cookie. Only the line was much longer at 2 Ellish Parkway. I would drive to the office after school to get my number. Then I would drive home to have a snack, do my homework, and then drive back to the office over an hour later just in time for my "zetz." That's what my father used to call it. Of course, our whole family would get adjusted.

Dr. Landi always talked about Reggie. He kept his spirit alive in that building. So when I went to Life Chiropractic College in 1982 and saw that Reggie was coming to give a seminar, of course, I had to attend. That's where I first learned about the 33 principles and the triune of life.

The seminar was on Reggie's famous "Letter N Layman's Lecture." Reggie taught me so much about chiropractic philosophy, purpose, communication, and public speaking. I was in awe of his unique style and legend, which came temporarily crashing down during one of the breaks.

I went to the bathroom, and while I stood at the urinal doing my thing, Reggie came and stood in front of the urinal next to me. Within a few seconds, he let out the loudest fart I think I had ever heard in my life. It caught me completely off my star-struck guard.

Then without flinching, Reggie turned to me and said, matter of factly, "It wasn't meant to stay inside." He gained his status back instantaneously.

The seminar was 8 hours long for this 1-hour lecture. At the end of the day, when Reggie took some questions, a student in the back of the room asked in a very wise guy fashion, "Reggie, you don't always have an hour to do a talk. What would you say if you only had a minute to convince someone to get chiropractic care?"

Reggie's answer changed my life. He said, "I would use the entire minute to convince that person to spend an hour with me."

I think about Reggie's answer to that question every day. It is why I write books, and articles, do videos, etc., to convince people to spend their whole life with chiropractic. We tell people all the time, "Your Innate Intelligence will organize around the thoughts you think, the choices you make, and the lifestyle you live." This is a 33 Principles-centered message that makes sense to many of the modern-day, misguided earthlings that we serve.

Reggie's explanation of providing chiropractic care for people with scoliosis is something I regularly use in practice. When asked, "Reggie, is it your goal to straighten the spine of a person with scoliosis?" Reggie answered, "Should we align the bones or the holes in the bones. When you adjust the subluxation, Innate will do its job to align the spine in the best interest of the nerves." As a young chiropractor, this was a powerful message, and people get it!

Reggie was a huge supporter of my work with *The Family Practice* and *The 100 Year Lifestyle*. In fact, in 2008, after *The 100 Year Lifestyle* was published, I did a seminar with Reggie and Ernie. I called the seminar "Three Generations at 2 Ellish Parkway." It was awesome. To share the stage with my mentors was very humbling.

After Reggie passed, I was invited to speak at the first-ever Life West Wave. I met Irene there and organized a conference call with her and Ernie, also called "Three Generations at 2 Ellish Parkway." It was a fun and inspiring discussion where the three of us shared some of our most meaningful memories that occurred in that historic location. We recorded this beautiful conversation, and if you'd like to listen to it, you can email me at admin@100YearLifestyle.com, and we will send it to you.

I feel so blessed to become close with two of my most important mentors. They taught me the importance of telling the story and being exceptional at it and that we need more chiropractors in the world. I believe that with all my heart.

Over the last 11 years, I have donated my time to deliver the Friday night keynote speech in front of prospective students and their families at Life University's Life Leadership Weekend. I have also done this talk at Life West's Champions Weekend. I always mention my mentors during this talk, which always makes me emotional.

B.J. said, "You never know how far reaching …" Reggie, Ernie, and all of the rest of us continue to work to make this a subluxation-free world. Their ripple keeps growing. It's an honor to contribute to this tribute and know that this ripple will continue for generations to come.

Thots on Dr. Reggie Gold
Eric Russell

On a recent podcast, I was asked about my introduction to the philosophy of chiropractic. Most of the time, people assume that I was a huge philosophy person in chiropractic college. In reality, I was not. My answer is always the same; I was technique focused in chiropractic college and was not interested in the philosophy of chiropractic until after I graduated.

I distinctly remember being about a year in practice and suffering from a little bit of burnout. I remember asking, "Is this it?" and was concerned about where my career was going for the next fifty years. However, I was very fortunate to ask the right question, "Why are some people so fired up about chiropractic and others are not?" This simple inquiry eventually led me to the answer of the philosophy of chiropractic.

In my quest to learn more about chiropractic philosophy, I asked a great friend of mine, Dr. Rob Sinnott, what chiropractors inspired him, and one of his answers was Dr. Reggie Gold. That conversation was my first exposure to Dr. Gold's teachings. I remember Dr. Sinnott vividly talking about following Dr. Gold around and learning as much as possible from him. Since I could not travel as much because I was starting a practice from scratch, I scraped up some money and bought the ten CD series by Dr. Reggie called "Reggie Gold Speaks on Chiropractic, Album #1, The Philosophy."

I distinctly remember driving to the office, listening to those CDs every day, and would get through the series in just a couple of weeks and then start all over again. Dr. Gold's message was crystal clear, and I felt like his CD series was a perfect lecture on chiropractic philosophy. His logic is evident; he was entertaining and had just the right amount of humor to keep you interested. And when you got comfortable, Dr. Gold would hit you with a point that would make you think. This lecture style is what made Dr. Gold one of the profession's best at articulating the philosophy of chiropractic. All steak and some sizzle.

I loved that CD set and listened to it from start to finish too many times to count. Unfortunately, about five years ago, I loaned it out and never got it back. However, as luck would have it, I found a set for sale and immediately purchased it.

As I listened to it with fresh ears, I was amazed. So many of Dr. Gold's teachings had become part of my teachings, and I was pleasantly surprised at how much influence his teaching had on me. I loved "The Valley of the Blind" CD for inspiration and Dr. Gold's *Triune of Life* book. Still, besides *Stephenson's Chiropractic Textbook*, Dr. Gold's CD set on philosophy is one of the most significant references for my philosophical perspective. I use his information every time I teach a class on the philosophy of chiropractic.

It is interesting to think about Dr. Gold because I learned so much from him, primarily by listening to his lectures. My interactions with Dr. Gold mainly happened when I was the New Zealand College of Chiropractic president from 2011-2013. I will never forget that one of the first events I attended while president was a chiropractic event in Peru. I shared the stage with a fantastic group of chiropractors, but the headline speaker was Dr. Gold. That weekend Dr. Gold was on point, and he had everyone's attention during his lecture. I was genuinely watching a master at work.

Another benefit of being president was hosting the college's annual Lyceum and hosting all of the dignitaries. A speaker would fly in the day before Lyceum, and it was my job to make sure they were taken care of. However, Dr. Gold was different. First of all, he had a standing invitation for every Lyceum, and he did not miss any of them. Secondly, he would arrive a good week or more before the event. Dr. Gold stayed at the same hotel and became friends with the owners. And thirdly, he would stop by my office for a quick hello, but Dr. Gold was then out the door wanting to hang out with the students, not some stuffy VIP dinner.

I remember asking a student who was spending time with Dr. Gold what they were doing that day, and their answer was they were having a yard sale, and Dr. Gold was going to help him price some items. I asked, "Are you sure this is what Dr. Gold wants to do?" The student answered that since Dr. Gold had an import-export business before chiropractic, he was more than qualified. Imagine my horror and surprise when they got into the car and took off. That was when I witnessed Dr. Gold having a moment of bliss, hanging out with chiropractic students talking philosophy and life, and not being treated like a VIP. Just the way he wanted.

I always tell chiropractic students that when they want to learn more, ask a chiropractor they like who their top three influences are and explore them. This exploration will give the student three new prominent chiropractic philosophers to learn from and get a better breadth of understanding of chiropractic philosophy. There is no doubt that Dr. Reggie Gold is one of my three. His teachings and lessons live on today through so many chiropractors around the world, including me. It makes me smile when I think, what a legacy!

Never Compromise Your Beliefs
Jack Bourla

Sometimes it is only during times of intentional retrospection that we begin to fully understand the role that others have played in our lives. We get busy with our to-do lists, practices, families, hobbies, and associations/organizations, and we forget to self-reflect and assign relevance to who we are, what we are doing, what we have done, and what we will do, and who helped to get us where we are.

Many chiropractors have been influenced by Reggie and Irene Gold, and I am no exception. When I think of the Golds, one word comes to mind that overshadows all other words: *conviction.*

Throughout his life, Reggie Gold stood for what he believed in and did so with absolute conviction. He was a superb communicator with a brilliant mind and a masterful ability to simplify the complicated. His command of language was second to none. As those of us who are fortunate enough to have listened to him or to have listened to his recordings, we stand in awe at how Reggie conveyed his thoughts and convincingly caused us to follow him, sometimes unknowingly.

The lesson I learned most from Reggie was this: to look at everything through a chiropractic lens. In so doing, we bring relevance and practicality to our chiropractic philosophy and principles. Whenever I watch a movie, I look at it through the chiropractic lens. When I listen to music, read a book, or have a conversation, I always bring it back to chiropractic.

Reggie exuded passion for chiropractic like few others. Nothing could stop him from achieving his desire for the world to know the capacity that chiropractic had to bring out the best in all people. Reggie believed that chiropractic was not a healthcare modality. He knew that chiropractic could help unleash possibilities in people who previously had vertebral subluxations. It was Reggie who promoted unapologetically that vertebral subluxations were a detriment to life's expression and a limitation of one's ability to experience their maximum human experience.

His convictions led him to so many adventures, which most of us read about in amazement. His stints at various chiropractic colleges, organizations, and offices revealed his character: he did not stop until he got done what he wanted to get done.

Reggie was a unique character. His life was a playground for his ambition. He was challenged by many. He challenged right back. And he never once wavered about what chiropractic could do for the world. He sat in confidence about what chiropractic could do for humanity. He was seen in public debates holding his ground because when one is as convicted as Reggie was, no one and nothing could shake him.

I remember one day attending The Wave, an event dreamed of and executed by Brian Kelly, then president of Life College of Chiropractic West. I walked through a hallway and passed Irene and Reggie, sitting on a bench, observing as they always did. The friend with whom I was walking wore a T-shirt with "Chiropractic Warrior" written across the chest. Irene called us over, and my friend whispered, "oh sh*t," thinking he was in trouble. Irene asked what "Chiropractic Warrior" meant, and as he stumbled to explain himself, Reggie said, "Whatever it means, never compromise your beliefs. Others will try to trip you up, but stick to the principles that animate the living universe, and you will prevail."

We walked away rather briskly, and when we were out of range, he said, "Reggie Gold gave me advice!" I thought to myself, just be glad he didn't kick your a$$. When it came to chiropractic, Reggie did not compromise or joke. He was all business, all the time.

Today, I sit in awe that I have served three terms as President of the International Federation of Chiropractors and Organizations, and I now serve as the Chairman of the Board of an organization that Reggie founded, the IFCO (then the FSCO) because he was unwilling to compromise the tenets of chiropractic. He wasn't one bit happy that other organizations were willing to jeopardize the purity of chiropractic, and he would not stand for that. He formed an organization that has seen many leaders take on his hope of keeping chiropractic pure, unsullied and unmixed, just as B.J. Palmer admonished us to do in his plea to "Guard the sacred trust."

We need another Reggie Gold today more than ever as we see chiropractic being sacrificed for so many reasons, none of which recognize the incredible profession that can change the world. I loved when Reggie would proclaim with such certainty, "If you are not out to change the world, everything else is Mickey Mouse!"

And with that veracity, I teach my children that all things are possible in life when they are clear of vertebral subluxations and that they must leave planet earth better than they found it.

To have any discussion regarding Reggie without recognizing the enormous accomplishments of Irene Gold would be an incomplete discussion. Irene is perhaps one of my favorite human beings. She demonstrates poise, grace, humility, strength, intelligence, certainty, humor, and determination.

Irene supported Reggie like no one else could. She believed in him, challenged him, and played her behind-the-scenes role because she saw the potential that chiropractic had to change lives. She is not a push-over, and her humility is her strength.

In addition to being a huge chiropractic advocate, she has helped thousands of chiropractors to pass their national board exams. She recognizes that the exams are not chiropractic, but they have been made necessary to enable a chiropractor to practice so that they may be conduits to improving society. I am one such chiropractor.

As I wrote in Irene's book, *Gold: A Lifetime of Love in Chiropractic*:

> The famous B.J. Palmer quote, "you never know how far reaching ..." could never be more appropriate in my life with respect to Irene Gold. I was an excellent chiropractic student, graduating at the top of my class as Valedictorian. I did extremely well on national boards Parts I-III. When it came time to take Part IV, I did not want to risk failing the boards. I was 42 years old, and failing the boards would mean delaying my license by at least six months. So, I enrolled in Irene Gold's Part IV review classes.
>
> She was remarkable. She actually made preparing for the mundane fun. We learned, laughed, and prepared. I knew the stuff cold. I was ready for anything they threw at us. Irene knew it. We had a rapport. She knew I was very prepared.
>
> Friday afternoon of the dreaded weekend came, and it was my turn to take the X-ray portion of the exam. The students were placed in a dark room with ten stations of films and questions related to the films. Each station was timed. When the examiners said "go," the students would each go to their assigned stations and begin the exam. When I arrived at my first station, I asked myself, "Is this a joke? Is this a human X-ray?" I panicked. I couldn't make out what I was looking at, and the timer went off; time for

> Station 2. But I had not yet answered the questions for Station 1.
>
> I went to Station 2 thinking about the questions for Station 1. I did my best to answer Station 2 and tried to answer Station 1 with the time I had remaining. I was still thinking about Station 1, and now even Station 2, and that continued for the remaining eight Stations, and I thought I was a dead man.
>
> After the X-ray exam was over, we were all herded into a holding room. During the cattle march to the holding room, I spoke with another student who did not take Irene's review course. He said the exam was a breeze. I told him I failed miserably and that I was not going to take the rest of the exam that weekend. Somehow, Irene found out about my decision, and she called me at home that night. She asked me what I thought of the exam, and I told her that I had failed. She told me I was "crazy" and not to be "silly." If I failed, she reasoned, everyone else failed. She insisted that I take the remainder of the exam.
>
> I listened to her, and I took the exam. My scores came back, and I killed all sections of Part IV. She was right. Had I not listened to her, I would have bailed from the exam and delayed receiving my license by at least six months.
>
> Here is the amazing thing: I ran into Irene and Reggie Gold at a conference 15 years later, and she stopped me in the hallway and recanted the entire story, verbatim, as though it had just happened. She remembers everything and everyone. Her memory is unparalleled. She remembers stories from 40 years ago in vivid detail. She is an unbelievable treasure to the profession. Her commitment to the students is so remarkable that everyone she touches benefits, just like Reggie.
>
> Oh, and that guy who boasted about passing the X-ray portion of the exam that day? He failed Part IV. He should've taken Irene's review course with me. (p. 128-129)

For those of us who have been shaped by the Golds, we are the blessed ones. Their selfless contributions to the profession, the colleges, the students, and the chiropractic organizations have caused a shift on this planet. It is our job to continue what they started because absent chiropractic in its purest form, the world will never know its true potential.

As the newly selected and sixth President of Sherman College of Chiropractic it is my duty to ensure that our school achieves its mission to educate and prepare our doctors of chiropractic who are focused on analyzing and adjusting vertebral subluxations. Reggie would be pleased to know that Sherman holds dearly to the tenets and principles of chiropractic. We will not waiver in our mission and vision to keep chiropractic pure, unsullied and unmixed for future generations.

Life Heals...Not Doctors
Pam Jarboe

In the early 1990s, I attended Life University in Atlanta, Georgia. I got involved with a club on campus called Point Zero. The club's purpose was to help all of us as students become better communicators of the philosophy and science of chiropractic. For some reason, I struggled to learn to communicate. My experience in chiropractic care had changed my brain, mood, and life. I knew a truth about health and life, yet often when I have a body knowing and a passion for something, I become spazzy when I attempt to convey my experience. Not spizzy, as true chiropractic enthusiasts would say, but spazzy. I would just feel wound-up and super passionate, but ungrounded and stressed when I tried to share the message.

I mention that I felt stressed because early on in my chiropractic education, I received a phone call from a family member who had recently had a baby. The baby had been born with something that they struggled to explain to me called torticollis (Insert eye roll!). My family member spoke intensely about this diagnosis. I listened and asked questions and learned that the doctors were recommending a surgery to cut the SCM on the elongated side by 1 inch, in order to allow the baby to hold its head up right. They felt that this incision would correct the "imbalance" this new baby was experiencing with his head.

In my spazzy and passionate way, I fought to get the baby checked by a chiropractor, and adjusted if necessary. My family members were horrified at the idea, and nothing I said could change that. I felt awkward and shy, and inadequate, and that my time in Point Zero Club might have failed me. This also brought on feelings that I had failed this baby. This baby actually received the barbaric surgery, and my relatives continued to think that chiropractors were quacks, and this was a responsible choice. My heart was broken.

For days I hid in bed, and felt like giving up. It was something I experienced often, when I tried to speak to "muggles." The chasm between what I KNEW, and the paradigms that I came up against overwhelmed me.

I finally decided to get out of bed and fight the good fight, and happened to attend Sherman Chiropractic College Lyceum. Reggie presented that weekend, and he embodied the confidence, intelligence, and wit that I longed for. I heard him, and all I could think about was how life heals ... not doctors. In his story, he talked about the innate intelligence of the body knowing exactly what was needed. He made a suggestion that we put iodine on a steak, wrap it up and see whether or not that steak heals. He reminded all of us in the audience that without a doubt, it is the body that heals. Specifically, the power of life heals.

This dramatic (there was often a bit of drama in his presentations!) distinction was extremely helpful for me at the time. Reggie's words helped me to communicate the profound simplicity of the message. What we do as chiropractors IS so profoundly simple. What I noticed is that Reggie was very comfortable with that profound simplicity. He repeatedly, and passionately communicated it.

Reggie Gold's devotion to chiropractic communication inspired me. It helped me to not quit, and that has had a massive ripple effect in my community, and in the global chiropractic community as I continue to speak and teach throughout our profession. I am daily reminded that *life heals*. Reggie's life, and passionate teachings, have lifted many lives even after his death. May we all have this type of far reaching, pure and enlivening impact long after we are gone.

Adjusting Subluxations
Ronen Mendi

Dr. Reggie Gold was an incredible professional and quite a character. Dr. Gold put reason and good scientific understanding into our profession by making sense of the art, philosophy, and science of adjusting subluxations. He taught how subluxation corrects and balances the body emotionally, chemically, and physically. Dr. Gold knew how to make the chiropractic message simple so that people would get it, so we don't spend time and energy arguing with other professionals about what we, as chiropractors, do.

We adjust and release the body's Innate (internal/inborn) force to function as it could and should. This is the sense of chiropractic. Dr. Gold also said, in a straightforward way, that adjusting the spine to function at its best is a lifetime endeavor. Not only when one isn't feeling or functioning well. However, that might be the point of entry or the beginning for many who begin chiropractic spinal life care. Since he understood how spinal adjustments strengthen spines and life expression, he demanded that people take care of their kids and families as well as themselves, especially before symptoms take over the reason for taking care of their health.

It was an honor for me to meet him and hear his message personally in so many professional meetings, seminars, and lectures, where he never hesitated to tell his story and spread his wisdom.

Let us never forget his enthusiasm about the message and his willingness to risk his license and reputation for the clear message that he named Spinology, the study and knowledge of the spine.

Reggie's straightforward message brings our profession to lead people, families, and humanity to future new health, best function, and potential manifestation. That vision is how we can contribute to a better world future. Dr. Reggie Gold was and always will be a chiropractor, teacher, and visionary. Thank you, Dr. Gold, for your leadership.

The "Big N"
Hans Salas

What you do for yourself vanishes when you die. What you do for the rest makes up your legacy. -Kalu Ndukwe Kalu

We have all come into this life to do something; all people are important in the world. Some people leave us teachings, and some leave a mark on the lives of others. Some people have dedicated their lives and efforts to be able to leave something for future generations, keep an idea alive, and make a change in the world far beyond their lifetime. There are opportunities where the legacy becomes a mark that transcends one person's lifetime. Chiropractic is no exception; Dr. Reggie Gold is part of this legacy.

I am part of a generation that did not have the opportunity to have contact with some of the brightest minds in the profession. Reggie Gold is one of those minds. Despite not being physically with us, his legacy continues to impact more people. I have no doubt that, in time, his legacy will continue to do so for the next generations of the profession.

We can consider this because today, thanks to our technology, we can access a lot of information, and we can find presentations of many legends of the profession; we can find several talks by Dr. Reggie Gold. We can learn and be surprised by his communication capacity and how he explained chiropractic to people. Also, through technology and face-to-face meetings, we can learn from other colleagues who were at his lectures. We can admire how Reggie's words and ideas impacted them. It has happened to me on several occasions when talking to my mentors and more experienced people when asking them about who was the person who most impacted or influenced them during their career. The name Reggie Gold is one of the ones I have heard the most. His unique form and style, his ability to communicate, his security and certainty when speaking, and the simplicity of explaining the importance of chiropractic for achieving each individual's human potential. He is and has been one of the voices that have generated the most impact.

What has been the influence of Reggie Gold?

I believe that his contribution, and his dedication to the profession, was his revolutionary act of questioning our basis and redefining our role, always maintaining that our goal is unique and distinct in the way that we serve the world.

One thing that made a big difference was that Reggie was the one who started talking and developing the thought about human potential in chiropractic. In doing so, I think he took a step towards the evolution of chiropractic without losing our essence and our "big idea."

Many people may agree that chiropractic is for everyone; the nervous system is present in all humans, and vertebral subluxation alters the communication and coordination of the nervous system. So, vertebral subluxation will never be a positive thing in the life and organic functioning of a person.

Reggie explains this very well in his essay on "The Chemistry of Life," the piece that has impacted me the most. His essay is valuable for this and future generations of the profession to maintain the chiropractic objective with certainty, emphasizing the importance of chiropractic in people's lives.

The essential step Reggie made was the evolution of the idea of "Getting sick people well." Chiropractic moved beyond this, not because it's a bad idea or a bad thing but because it's incomplete. Chiropractic care is for everyone; all people should be able to access regular and lifelong chiropractic care for the optimal functioning of the human body. We do not diagnose pathologies, that is a role of the practice of medicine, and if our goal is to make people feel better or that sick people get well, we are using the name of chiropractic to practice medicine. Chiropractic care is for healthy and unhealthy people, regardless of their state or their perception of health. Chiropractic goes to something much bigger, and that has to do with life, organized functioning, and human potential.

As we already know, the nervous system plays a key role in the organization and coordination of the human body. We also know that the ability to adapt has an intimate relationship with the state of the nervous system, self-healing, or self-regulating processes. The nervous system also governs the functioning of the physiology of living organisms that must be kept at "normal" levels to be in a state of equilibrium, or internal homeostasis, which allows human adaptive mechanisms to function. If we take the example of a person who suffers harm or injury due to some kind of mechanism; whether physical or mechanical, chemical or metabolic, emotional or psychological, it is known that the primary response mechanism is carried out through the immune system; but coordinated by the nervous system. The nervous system triggers an inflammatory process and seeks to respond to damage for multiple reasons, such as reporting the presence of damage, increasing blood flow in the area to accelerate the presence of chemical and hormonal elements, initiating a cascade of reactions. These reactions control and contain the damage, generate a bridge of tissues and perform a healing process so that the tissue can be regenerated, repairing the damage over time. Can you imagine if all those response mechanisms had an alteration in the communication system? What if the response of a person's body was slower? How long would the body struggle to solve that problem?

The presence of vertebral subluxations alters the internal responses and communication of the body. In "The Chemistry of Life," Dr. Reggie Gold explains, in a simple way, the complexity of self-regulation of the human body through the chemistry of the body and how it works. He described this as "body chemistry," which explains how human potential and its ability to function depends on the balance of internal chemistry and how the presence of vertebral subluxations affect the coordination of glands and the chemical regulation of the body. This inevitably leads to a limitation in the ability to adapt, affecting performance and human potential, described as his concept of the "Big N" (Figure 1).

Figure 1
Description of Reggie Gold's "Big N"

1. Chiropractic takes care of human performance.
2. Every level of human performance is controlled by the chemistry of the body.
3. The chemistry of the body is controlled by the glands that are responsible for making chemicals.
4. All glands are controlled by the nervous system.
5. The nervous system is protected by the spine.

When vertebral subluxation occurs

1. A vertebral subluxation is a vertebra over which the body has lost some of its control.
2. A vertebral subluxation irritates the nervous system.
3. Nerve irritation alters the function of the glands.
4. Inadequate glandular function alters body chemistry.
5. Altering the body's chemistry decreases performance.

When a chiropractic setting is applied

1. Chiropractic adjustment restores vertebral positioning.
2. Proper vertebral position removes nerve irritation.
3. Restores nerve control for normal glandular function.
4. Proper glandular function produces a chemical balance of the body.
5. The proper balance of the body's chemistry increases performance.

When I was invited to participate in this beautiful project to honor the legacy of Dr. Gold, many things came to mind. Some that I considered were; his career around the world, sowing seeds in the past Sherman College of Straight Chiropractic, his congruence in “The Great Debate,” his “The Valley of the Blind,” *The Triune of Life*, and his overall contribution to the growth and development of the profession. However, for me, the development of the “big N” concept has been the way Reggie Gold has most influenced my career. It impacted how I explain and communicate about chiropractic in a simple but profound way.

Thanks to Reggie’s work and effort throughout his life, new generations have learned that chiropractic focuses not only on the body’s health potential but also on each of its activities and functions. Our profession relates to all levels of human performance because each level is controlled by its internal chemistry. In short, the body produces chemicals for its operation and internal regulation, which allows the ability to adapt or adaptability, which is central to the objective of chiropractic. Chiropractors seek to assist the body In adapting and expressing itself more effectively by correcting vertebral subluxations that generate nerve interference in the neuro spinal system. Clearly, the body can also adapt better without disease, but treating disease is not a chiropractic goal. Higher performance and reaching an optimal life potential allow a greater ability to adapt, which is the purpose of chiropractic. In other words, our goal is to allow every organ, tissue, and cell of the human body to communicate better through the nervous system. This is so that the process of adaptation occurs more effectively, and the human body heals and repairs itself better when the nervous system is free of vertebral subluxations.

Our profession is in a critical situation where our actions will lead us on the right track or the wrong path. History advances day by day and is marked by the actions we take every day. It is important to look more closely at the past, to know our roots and the legacy left to us. We should follow Reggie’s example and leave future generations a path they can follow. The responsibility has now fallen on us, and we must continue the legacy left to us by Reggie and others.

References

Gold, R. (1971/1972). The chiropractic expert series: Part 2 - Body Chemistry https://youtu.be/15nLfzRBWo4.
Gold, R. (1979). The great chiropractic debate. https://youtu.be/zRRNzlKMLYk.
Gold, R. (1972). *The valley of the blind – Lay Lecture*. https://youtu.be/VZd8_BAHVGM
Salas Redlich, H. (2021). *Legacy: The art behind a chiropractor*, Vol 1.

My Life Turned 180 Degrees
Monique Andrews

Every once in a rare while, you meet someone who changes the trajectory of your life. You know it when it happens because nothing after that moment is ever the same. I recall when it happened for me with vivid clarity on a chilly March afternoon in 1999 in Davenport, Iowa. The first time I ever heard Reggie Gold speak.

I was in my third trimester at Palmer college when I met Reggie Gold for the first time. As a bench neuroscientist who was yet to get "The Big Idea," I was more than skeptical about what this chiropractic philosopher had to say. Reggie was on campus to speak, and with equal parts curiosity and doubt, I sat down at a packed house to listen to Reggie give his *Chemistry of Life* talk.

My life turned 180 degrees on its axis that afternoon, and I would never be the same again. I walked into that room a naive mechanist and walked out a principled CHIROPRACTOR. Not only did I get The Big Idea, but I also gained a love for our philosophy and our unique language. Reggie sparked in me a deep desire to master the art of communication.

Reggie was beyond an exceptional orator, he was a visionary and a master at making the message simple, and I wanted to be just like him. A good teacher makes you want to learn more. A great teacher makes you want to inspire others. Reggie made you want to change the world!

The most important thing I learned from Reggie was to keep it simple. We have all heard that speaker who is more interested in you knowing how smart they are than in teaching you something. Nothing is less inspiring. Reggie never made it about himself. His number one goal was to spread the chiropractic message in a way everyone could understand. I modeled my teaching after him and the greatest compliment I get today is that I can make the most complicated material sound so simple.

I went on to develop a deep personal relationship with Reggie. He was tireless in his efforts to help students and was instrumental in us bringing the student philosophy triunes to Palmer for the first time ever. He never said no to students. Another lesson of his that I embody to this day.

I carry so many lessons that Reggie taught. While "just keep it simple" is perhaps the most enduring for me, Reggie also left us one other precious gift that I still cherish today ... the woman behind the man - Irene Gold. Not only as formidable of mind as he was but with a generosity of spirit that exceeds parallel. In one word – GOLDEN.

Some of my most treasured Reggie-isms ...

> "Chiropractic is different not because of what we think, but how we think."

> "No doctor anywhere ever cured anybody of anything."

And my personal favorite Reggie response, a question I often ask myself, when asked: "*which technique is the best for ________ ?*"

> It doesn't matter if you hit them in the ass with a shovel – chiropractic works every single time."

Reggie Talked the Why
Bob Tarantino

He is in the front of the room, standing with one foot on the seat of a chair, getting ready to speak. It is the year 1969, and I am two years in practice and failing miserably. I graduated in 1967 from The Chiropractic Institute of New York, located in New York City, and to the time of my opening a practice, I was not taught how to run a practice. My best friend, Dr. Joseph Intelisano, insisted that to become more successful in the practice of chiropractic, I had to experience the teaching of two men, Dr. Sid Williams and Dr. Reggie Gold. I found that both men profoundly influenced my life from that time on. Dr. Sid talked about *the how*, and Dr. Reggie talked about *the why*.

He begins to speak and instruct his listeners on the philosophy of chiropractic. I have always thought of these words as the golden tones of the song that is chiropractic.

We are packed into a recreation room in his home on Ellish Parkway in Spring Valley, New York, hundreds of us sitting and listening. Irene, his wife, was so gracious to host this madness. My wife Evelyn and I always arrived early to get a seat in the room, while others were forced to just hear his voice from other rooms in the house. We attended these Saturday meetings monthly for years, always getting home when the sun was coming up. Most times, we traveled with our friends Dr. Gabe and Arlene Ricciardi and Dr. Joseph and Lynn Intelisano. In the previous decade, the practice of chiropractic's scope was being changed from the removal of vertebral subluxation for its influence on the nervous system as its primary focus to a more allopathic approach. Chiropractors were mainly focusing on relief from musculoskeletal conditions. Chiropractors, including myself at that time, were like medical doctors, treating musculoskeletal discomforts. We were not taught the philosophy of chiropractic and why the correction of existing vertebral subluxations was vitally important to the function of the human body.

Here comes Reggie, speaking so eloquently with his British accent, painting verbal pictures, and explaining *the why of chiropractic*, the philosophy. Reggie taught us why everyone should be under the regular care of a doctor of chiropractic, who will locate, evaluate and correct any existing vertebral subluxations and their interfering effects on their nervous system. He taught us to make it affordable to all; hence we had a fee system that allowed our families to pay what they could afford each week. We were chiropractors and practiced only chiropractic and were no longer using modalities or treating symptoms. We were taught that vertebral subluxations interfere with that person's ability to experience their body's innate potential. We were taught that a human body is far better without vertebral subluxations. We were also taught that it is imperative that we tell others and explain to them how important it is that families be under regular chiropractic care. This was what I needed in those days to understand how important chiropractic is to humanity. I was out to change the world, thanks to Reggie Gold.

We adopted this philosophy in our lives, and it changed our family's life and the thousands of families we have influenced in our practice. Because of Reggie's influence, we gave regular weekly orientation lectures to all new families. Our practice grew to one of the largest practices in New Jersey, regularly serving over 700 patient visits per 3-day week.

Of course, we all know by now the *Reggism*, "If you're not out to change the world, everything else is just Mickey Mouse." We are changing the world exponentially through our practice members and their families.

Reggie's words and influence have also been responsible for so many things we have today. Because of his *Triune of Life,* we have a better understanding of the chiropractic philosophy, and we fight to protect our legacy. An army of dedicated chiropractors whose sole purpose is to change the world were born out of his words. I was fortunate to be one of seven chiropractors, including Dr. Gabe Ricciardi, Dr. Joe Donofrio, Dr. Frank Centrelli, Dr. Bob Sottile, Dr. Ray St. Miklossy, and Dr. Joe Intelisano, who, in the early 1970s formed the Garden State Chiropractic Society. This small group of chiropractors greatly influenced the founding of both Life Chiropractic College and Sherman Chiropractic College, as well as many philosophical groups and societies in existence today.

Reggie's teachings also influenced areas we tend not to associate with philosophy. In 1989 the New Jersey Chiropractic Board of Examiners was being voted on in the New Jersey Senate. Up until that time, the New Jersey laws governing chiropractic required that in order to treat an individual in our office, we had to show a concomitant symptom associated with the vertebral subluxation adjusted. Because Reggie and Sid influenced the groups, many of their followers went to our state capital in Trenton and became belligerent, forcing the law to be rewritten to say "the presence of a vertebral subluxation, absent any symptomatology, was reason enough for a chiropractor in the State of New Jersey to treat a patient." Up to that time, adjusting children and even family members was subject to disciplinary action. Neither Reggie nor Sid knew their influence changed the laws in New Jersey.

On a lighter note, many years ago, I had a very successful Jewish practice member named Billy Rifkin. He was so popular and influential to many people that he told his friends that in order to "hang out with him," you had to be subluxation free. Needless to say, he helped my volume of patients grow. One day he gave me a gold pendant to wear on a gold chain. The pendant was a Chai. He explained that the Chai was a Hebrew symbol that stood for Life, the number 18, and the unspoken "god."

Reggie saw this symbol around my neck one day and said, "Tarantino, you're not Jewish. Why are you wearing the Chai?" After I explained that it could mean Chai-ropratic and we make *life* better. He smiled and said, "Nice!"

The next time we were together, he had a Chai larger than the size of a silver dollar around his neck on a big gold chain. Of course, it was made of solid gold and as part of the Chai, he added the "adjusting hands in a Palmer arch." So many people wanted them, he made replicas, and we all wore them constantly.

One of the most important lessons I have learned from my friend Reggie was his insistence that we must use our lexicon. Words to him were so important. Terms, for example, like "treatment," "treatment rooms," "god," as it relates to Innate or Universal Intelligence, were misleading to the public and must not be used when discussing chiropractic.

In closing, I want to thank the editors for allowing me to share some things relative to my association and friendship with both Dr. Reggie and Dr. Irene Gold. Reggie remains in my heart, and I will be ever grateful for the influence he has had on me and my family.

THE THIRD PARADIGM

Reprinted from Dynamic Chiropractic
April 3, 2000 - Volume 18, Issue 8

The Third Paradigm
Reggie Gold

As I read the scientific writings of other chiropractors, I am sometimes aware of their tendency to so complicate ideas with technical jargon and convoluted thoughts that the main point of the article becomes lost or obscured.

This is not criticism, but a realization that the authors are chiropractors first, scientists or philosophers second, and writers third. They undoubtedly have great expertise as chiropractors and scientists, but cannot transform ideas to simple writing that is easily understood by those who are not as dedicated to the subject matter.

To capture the interest of the casual reader and prompt further investigation, which is presumably the goal of the author, requires simplicity. The average chiropractor does not necessarily have an avid interest in new theories and ideas, so the author's first job becomes to arouse interest. A simple, straightforward presentation of ideas is likely to create understanding, which alone can cause interest and result in further investigation on the part of the reader.

In an attempt to follow my own advice, I shall offer a simplification of my own chiropractic theories for your consideration. When I am faced with a problem of logic or ethics, my methodology is to reduce an idea to its simplest possible expression. When all the camouflage and obfuscation is removed, an idea stands alone, and its strengths and weaknesses become patently obvious. Simplicity promotes clarity and makes avoidance of issues very difficult, leaving ideas to stand or fall based solely on their merits.

Here, then, is chiropractic's number one issue in its simplest form:

There are three paradigms of chiropractic thinking. Each chiropractor must choose one to live by or else exist in a clouded world of half truths, where refusing to face facts results not only in an inability to talk about chiropractic with clarity, but also to practice it.

Paradigm one maintains that chiropractic cures all disease. This paradigm is evident in an advertisement which B.J. and D.D. Palmer ran in the Davenport Times in 1902, which proclaimed, "You have no right to be sick when chiropractic cures all disease." Practitioners of this paradigm, though few and far between, would live by such slogans as, "The power that made the body heals the body." They neglect to mention, however, that while it is true that the only power that heals the body is the power that made it, sometimes even that is not enough. Some people are beyond healing. The pretense that all sick people get well when properly adjusted merely holds us up to ridicule. Other slogans claim that "chiropractic gets sick people well" without adding the necessary word, "sometimes," which would make it true. This slogan, incidentally, even if true, would offer chiropractic care only to sick people and deny it to those who are not yet sick with clinical or laboratory symptoms.

A second paradigm of chiropractic thinking and practice holds that only some sick people get better when their vertebral subluxations are corrected. Because of the nature of their disease, or the advanced stages of it, others require medical intervention or adjunctive therapy.

This paradigm of treating some and referring others sounds logical and caring, and is most likely to earn us the respect of the community of health care providers. This paradigm represents the thinking of the vast majority of chiropractors. Though there is disagreement how patients should be treated, when to refer, and which treatments to administer in the chiropractic office, the second paradigm is heartily subscribed to by the two largest national associations.

Since both organizations agree on this major issue, it makes one wonder why we have two separate major organizations. If they both agree to treat some diseases and refer others, what are they disagreeing about?

There is, of course, one slight problem that arises when deciding which patients and diseases to treat and which to refer: all treatment or referral decisions are dependent upon diagnosis. Diagnosis is the one great area of weakness in this practice paradigm. Diagnosis is, after all, the greatest challenge and the area of greatest risk of mistakes being made. Yet chiropractors, who receive much less diagnostic training than MDs, think they are competent to diagnose for purposes of referral. How is this possible when they:

- denied by law the use of all diagnostic methods that invade the body chemically or surgically;
- generally learn diagnosis out of textbooks without ever seeing cases of the diseases they purport to identify;
- frequently learn diagnosis from other chiropractors who also

learned from textbooks and have never seen cases of the diseases;
- often couldn't pass national board exams in diagnosis without a crash course before the exam.

Some say that to practice without diagnosis would be dangerous. I suggest that nothing is more dangerous than incompetent diagnoses. Every year tens of thousands of sick people visit chiropractors of the second paradigm. People seeing chiropractors complain of a variety of problems, which could be the manifestation of vertebral subluxation, or could just as easily be symptomatic of something else, possibly a life-threatening disease. Instead of practicing chiropractic, the paradigm two chiropractor does a medical diagnostic examination, followed by a medical report of findings in which the DC claims to have identified the cause of the problem.

And with such blithe and dangerous comments as, "We do not treat the symptom, we correct the cause," the DC proceeds to offer treatment, which delays medical care for what may be a life-threatening medical emergency.

Was that backache really caused by vertebral subluxation, or is it perhaps a manifestation of prostate cancer, kidney stones, or referred angina from an impending heart attack? Is that headache caused by subluxation or is there an aneurysm at the Circle of Willis, or a brain tumor causing the symptom? How good is the chiropractor's diagnosis?

Another point to consider is that while thousands of people go to chiropractors every day, but millions more stay subluxated because they have no symptoms. For 104 years we have exposed people to the limited understanding of chiropractic that results from paradigm two. The treatment of some diseases by adjustment and the referral of others based upon our diagnostic knowledge is not chiropractic at all, it is the practice of manipulative medicine, and it is even more dangerous than paradigm one.

Paradigm one is obviously stupid, so stupid that nobody really believes it. Nobody believes that all disease is caused by vertebral subluxation, so nobody gets hurt by it except the chiropractor who tries to make a living at it. Paradigm two, however, sounds logical. It is saleable and, subsequently, dangerous. If paradigm one is stupid, and paradigm two is dangerous, let us consider a third paradigm.

This paradigm makes sense to me. It is a paradigm that thousands of chiropractors practice on their families, yet neglect to offer the public. Paradigm three is neither based upon a claim to cure all disease, nor an attempt to prejudge which diseases might become cured if vertebral subluxations are corrected. In fact, it has no disease treatment basis at all. It is totally nontherapeutic in its intent and practice.

Chiropractic holds that a vertebral subluxation, by its very existence, inhibits the body's ability to fully express its inherent potential. Every vertebral subluxation, by definition, includes some alteration of nerve function from perfection to something else. Vertebral subluxation is, at the very least, a change in the body's structure, and every scientist knows that a change in structure must inevitably result in a change in function. Therefore, all vertebral subluxations must result in altered function. In short, people with vertebral subluxations would be better off without them.

It does not matter if a subluxated person has a disease or if any disease would be best treated by manipulative medicine or some other treatment. The presence or absence of disease is irrelevant. Every human being, sick or well, newborn or aged, regardless of nutrition, exercise, occupation, sex, race, religion, and all other factors of life, is better off without vertebral subluxation. Why then do some chiropractors and organizations want to limit chiropractic correction of subluxations to certain categories? Is the person with AIDS or terminal cancer better off left subluxated? Should an infant with a vertebral subluxation but no determinable disease symptoms be left subluxated until symptoms occur? Symptoms are the last stages of malfunction, not the first.

By the time symptoms have occurred, years of opportunity for repair may have been lost. Why not correct vertebral subluxations when they occur, rather than wait for years of damage to produce symptoms?

To restrict chiropractic to sick people is as stupid as restricting vitamin C to people who have a cold. Furthermore, to treat disease by manipulation is necessarily to delay alternative treatment and thus, possibly endanger a life.

The third paradigm of chiropractic practice is the only that makes sense. It makes so much sense that thousands of chiropractors use it for themselves and their own families, yet because medical insurance does not pay for it, they do not teach its value to the public at large. We live in a country that spends billions of dollars a year on the treatment of sickness and disease, but precious little on health. Our chiropractic profession is supposed to lead the world into a new and more intelligent way of thinking, not follow the mistakes of the past.

Paradigm three is not about health and sickness. It is about the recognition that vertebral subluxation causes more than just lost health potential and loss of every human potential. The nervous system is the coordinating system whereby the countless billions of body cells interact in harmony to express mind, body, spirit, emotion, artistic talent, speed, stamina, coordination and family relations. Vertebral subluxation is a cause of disharmony to this beautiful thing we call life.

Paradigms one and two are about backaches; paradigm three is about life. We can choose to conform to the errors of the past, or we can step proudly to the forefront and lead the way into the future.

Carry It On
Nalyn Russo Marcus

The foundation of my grasp of the chiropractic principles comes from my time with Reggie Gold and his impact on my life. It was such a privilege to hear him speak and lecture so often at Sherman, on the Lyceum stage, and at New Beginnings seminars. It was at Sherman's Lyceums, however, that the impact was the most lasting because my yearly talk was often the warm-up for Reggie to speak and share his amazing philosophy talk.

My talk began at some point while in school; my story of how I came to Sherman was a great educational presentation to potential students. I presented my story annually, being an "older" student who could not return to her home state due to accreditation issues. I spoke to the students and parents to warm them up for Reggie's talk. This was the program on career day at Sherman for years. I never realized how truly amazing it was to share this time with him. Later, on Sundays, he'd encourage us all to share on the stage about how Lyceum impacted us. I don't think we ever realized how that would influence us to share the story with our own future audiences and new patients.

For years we ended the weekend with a rendition of Catherine Ridell-Silva's "Carry it On." On the years she wasn't present, Reggie would seek me out to assist and piece together the melody and lyrics. The song was so important to capping off the Lyceum spirit of bringing chiropractic to the world. I would round up the other voices. It was easy to see that this song was vital for Reggie because it embodied the essence of the urgency to instill the message B.J. conveyed.

Later on, after graduating in 1990, as we brought our son to every Lyceum, it was a special delight to witness the almost grandparent relationship fostered between Ben, Reggie, and Irene. To this day, we have loving memories of our talks and times together. Some were snippets as we all waited for the same flight back to Philadelphia or at the afterglow picnics at Dick Plummer's. When you're learning over decades and being instilled with the triune so clearly, it would never dawn that one day the teaching would be passed entirely into our sacred trust.

Reggie graduated to the universal plane but left countless lessons in all our hearts to "carry it on."

A great memory was when Reggie asked me, as a newer graduate, to adjust him at his home. What a humbling honor. Thank you for seeing something in me that I didn't see. You believed in me and let me feel it. I am a proud pupil now sharing the message and guarding it well.

Profound Influence
Phil McMaster

It was 1980. I was 17 years old, and Dr. Reginald Gold was about to profoundly influence my life.

It was not a direct influence in the strictest sense. In fact, I didn't even know who Reggie Gold was until quite some time later. I was in high school, at a stage where I was wondering what I was going to do with my life once I'd finished playing rugby, cricket, and tennis at school. I had a strong interest in the body and its function from a sporting performance and injury point of view, which led to me applying to physiotherapy school—I was accepted.

As fate would have it, I saw a sign on a high school noticeboard announcing a presentation on chiropractic as a career at a local chiropractor's office. In my ignorance, I considered going to it worthwhile because I thought I was enrolled in essentially the same sort of thing at physiotherapy school.

An American 12th-quarter student from Sherman College of Straight Chiropractic delivered the career talk. Jay Goodwin was visiting New Zealand and finishing his chiropractic externship here. He talked about a form of intelligence that was the organizing influence of all things in the universe and a similar intelligent organizing influence that was specifically exclusive to the organization of living things. He also spoke of the influence of the nerve system in terms of overall performance, control, and health of the body and the importance of the relationship between the spine and nerve system.

He explained that by promoting and maintaining the function of the spine and nerve system in an optimal state, the natural flow-on effect is a body that is better able to look after itself in its environment more accurately—regardless of its symptomatic state. I was transfixed! I was hooked! This is what I wanted to do! This was a significant moment of clarity for me.

So, how did Reggie influence my decision to dedicate the rest of my life to the practice of chiropractic and the education of my patients and students of chiropractic? It was not until well after arriving in Spartanburg, South Carolina, about a year later, that I realized the talk Jay Goodwin gave that night was a version of Reggie Gold's original "Layman Lecture." Of course, Reggie was one of the original teachers at Sherman College and taught countless students how to deliver a layman lecture using his delivery as a template. There are now many different iterations and versions of his "Layman Lecture" still being used today by many chiropractors worldwide. Most current versions could trace their origins to Reggie Gold's original lecture, which he presented thousands and thousands of times. That fundamental message, passed on by an oratory master and delivered by one of his students, was a defining moment in my future. This was not going to be the last time that Reggie Gold would influence me.

Reggie had left Sherman College by the time I arrived in 1981. His influence was still very apparent throughout campus life. Even though I still had not met the man, I felt a strong connection to his message. His legacy was clear to see around the campus. I chose to go to Sherman College because of the emphasis placed on teaching chiropractic philosophy there. From very early in the college's history, Thom Gelardi knew that he needed people who had exemplified philosophically driven practices to help him build a college that was committed to the same. What an inspired choice to ask Reggie to leave one of the most successful practices ever seen to help lead the philosophy department. His oratory genius and acute understanding of the philosophy of chiropractic ideally suited Reggie to his role at Sherman. A case of 'cometh the hour, cometh the man,' I say!

My roommates, while attending college in Spartanburg, Brett Ireland, who was also from New Zealand, and Gary Rixon from South Africa, unlike me, were both aware of Reggie's oratory prowess before arriving in the USA. They both had cassette tape recordings of some of Reggie's better-known work. These were given to them by their respective chiropractors. We would spend many evenings listening to "The Valley of the Blind" and other of Reggie's best recordings. Great discussions long into the night would ensue. We were bonded for life by such experiences, and many more passionate discussions were to take place for the rest of our practicing lives.

Reggie's articulation of the principles of chiropractic, with his associated analogies and anecdotal stories, profoundly affected me. The messages were all so simple and logical when Reggie said them; I was envious of his ability to connect with so many people on so many levels—something I wanted to emulate. Here's the thing about Reggie, he was always himself. Reggie never tried to be or pretended to be anyone other than Reggie! He was authentic. He was genuine, and he was consistent.

Hearing of Reggie's famous practice in Spring Valley, New York, with the huge numbers of people he served and the positive impact he had on the surrounding communities, inspired me to take a similar approach in my practice on returning to New Zealand after graduating in 1985. Reggie's *box-on-the-wall* payment system appealed to me. It seemed to me that because chiropractic care was based on a more proactive, vitalistic approach to health, we should offer a fee system that was consistent with that approach rather than adopting the more commonly used medical-based fee system. A box-on-the-wall approach was not an option in New Zealand, where it was considered illegal by the Inland Revenue Department. So, a different approach was needed. I often thought of chiropractic care and its benefits, similar to going to a gym for physical fitness and well-being. If you are diligent, regular, and consistent with your efforts in the gym, you are likely to see benefits from that. If you want to continue to see the benefits, you need to continue to put in regular effort. A monthly or yearly fee system seems to make sense as a fair exchange for this type of approach, so my version of Reggie's box-on-the-wall was a fee that was paid for a full year of chiropractic care which allowed for unlimited visits as was deemed by the chiropractor. If the patient wanted to get checked in addition to the pre-arranged appointments, they could do so. This approach was an endorsement of the same reasons for Reggie adopting his fee system.

Another motivating factor for organizing my office in this way came from Reggie's concept of the three paradigms of chiropractic care. The first paradigm is based on the premise that *you have no right to be sick when chiropractic cures all disease*, so the approach is that chiropractic cures all disease! The second paradigm is the more commonly practiced approach whereby *only some sick people get better when their vertebral subluxations are corrected.* It is a suitable treatment-based model for third-party/insurance payers. I would suggest that having a fee system based on third-party insurance payments and not one that supports regular, whole-family care is why most practices operate predominantly in second paradigm.

The third paradigm, however, is based on the presumption that every vertebral subluxation includes some alteration of nerve function away from optimal and, as such, should be corrected regardless of symptoms or disease. In other words, everyone should be able to access chiropractic care for the correction of vertebral subluxations on an ongoing basis for optimal expression, regardless of their state of health or symptoms and disease. I wanted to base my practice on this model.

The third paradigm represents the type of care I had always observed chiropractors providing for their families. Presumably, they would provide the best possible care for their family members. Why were they not providing the same care to their patients?

Reggie was committed to correcting vertebral subluxations wherever and whenever and so had a fee system that supported that desired outcome. I wanted the same thing. Reggie's influence contributed to creating the chiropractic practice of my dreams that endured for over 27 years as one of the busiest, most successful practices in New Zealand. I am very proud of that. The community I served benefited from having the opportunity to access affordable chiropractic care for the whole family. I had the good fortune to be very busy doing what I most loved, earning a great living, and enjoying a wonderful lifestyle.

I have taught philosophy at the New Zealand College of Chiropractic every week since its inception in 1994. Of course, the hours and hours of listening to Reggie's tapes and subsequent conversations with Reggie, more latterly, have strongly influenced my teaching of the philosophy of chiropractic. Other influential teachers, such as Dr. David Koch, have also contributed to my teaching of the philosophy of chiropractic. I am sure David would also acknowledge the huge amount of influence Reggie had on his thoughts and approach to chiropractic philosophy.

The study of Reggie's thesis on *The Triune of Life* was a staple on the academic calendar throughout the philosophy curriculum. David Koch gifted me a hardback version of this piece that I treasure and refer to often.

During my time as the Chairman of the Board of Trustees of the New Zealand College of Chiropractic from 2003 to 2013, my contact with Reggie increased as we often caught up at conferences and seminars and, most notably, at Sherman College's Lyceums. I encouraged him to attend our Lyceum events in New Zealand. So for several years in a row until his passing in 2012, Reggie was a regular feature at Lyceum and in various classes at the college during the week leading up to the event. Reggie lectured in my philosophy classes and basically just hung out with the students in the Gold Lounge - the student's lounge at the college.

It was during one of these classes in 2011 that something extraordinary happened. Reggie was lecturing on the triune of life when, to my eye, he appeared to stammer over his words a little and held an unusually long pause during his delivery. To most of the students, nothing seemed unusual or indifferent, but to me, being used to his normal style and delivery, this was not usual for Reggie. I called a 10-minute break from the class and went to Reggie to ask if he was ok. He said that he felt he had just experienced another transient ischemic attack. He had already had a stroke prior to coming to New Zealand that year and was advised not to travel internationally, but of course, he was determined not to miss Lyceum. So typical of Reggie, he asked me if I would check him, which I did. I adjusted him, and then when the 10-minute break was over, he launched himself back into the lecture and didn't miss a beat. Afterward, I took him to his hotel, and he was exhausted. This was a classic example of Reggie's unbelievable commitment to delivering his message. A message that he knew so well and articulated like no other.

Almost every aspect of the chiropractic profession over the best part of the last 65 years has in some way been influenced by Reggie Gold. His eloquence and his ability to make the complex simple have given many chiropractors a template for success in practice and in the education of thousands of chiropractors worldwide.

I consider myself very fortunate to have had the opportunity to get to know Reggie and Irene Gold very well, especially in the last few years of Reggie's life. I feel honored to consider them both good friends and mentors.

The Gold legacy runs deep. Their influence on the chiropractic profession is immeasurable.

Reggie Ruined My Life
Christopher Kent

My first encounter with Reggie Gold was at Palmer Homecoming 1970. This event was very well attended, as it was the 75th anniversary of the discovery of chiropractic. I was in the first quarter of my first year as a student. One of my dorm buddies was to become a second-generation chiropractor and had been attending Palmer Homecomings since he was a child. He helped shape my early understanding of chiropractic by introducing me to *The Bigness of the Fellow Within*. He was excited about Homecoming, or Lyceum, as his dad referred to it.

The event was set to begin, and as he perused the schedule. He stopped reading suddenly and said, "You've got to come and listen to Dr. Gold." I had no idea who he was talking about, but I accompanied my friend to the event. A man appeared dressed in purple and white (Palmer colors) with mutton chop sideburns and a sort of hybrid British/New York accent. He seemed both imposing and, to a naïve student, a bit bizarre.

That talk defined the direction of my life. He said many things, and when the allotted time expired, several of us followed him to a student's apartment, where the lecture continued. His energy and resolve were not bound by the lateness of the hour. Two statements resonated with my 18-year-old mind. "If you aren't out to change the world, everything else is Mickey Mouse." The second was a question. "If you were the last chiropractor on earth, would chiropractic survive?" In challenging times, I have quipped, "Reggie ruined my life with that statement." It became, and remains, my obsession.

The Boatman of Our Profession
Aram Gomez

Talking about Reggie Gold´s legacy is not an easy job. Many people say that the greatest man in chiropractic history is B.J. Palmer, but I dare to express that Reggie has the same importance for the profession. Why? He gave his mind, body, and soul to take the profession to the highest level and also to protect the principle of chiropractic.

Why do I say Reggie has the same importance as B.J.? In my opinion, after B.J.'s departure, the profession was completely lost for a long time. With no boatman on board, the chiropractic ship was going in a different direction and crashed with a big iceberg known as the therapeutic side. Our pillars were being broken slowly. Reggie was the man that took the rudder and became the boatman of this profession.

When I was a student, I was totally oriented by my college to the therapeutic side of the profession. One day I heard some ICA people talking about chiropractic philosophy, and I realized this was something different than I learned in school, but it also sounded very weird to me to listen to an almost religion mixed with philosophy. Regardless, I took the traditional straight chiropractic teachings and started to study the Green Books. One day I heard "The Valley of the Blind" spoken by Reggie, and on that day, chiropractic truly made sense to me. I understood that philosophy was not mixed with religion, and I learned from Reggie the purest form of chiropractic, objective straight chiropractic. I started to listen to all of Reggie´s audio recordings. I was most impressed by his communication skills. After watching "The Great Debate," I especially remember feeling profound passion watching Reggie defeat the medical doctors in front of everyone. I can truly say that I felt that he transmitted his passion to me just by watching and listening to him.

After I listened to him, I felt more connected to Reggie´s purpose than with the Green Books. I felt he had a mission, and his mission was to protect the chiropractic principles and transmit them to everyone around the world. He was the guardian of our profession, and no one stood up like him. He didn´t care about being diplomatic with others and chose not to be silent if someone in front of him was doing wrong for the profession. He declared war on the mixers, the traditional straight thinking, and to all the hypocritical organizations that sell out our principles. When he saw that the profession needed him in a full-time way; he didn´t think about it, and he sold his home and practice and gave all his energy to open the only objective college today - Sherman College of Chiropractic, he opened his house to give free talks to future chiropractors, founded the ADIO Institute, Pennsylvania College of Chiropractic, and created Spinology, which became another name for an unadulterated way to deliver pure chiropractic.

I also felt inspired when I read how Reggie resigned from ICA and decided to form a new organization, the FSCO, which today is the IFCO. When I heard that this organization was founded by him and the reasons why he resigned from ICA, I immediately joined to assist his mission. His work inspired many of the legends of our profession.

I had the opportunity to teach Reggie's article "The Third Paradigm" during the Academy of Chiropractic Philosophers Program and also to the World Congress of Chiropractic Students. Whenever I teach this article, there is always someone at the end of the talk that approaches to say, "I changed my mind, and I want to change to straight chiropractic."

I had the chance in 2019 to give a talk at the Berkshires, and Irene Gold was there. I was so influenced in my talk by Reggie that at the end, she approached me and said, "I´m very proud that you follow Reggie´s work, and I have not heard a talk like this in a long time." I felt very blessed that day.

I did not have a physical association with Reggie, but I have had an association with him through his teachings, and I consider myself his student. When I started to practice, I would listen to Reggie´s tapes inside my office, and this inspired me to communicate the powerful message of chiropractic based on locating, analyzing, and correcting vertebral subluxations (LACVS). I try to focus on helping people to express Innate Intelligence at 100%; as he mentioned, "Nature needs no help, just no interference."

Reggie referred to chiropractic as a profession about life, not as a health profession. He tried to move from the health paradigm to make chiropractic unique and not be confused with other professions.

Reggie is an example of how to give everything for the good of the profession. We owe him for objective straight chiropractic and teaching us how to communicate about it. Thank you, Reggie.

The Philosophy of Chiropractic Is So Bloody Simple

Isobe Hirofumi

I sincerely thank Dr. Reggie Gold for his outstanding contributions to the profession. He was a great leader, philosopher, and author of chiropractic. He contributed to protecting the profession and promoting its unique value of adjusting vertebral subluxations nationally and internationally through his visits, teachings, and writings. In fact, he visited my home country, Japan, in 1980 to promote chiropractic.

Dr. Reggie Gold's pictures were in many classrooms and hallways when I was a student at Sherman College of Chiropractic in South Carolina. A large statue of Dr. Gold was placed at the college entrance, and we learned about him in chiropractic history and philosophy classes. It was well known that he was one of the best supporters of Sherman College. The founder of Sherman College, and my dear friend and mentor, Dr. Thom Gelardi, often told me how much Dr. Gold's contributions mean to him, the college, and the profession. Dr. Gold often visited to teach the philosophy of chiropractic to the students and the faculty members at Sherman College.

All chiropractors and students must read Dr. Gold's book, *The Triune of Life*. This book should be available at all chiropractic schools in the world. Fortunately, this book on *Reggie Gold's Philosophical Legacy,* includes the entire second edition. *The Triune of Life* includes a comprehensive explanation of universal and chiropractic principles and the nature of reality. It describes clearly how the body can maintain itself through its connection between intelligence and matter via force. Intelligence continuously creates and animates the power. The book also describes the limitations of matter and highlights the dire importance of nerve energy flow. *The Triune of Life* also guides chiropractors to educate their patients about why and how adjusting subluxations can enhance their overall wellbeing through proper nerve supply, not just the relief of symptoms.

This objective of chiropractic is captured in Reggie's chapter from the book *Chiropractic Revealed: One on One with the Great Masters of a Misunderstood Profession,* where he writes "Chiropractic does not cure disease and it is not meant to cure disease. Chiropractic allows the body to function at a higher level." (p. 112)

Dr. Gold's life work has shown me that each chiropractor has to have leadership and should stand firmly for the profession. In 1979, Dr. Reggie Gold and Dr. Terry Rondberg were on a TV show to debate chiropractic with two MDs, Drs. Jerome Williams and John Grant. I was impressed by Dr. Gold's clear presentation of chiropractic on national television. Dr. Gold's relentless public passion and pride for principled chiropractic made a lasting impression on me, and I strive to perpetuate this passion. He conveys this in the chapter from *Chiropractic Revealed* when he writes,

> This is why I say the only hope for chiropractic in the future is to divorce itself from that medical image. We need a lot of hard-nosed chiropractors who really understand the big idea and are prepared to work on changing the world's opinion of chiropractic. (p. 116)

I appreciate Dr. Gold's efforts to educate and train straight chiropractic leaders at Sherman College and ADIO Institute and for passing Gold chiropracTIC insights and techniques to us. He also writes:

> The philosophy of chiropractic is so bloody simple. The problem is that it's too simple for most chiropractors to understand. Most chiropractors think that it has to be complicated, and they think there's a lot to learn. There's almost nothing to learn. (p. 120)

Reggie Gold's legacy will live on through many of his students and colleagues. I am one of those "hard-nosed chiropractors" who will always stand for the power of the chiropractic adjustment and the chiropractic profession. From studying Drs. Palmer, Gelardi, Gold, and others, I understand the big idea, and I'm working hard to educate Hokkaido, Japan, about chiropractic. I am honored to be a part of this TIC revolution and its movement for a chiropractic future that Dr. Reggie Gold would be proud to see.

**This essay was graciously edited by my life and business partner, Clara Sughrue Isobe.*

If You Were the Last Chiropractor
Valerie Pennacchio

Reggie Gold!!! Just typing his name brings a smile and a tear. A smile because of all the memories of the times I shared with Reggie as a student at his feet, so to speak, and a tear because I miss him. The tear is selfish, of course.

The first time I was in Reggie's presence was when I came to Sherman College, considering a career as a chiropractor as my "field chiropractor" (which is what we used to call the chiropractor who inspired you to study) told me, "Sherman was the only place to consider studying."

I was picked up at the airport by Dave Courtney (a 5th quarter student at the time) and the husband of Pam Courtney, Financial Aid Director at Sherman. His car was covered with inspirational quotes in what I later found out was B.J Script. I mention this because he and Pam invited me (and my partner at the time) to stay with them instead of at a hotel, AND there was a huge gathering at a very special instructor's home that night, and they wanted us to go. Although we were like deer stopped in headlights, we said yes, of course. The night continued with a huge gathering at Reggie and Irene's home with lots of students that were welcoming and fun. Reggie was swimming and being playful with the students. I couldn't believe the comradery I was witnessing (being from a rough part of New Jersey). Later, talking to Pam and Dave, I realized that I had met Reggie briefly once before when my chiropractor back home, Gabe Ricciardi, brought us to an evening presentation promoting the opening of another chiropractic college in Pennsylvania, which was to become ADIO Institute of Chiropractic and later the Pennsylvania College of Chiropractic. His presentation was so inspirational I wanted to sign up that evening, but Gabe encouraged us to check out Sherman too. And that was the beginning of Reggie's (and Irene's) influence in my life.

When I was a student (a geek), I came across his speech entitled "The Valley of the Blind." This presentation has fueled my chiropractic life since I first heard it. Being pumped up and aggressively advocating chiropractic, I was determined to know all I could about the profession and the philosophy underpinning it. Reggie's presentations were my daily diet. After graduating as a chiropractor, I was honored to be asked to teach at Sherman and was THRILLED when Thom Gelardi asked me to give a health talk at his house for prospective students. It was nerve-wracking to talk about chiropractic with Thom and Betty in the audience, but that was just a dress rehearsal for the time Reggie Gold sat in my philosophy class. I thought I was going to pass out but decided I would continue and be myself knowing for sure if it was necessary, Reggie would give me constructive criticisms after class, and I was eager to learn how I could present the material better. After class, I held my breath as he walked towards me. He was very gracious to this fledgling philosophy teacher and even complimented me on how I engaged the class. I was flying from his praise.

"The Valley of the Blind" became something that I played for my students in class so that we could have a lively philosophical discussion after they listened to the entire presentation. At the end of this particular version of this presentation, he asked the question, "If you were the last chiropractor would chiropractic survive?" That question has been with me on a daily basis. There are days in my practice and also in the classroom (as I am still honored to be teaching philosophy to young chiropractors) that I am secure that I have done what would have made Reggie proud, and then there are days that I wish I still had him to bounce some ideas off of, hoping he'd kick me in the bum and get me back on track. I still listen to this "Valley of the Blind" presentation. If you haven't heard it, I highly recommend it – he's inspirational no matter what he is presenting, but this is very special to me. I'm not the only one that finds this inspirational. I was in the audience once when he asked the crowd what they wanted to hear, and people started to yell, "Valley of the Blind," like at a concert yelling the name of a song you want to hear. It brought tears to my eyes to realize how influential this essence, this man, was not only to me but to so many. I have been richly blessed in my 40 years in chiropractic to have been in Reggie's presentations in the USA and New Zealand. He often graciously accepted my invitations to speak in my philosophy classes, and every time I listened to him, I was that "kid" at the master's feet. Thank you, Reggie (and Irene, for being so generous with your time). I am who I am in chiropractic because of you, and I'm eternally grateful.

This is the Real Chiropractic
Ahn Sung-Hyun

The chiropractic journey in Korea is still ongoing, and the chiropractic philosophy is at the center of the journey.

My academic interest in chiropractic philosophy began with a small girl who was my patient. It was 14 years ago, but I can still vividly remember that day. In the summer of 2008, a woman visited my chiropractic clinic for back pain. She had a 6-year-old daughter. The girl sat in my doctor's chair and ate candy while her mother was receiving a chiropractic adjustment, and at the end of her mother's treatment, she smiled and gave me a candy with her small hands.

One day, the mother visited the clinic alone without her child. I asked her if there was anything going on with her daughter. The mother said that the father was taking care of the child at home because the child was not feeling well due to otitis media. Half worried and half curious; I asked the mother about the child's history and treatment record for her otitis media and sinusitis. I was told that the child was continuously being treated for otitis media and sinusitis for one year at a university hospital and is currently considering otitis media ear tubes. While getting ready to go home, I saw the candy on my desk and wondered if there was anything I could do to help the child. I called my chiropractic professor from my university. I told the professor about the child's condition and asked, in a confident voice, if her condition could improve through chiropractic. The professor yelled at me, asking if I had forgotten the philosophy of chiropractic. Of course, I remember the theory of the Meric System and subluxation from school, but unfortunately, a case like this girl's was a first for me. After listening to the professor rant in an aggressive voice for 10 minutes, I decided to recommend chiropractic treatment for the girl.

When the child's mother visited the clinic again and finished her treatment, I carefully advised her to try chiropractic treatment for her daughter because there were previous case studies in which otitis media and sinusitis improved with it. The child's mother readily consented, and I began treatment with all my heart. I constantly sought the advice of nearby chiropractors and prayed for her. Surprisingly, after two weeks, her symptoms gradually began to improve. Three months later, to my surprise, she no longer had otitis media and sinusitis.

After that, I started to search and read the history of chiropractic and various chiropractic philosophy books again, reflecting on whether I was practicing chiropractic properly. At that time, it was impossible to purchase chiropractic books in Korea, so I purchased books from American bookstores or eBay through the Internet and received it by airmail. At times, I had to pay more for airmail than for the books.

Then, while looking for chiropractic information on the internet, I came across Dr. Reggie Gold's 1979 "Chiropractic vs. Medicine Debate" video. As I watched the debate between Dr. Reggie Gold and the Medical Doctors, I couldn't control my excitement and shouted, "This is the real chiropractic." I instantly bought Dr. Reggie Gold lecture videos and books and watched and read them without a break. Watching his videos and reading his books helped me create a compass for my chiropractic journey on how to put it into practice correctly.

Currently, according to the World Federation of Chiropractic, chiropractic is being practiced in 95 countries. In each country, chiropractic is practiced according to the situation of each country. However, the situation is not the same as in the United States. For example, chiropractors in the United States can use x-ray equipment, but in countries such as Japan and Hong Kong, chiropractors cannot use x-ray equipment according to their medical laws, so we need to seek cooperation from the MD. In addition, out of all the countries in the world, Korea cannot practice chiropractic without a medical license. Of course, chiropractic is not taught in medical schools.

In Korea, about 200 chiropractors who have been trained in chiropractic in the US, Australia, UK, Korea, Japan, and other countries are trying to practice chiropractic with the same mind. Although we have learned chiropractic from different countries and different schools, we have all learned the philosophy of chiropractic and we are trying to practice the correct chiropractic despite our situation.

In 1991, Dr. Reggie Gold said one of his memorable quotes: "Chiropractic does not need a philosophy. It is a philosophy." As the saying goes, I hope that chiropractic and philosophy will be practiced together around the world.

Lastly, I want to express my gratitude to Drs. Reggie Gold, George B. Curry, Yong-Gu Kenneth, and Jong-Il Bae, who became my pillars to practice chiropractic in Korea, as well as to my wife Young-ran, my daughter Hyun-seo, and my son Jun-seo, and to Dr. Simon Senzon, who gave me this honor today.

What Would Reggie Do
Sharon Gorman

I was a first quarter student at Life Chiropractic College, and Reggie came to Atlanta to talk to the students about philosophy. I went along with my roommate to some local hotel meeting room. Reggie made a lot of sense, so much sense.

I grew up around chiropractors and was taught how to think about chiropractic by some very smart and successful men. Most of them learned what they knew from Reggie. I listened and accepted all they told me about chiropractic, and I was on a very principled path from the very beginning. I never questioned. I was still a teenager. Who was I to question? They were so passionate. I believed. I sometimes felt inadequate when other students questioned my philosophy because I could tell them what I believed but not why I believed it.

The next morning a few students hosted Reggie over at their apartment for breakfast. Somehow, I was invited. After we ate, Reggie asked us if we had any questions from the night before. I asked a question which led to another question and another and another. By the time I left that apartment, any holes I might have had in my philosophy were filled.

Chiropractic went from a system of beliefs to the most logical philosophy I had ever heard. There were no holes. No questions that couldn't be I answered. I stopped believing, and I started knowing. I still know – over 40 years later. Not only was Reggie a master communicator he also had a brilliant mind. He could think on his feet. That morning changed my life.

Many years later, I was practicing in the Poconos. Thanks to that incredible morning some ten years earlier and the phenomenal guidance of my mentor Dr. Jim Sigafoose I already had four offices that were seeing thousands of patients a month.

One day, I drove down to Philly to have lunch with my friend Judy Nutz Campanale. When I spoke to Judy the day before, she asked me if it was okay that she asked Reggie to join us. Of course, it was okay; it was way more than just okay. I remember it like yesterday. Judy drove, Reggie was in the passenger seat, and I sat in the back, in between the seats leaning forward because I didn't want to miss a word. Reggie knew about my success and actually had attended a few of my open houses in the past. Reggie asked me a few questions about my practice, and then he told me that I shouldn't take insurance in my practice any longer and that I couldn't really practice chiropractic the way it should be practiced if I took insurance. I got defensive. I wanted him to approve of my practices, and we went back and forth for a while. Sort of talking in circles. I told him that at the time, I had five associates, and I wouldn't make enough money to pay them all if I didn't take insurance. I told him that if I had one high-volume practice and didn't take insurance, I would be fine, but I couldn't keep these docs employed and paid long enough to make them strong enough to survive without insurance. This was in the late 80s, and most of my actual collections came from insurance. He finally conceded that he saw my point about the associates but clearly still didn't agree with me, so we agreed to disagree.

Now so many years later, I was pushed into a position of not collecting very much from the insurance companies (as many of us have), and I can now see that I could have done it without insurance back then too. I now take very little insurance, and I am still thriving. I couldn't see it then and certainly wouldn't have created that kind of practice because I couldn't see it until the insurance climate changed and I was forced to not take the path of least resistance. Well, that is the past.

Throughout my career, I have many times asked myself, "What would Reggie do?" when making a decision on how to run my practice? One time I heard Reggie speak in New Jersey, and he said that he knew most chiropractors would not practice the way he did, but he hoped to move the philosophical line. Most wouldn't be as extreme as him, but they would strive to be closer to that line. I strive for that every day.

Shortly before Reggie passed, I went to visit him. Toward the end of our visit, he moved his sheet and pointed out the swelling in his lower legs, and he said, "I can't live like this much longer." He stared into my eyes, and I stared back. Both of our eyes were filled up. It was his way of saying goodbye. He then said, "Would you adjust me?" and I did.

I left shortly after, never to see him alive again, but as always, I took a piece of him with me. So many carry so many pieces of a man who spent a life well lived full of purpose and meaning. As they say, guard it well.

His Essence
David Serio

Reggie's entire essence is a perfect metaphor for Chiropractic. He was a deep, profound thinker, yet his expression was that of simplicity and conviction for the betterment of humanity. Reggie was a teacher to some, a Chiropractor to others, to some a friend, a husband to the beautiful Irene, and a mentor; Reggie was so many things to so many people. I want to give you a glimpse into the Reggie that I came to know and love as a young student.

I was in my first quarter at Life College, and someone told me, "David, you must come with us. We are going to see Reggie; he was banned from campus, so we must go to see him at another school." I was sold even though I had never heard of this Reggie person before. We entered a crowded auditorium, and there must have been about 200 people there. I had to sit way in the back, and there was this amazing energy and feeling in the air. It was noisy, and people were excited.

Reggie stood up as only he could, his classic pose, foot on a chair, looking off a bit, head on an angle before he addressed the crowd. As he started to speak, I was mesmerized by the way he spoke, his tone, his words, and the energy of his movements. It was as if I was literally watching a modern-day Socrates. Everything he said was so logical, simple yet deep, and he had my mind exploding. When the talk ended, I walked right up to him and said without thinking, "Reggie, I'm David. Will you be my mentor?" He looked at me and said, "Which school are you attending?" I said, "Life College," his answer was, "First, you must transfer to Sherman College of Straight Chiropractic." I followed his advice, and the next time I saw him was at Sherman College of Straight Chiropractic, as it was called at the time, and he said the answer to your question is "yes."

From that point on, we developed a mentor-to-student relationship, and I spent as much time with Reggie as I could during my Sherman years and beyond. As I grew to know him as a young student, he came to represent for me courage, conviction, boldness, and logic. He was a master communicator, thinker, philosopher, teacher, and speaker. He loved the principles of chiropractic and traveled all over the world to ensure that chiropractors were exposed to its essence. He once told me, "Never turn down the opportunity to speak; it does not matter the organization, school, or venue. If you have a chance to share your message, say yes." I have followed his advice ever since.

For Reggie, chiropractic was so much bigger than health. For example, there was an all-school assembly at Sherman, and the college just put these big brand new, beautifully well-crafted letters outside the building of the student clinic that said, "Sherman Health Center." Reggie stood up for his all-school assembly in which every teacher, administrator, and student was there and said, "Who's brilliant idea was it to name the place where we adjust lives the Health Center?" with such a sarcastic tone that only Reggie Gold could deliver. Reggie then proceeds to give this amazing talk about how chiropractic was not about health. Yes, Reggie was not afraid to speak his mind; he was bold. Yes, he had the ability to get people to think that was second to none. He could push buttons like no other and then give his argument for why he just said what he said, and it was so perfectly crafted that it would open minds and get so many to question their actions.

His brilliance extended into his ability to bring a sense of humor to situations in ways I have never encountered in anyone else. That being said, Reggie, in every way, was so unique. There was an IFCO student global event held at Sherman with an amazing lineup of speakers. I was standing next to Reggie in the back when one of the speakers said, quantum physics is proving that we really don't even know where the spine begins and ends. Reggie blurts out, "That's why we have Guyton's physiology book; it's pretty clear right there in black and white where the spine begins and ends." The room burst out into laughter.

Reggie was a brilliant communicator. "The Valley of the Blind" is by far one of the greatest talks in and out of chiropractic I have ever heard. It is communicated with such brilliance, it is poetry, and crafted in a way that transcends time. His ability to pause in just the right place and the words and tones that he chooses are second to none. His "Lay Lecture" has changed so many lives, including chiropractors and lay people. I believe his genius as a communicator was that he was able to reach your heart, emotions, and head at the same time. I don't know of many other people in or out of chiropractic that have or had that ability. Reggie's mastery of communications wasn't limited to his speaking abilities. The entire reason for this book is he left behind one of the greatest works in chiropractic. His masterpiece version of *The Triune of Life*. I'm sure many of us wish he had written much more so we could forever read his brilliance flowing through the pages of a book.

The world of chiropractic is forever changed by his presence, and what I believe are some of his greatest contributions. First and foremost, all of the students that Reggie impacted as a teacher. So many of the great chiropractors in our profession were direct students of Reggie's. I personally never had the honor of being in one of Reggie's classes, but I had heard that when he taught at Sherman College of Straight Chiropractic, people would leave their other classes to go and hear him again and again.

He clarified and refined the philosophy of chiropractic. He was a thinker and questioned everything. He once told me that he questioned every principle and would try to find a fallacy in them and could not. That's what a philosopher does; they question, refine, and search for the very essence of truth. Reggie Gold distilled the philosophy of chiropractic into its purity. He cleared the incongruencies and shed light on their profound simplicity. He transmitted the logic of the depth and latitude of chiropractic.

I had a chiropractic assistant in Buenos Aires, Argentina, for many years who had never heard of chiropractic before meeting me. During her time as my assistant, she had heard about forty different chiropractors speak over the years. I once asked her who her favorite was and why? She said, "Not even close, Reggie Gold." When I asked why she said, "All of them were inspiring, but Reggie not only connected to my emotions, but I understood chiropractic so clearly after his talk I wanted to share it with everyone and could explain it to everyone." He kept the message simple and as clear as a perfectly shining diamond.

Reggie evolved until the very end. He was always finding new ways to help shed light on the state of chiropractic. I believe the first time he shared his idea of the three paradigms of chiropractic was at an IFCO event in North Carolina. I was sitting next to a few chiropractors that had heard Reggie for over twenty-five years, and they said he never stops growing and looking for new ways for us to understand chiropractic better. That talk was brilliant and opened so many minds into what was the current state of chiropractic at the time.

Reggie had courage. He once told me, "David, you need to be a little crazy to be a straight chiropractor because we are an about-face to everything the world knows." I will never forget that because his next line was, "So you will be just fine." We both burst into laughter so hard I was crying. But I believe he really meant to have the courage to be different and not to care what others thought. Anyone that ever saw

"The Great Debate," where Reggie debates a few MDs, can feel his courage. I believe courage was one of Reggie's greatest qualities.

His level of conviction about the principles of chiropractic and his ability to transmit this to others was second to none. I am sure there are thousands of chiropractors who are so deeply grateful for the conviction they have for chiropractic because of Reggie. He was and is chiropractic. He lived, breathed, and expressed chiropractic. There was no fallacy in his level of conviction. Tony Robbins was once asked, "What is the one quality that someone needs to have success in selling a service, product, or an idea?" Tony said, "Conviction." This is why Reggie had so much influence on so many people. His level of conviction was out of this world.

The last time I saw Reggie was in Peru at an IFCO convention. I will be forever grateful to Dr. Liam Schubel for putting on this event because the weekend was magical. Reggie was struggling somewhat with his health, yet there he was; he traveled all of the way to Peru. He was walking slowly towards the stage, and I had never seen him before in this state. As soon as he took the stage, he lit up, his energy shifted 360 degrees, and he went on for hours, sharing stories from his Palmer days, and Reggie gave one of the greatest talks I had ever heard. His presence and what we witnessed that day was a testimony to the spirit that flows through us when we are living our purpose.

On a side note, it was 7:30 a.m. that morning, and I was going on stage at 8 a.m. and happened to stop to chat with Reggie. He had a huge burning hot cup of coffee and accidentally spilled it on my freshly pressed pants. My legs were on fire, and I was soaked, and he said, "Looks like you're going to have to change those pants." We all burst out laughing, and it took the focus off the burning hot coffee on my leg.

I just adore Reggie and could go on and on about so many of the things he did for me personally to help me in my career and practice. He had a huge heart for service and gave freely of his time, energy, and money. I personally witnessed him donating to many chiropractic causes and schools. His legacy will live on through many of us for generations and generations, and chiropractic will be forever impacted by Reggie Gold.

The Triune of Life, in my humble opinion, is one of the greatest pieces of the philosophy of chiropractic, and Reggie's contribution to this universal truth has had an impact on every aspect of my life. The more I study this piece of art in the written word, the deeper it penetrates my consciousness and every aspect of life. I believe that *The Triune of Life*, in the way Reggie presents it goes so far beyond any box that we as a profession have put ourselves in.

This, I believe, is perhaps Reggie's greatest contribution to the great profession of chiropractic. His idea was that chiropractic was about life in all its expression and that health was putting chiropractic in yet another box. *The Triune of Life* is his masterpiece which is the foundation and cornerstone for this legacy that he left behind. I have come to the realization that the triune of life can be applied to success, life habits, all aspects of a Chiropractic practice, and so much more. The triune of life is literally the architecture for life and all aspects of its existence and expression.

In *The Triune of Life*, Reggie clarified where clarification was needed. He went deep where depth was needed. He simplified where simplification was needed. He brought the philosophy from textbook to the reality of life. For me, this was the epitome of Reggie's brilliance. The ability to take something abstract and express it in a way where this immense idea becomes a useful reality for the betterment of all life. Many would laugh at his saying, "If you're not out to change the world, you're Mickey Mouse," but it would hit me so deep inside. In my opinion, Reggie was right. What are we here for if we are not out to change the world? And what better vehicle than chiropractic?

Our service is so unique, and here is where I personally believe the genius of Reggie shines to its maximum. Reggie saw chiropractic as either therapeutic or non-therapeutic. This always made so much sense to me. He would say, "If you are diagnosing and treating sickness, symptoms, and or disease, you are practicing medicine." He was way ahead of his time in this thinking. From a reality perspective, he is totally correct; medicine is the diagnosis and treatment of symptoms, sickness, and disease. From a marketing perspective, his thinking was brilliant because if you enter the market of treatment, you are competing with everyone and anyone in this arena, and in this market, the kings are the Medical Doctors. But if you are practicing chiropractic in a non-therapeutic model, you are unique, not competing with anyone, and you have the entire world to serve.

I personally think his logic and thoughts and expression on the clarity of non-therapeutic chiropractic is so simple and logical and brings infinite possibility. If we as a profession embraced this idea, everything would change. From the way, our educational systems are set up to the cost of education to our personal practices. I personally believe his idea of non-therapeutic chiropractic is the path to saving our profession. There are so many upsides, including economic ones. His expression of this idea was and continues to be his unique ability to distill the universal principles of chiropractic into simple, logical, profound, and realistic ideas for the evolution and preservation of chiropractic.

I will be forever grateful to Reggie Gold for touching my life, career, and vision for Chiropractic. I have tried my very best to honor his legacy by living the teachings he passed on to me and passing them on to others, so his legacy stays alive for generations. Reggie's greatness and his reach in chiropractic and without will continue to unfold as time goes on, and his genius will continue to shed its gifts upon those seeking truth, clarity, and excellence within chiropractic.

Chiropractic For Generations
Kim Stetzel

I consider myself extremely fortunate to have grown up under chiropractic care. My father, Edward Rahuba graduated from the Chiropractic Institute of New York in 1959. (The Chiropractic Institute was a small Chiropractic College in New York City that was in existence from 1944 – 1968.) Technique was an important core of the education, but chiropractic philosophy less emphasized.

A few years into practice, the friend who had steered him toward chiropractic, Bruce Merritt, went down to Dynamic Essentials (DE) in Atlanta, got turned on by the philosophy, and convinced Dad he needed to go as well. From that point, he was hooked.

At the time, Reggie was a featured speaker and a huge draw at DE. Since we lived in northern New Jersey and Spring Valley was just across the border, Dad and a growing band of chiropractors from the area took advantage of the monthly philosophy meetings that Reggie held. Their understanding of chiropractic and its philosophy grew along with their excitement about chiropractic.

One primary lesson that Reggie inspired in so many was the importance of giving a weekly workshop for new people in practice, their spouses, families, and friends. This weekly talk was the key to helping new practice members more fully understand chiropractic, why it is not a treatment and why all people need to have their spines checked. Reggie recorded his own talk and made it available as a reel-to-reel movie. For my dad, this was huge! Dad was great speaking to people about chiropractic one to one, but he could not bring himself to get up in front of a group and speak. Reggie's movie allowed him to educate and inspire his practice, as well as a good number of young folks thinking about chiropractic as a career. I was one of those young folks.

I knew from an early age that I wanted to be a chiropractor. Reggie's influence on my dad and his friends had much to do with that. One thing I knew, though, was that I was going to have to learn to get up and speak in front of people and so I took every opportunity to take public speaking classes from junior high onward. Whenever we had to do a persuasive speech, it was always about why everyone would benefit from chiropractic!

When possible, I created opportunities and brought Reggie's movie into my biology class and was even able to show it to a few other classes as a result!

That movie and "The Valley of the Blind" record (so dating myself) were foundational in my understanding of chiropractic and my drive to make a difference through the profession.

Years later, Reggie taught me another important chiropractic lesson – through a cassette tape that Dad had recorded at a DE meeting. In 1981, when I started Chiropractic College, Life and Sherman were my two choices. I went to Life because, at the time, it was accredited by CCE, which would allow me to practice in any state after I graduated. However, while in school, we would head up to Sherman Lyceum for philosophy and fellowship. At the time, I really didn't understand the philosophical nuances between traditional "straights" and objective "straights." My belief was that if what you did in the office was adjust and nothing else, you were a straight chiropractor. If you added other therapeutics, modalities, or adjunctive procedures, you weren't. A number of years after graduation, I listened to a cassette tape Dad had made of two speakers at a DE meeting. One side had a popular platform speaker talking about how diabetes and other maladies would be cured when a person received chiropractic care. The other side featured Reggie's talk about chiropractic being a non-therapeutic profession. He spoke about "The Chemistry of Life" and the chiropractor's intent of detecting and correcting subluxations because they interfere with the fullest expression of innate intelligence in the individual. It was enlightening to hear these two different viewpoints on Chiropractic and better grasp the importance of intent.

Reggie helped me see that miraculous changes can and do occur when innate intelligence is again free to communicate with the tissue cells. The miracle isn't the chiropractor's job. Our job is to detect and correct the interference by adjusting subluxations. Which, in and of itself, is a huge service!

I am greatly appreciative of the immense philosophical contributions that Reggie made to this profession and to my understanding of chiropractic. I believe that he fostered an expansive and all-encompassing role for chiropractic and for chiropractors to influence the well-being of the planet.

ENCORE
Claude Lessard

Definition of "encore" from Merriam-Webster Dictionary:
1: a demand for repetition or reappearance made by an audience
2a: a reappearance or additional performance demanded by an audience
2b: a second achievement, especially that surpasses the first

It was 2 p.m., a sunny October afternoon in 1973, Broadway and 72nd Street, New York City. Disillusioned, I had just withdrawn from St. John's University in Jamaica, New York, where I was enrolled in pre-med; I was thinking about what I would be doing for the rest of my life. Rather unexpectedly, I ran into a friend of mine who introduced me to then, a ninth-quarter student at Columbia Institute of Chiropractic, Irene Gold. We spoke briefly, and she handed me an application encouraging me to enroll at the new Sherman College of Chiropractic in Spartanburg, South Carolina. That afternoon is an iconic memory of mine.

A few months later, Reggie is standing outside the Bell Telephone building on Main Street in Spartanburg. He was the first person I met without a southern accent. I was grateful. Originating from Northern Quebec, my French Canadian upbringing fashioned a very limited spectrum of vocal yelps. Reggie welcomed me and told me to register at the front desk inside. This was the beginning of an almost forty-year relationship. There is much I could write, so many anecdotes, some personal, some public, but instead I will fast forward and only share his "ENCORE" with you.

Reggie Gold, the chiropractor, the rebel with a great and unstoppable imagination who questioned even the highest authorities in chiropractic, such as B.J. Palmer, was ALWAYS about making a difference. Reggie was able to *see* what was not yet visible. He saw in his imagination what was hidden in plain sight.

Reggie, the visionary, asked Irene to call me; he knew he was dying. It was Saturday, March 5, 2012. I drove to their residence in Bala Cynwyd, Philadelphia. Irene showed me to his bedroom and left the room. Reggie was sitting on the edge of his bed, with his shaved head looking down at his feet. There was a chair in front of him, and there I sat. I said, "Hi Reg. It's good to see you." There was no response. I figured that perhaps he had not heard my greeting, so I spoke again, "Hi Reg. I'm happy to see you." No answer from him. Now, I felt somewhat perplexed and a bit nervous. I waited for about two minutes. The silence was deafening.

I commented on how I was and how the family was doing, but nothing by way of registering my words was given to me.

I switched gears, declaring how much he meant to me and my gratitude for his generosity in having invested so much of his time, energy, money, and love through the course of some forty years. Like a litany, I recalled many significant moments in chiropractic that we shared: Our starting the FSCO, the SFSCO, and formulating their Constitutions (1975), our orchestrating the "Spirit of '76" at Sherman (1976), our founding ADIO Institute of Straight Chiropractic (1978), drafting the ADIO analysis (1979), our discussing early Spinology in Yardley (1980), and so many others.

Ten minutes into this monologue, there was absolutely no sign of Reggie's having taken in all I'd said. I don't know how a few minutes can seem like an eternity, but they did. Was he hearing me? He didn't seem to be struggling for words; there simply weren't any.

Rising from my chair, I walked to him and kissed the top of his head. And at that moment, I remembered a reaction he had to something I'd said in 1996 with which he vehemently disagreed. I felt anger welling up in me and said in a loud voice, "Reggie, you once told me, 'Think, dammit, Claude, think!' YOU stop thinking now and say something, dammit! You asked Irene to call me, and I came right away! Why did you want to see me? What do you want to say?"

At that moment, Reggie lifted his head. With his brilliant, piercing eyes, he looked STRAIGHT at me for what seemed to be a long time. I even detected that signature smirk on his lips. He said ONLY two words and then lowered his head.

Reginald Rafael Gold passed away a few days later.

French, is my native tongue. This "Encore" has meaning as it exemplifies Reggie; a true leader, always charging **ALL OF US** together without condemnation.

These are Reggie's parting words. They bespeak his trust and confidence in the future of chiropractic:

"CARRY ON!"

REGGIE GOLD
Philosopher of Chiropractic
16 DECEMBER 1925 – 24 MARCH 2012

ABOUT THE INSTITUTE CHIROPRACTIC

THE INSTITUTE CHIROPRACTIC is dedicated to the publication of important books and media, which shed new light on topics such as chiropractic history and philosophy, spirituality, enlightenment, philosophy, integral theory, and subtle energies. The White Book Chiropractic Series is designed to bring forth important works from the history and philosophy of chiropractic, publish original new works, and inspire dialogue. Membership in The Institute Chiropractic is open to chiropractors and chiropractic students. Membership includes extensive online learning, scholarly discussion, and professional connections with the leading chiropractors around the world, those dedicated to acknowledging the profession's history, fostering a discipline of philosophy in the profession, and leading chiropractic into the future.

For more information on The Institute Chiropractic visit
www.institutechiro.com

Made in the USA
Middletown, DE
10 October 2023